THE EXISTENTIALIST LEGACY AND OTHER ESSAYS ON PHILOSOPHY AND RELIGION

James Woelfel

University Press of America,® Inc.
Lanham · Boulder · New York · Toronto · Oxford

Copyright © 2006 by
University Press of America,® Inc.
4501 Forbes Boulevard
Suite 200
Lanham, Maryland 20706
UPA Acquisitions Department (301) 459-3366

PO Box 317
Oxford
OX2 9RU, UK

All rights reserved
Printed in the United States of America
British Library Cataloging in Publication Information Available

Library of Congress Control Number: 2005938639
ISBN-13: 978-0-7618-3409-0 (paperback : alk. paper)
ISBN-10: 0-7618-3409-5 (paperback : alk. paper)

⊖™ The paper used in this publication meets the minimum
requirements of American National Standard for Information
Sciences—Permanence of Paper for Printed Library Materials,
ANSI Z39.48—1984

To the Memory of My Parents

Mary Frances Washinka Woelfel
1908-2002
Warren Charles Woelfel
1909-2001

Contents

Preface		vii
1.	The Existentialist Legacy	1
2.	Existentialism Today	25
3.	Existentialist (Mis)Interpretation: Iris Murdoch	39
4.	Existentialism and Feminism: Simone de Beauvoir and Mary Daly	57
5.	Existentialism and the Problem of Freedom: Viktor Frankl	81
6.	Three Philosophical Autobiographies: Rousseau, Mill, Camus	93
7.	Pascal's Wager, Past and Present	107
8.	Evolution, Theism, and Naturalism	111
9.	The Faith of a Heretic: Walter Kaufmann	129
10.	Two Types of Religious and Secular World-Orientation	143

Preface

The Existentialist Legacy and Other Essays on Philosophy and Religion is a collection of ten essays on topics in the two primary areas of my research and teaching: existentialist philosophy and the philosophy of religion. The essays I have selected for this volume span more than twenty years, although all but a few represent recent and current work and the older ones have been revised and updated—in some cases, very substantially. Six of the essays have never appeared before in published form. In writing and selecting the essays for this volume I have often had students explicitly in mind, reflecting on issues that have arisen over many years of teaching and to some extent trying to address their questions.

The common thread running through these otherwise varied reflections is a way of approaching issues in philosophy and religion that reflects my career-long indebtedness to the methods and emphases of the existentialist movement in philosophy. The existentialists' enduring contribution is a richly textured *humanism*: careful description and analysis of common features of the concrete "life-world" experienced by human beings as subjects, and a critique of all forms of reductionism and objectification as complete accounts of what it means to be human. Within that framework, my appropriation of an existentialist perspective is by no means uncritical, as some of the essays in this volume make clear.

The topics and issues I address in the essays reflect what has been for me the inseparability and overlapping between the two areas of my research. I introduce the point of view in the title essay, "The Existentialist Legacy," by briefly recounting the story and main themes of existentialist philosophy, proposing a "Kierkegaardian model" for understanding the existentialist tradition. In "Existentialism Today" I extend the existentialist story to a contemporary intellectual context shaped by the new sciences of human nature and by postmodernism in the humanities. In the third essay, "Existentialist (Mis)Interpretation: Iris Murdoch," I examine philosopher and novelist Murdoch's appreciative, critical, and—it must be said—confused and inaccurate interpretation of existentialism, as exemplifying a chronic misunderstanding of the existentialist movement on the part of scholars, writers, and popularizers alike. I go on in the fourth essay, "Existentialism and Feminism," to examine the natural and fruitful relationship between existentialist and feminist thought, focusing on two eminent "second wave" feminist existentialists, Simone de Beauvoir and Mary Daly. In the fifth essay, "Existentialism and the Problem of Freedom," I offer a critical appraisal of the "high" existentialist doctrine of freedom using the test case of Viktor Frankl's psychologically-informed Holocaust memoirs. I find a more adequate vocabulary in the language of "possibility" with its roots in Kierkegaard's analysis of human selfhood and in William James's discussion of determinism and indeterminism.

"Three Philosophical Autobiographies," the sixth essay, is a study of three influential philosophical autobiographers—Jean-Jacques Rousseau, John Stuart Mill, and Albert Camus—designed to show what we can learn not only biographically but also philosophically from philosophers' accounts of their lives. From an existentialist perspective autobiography is a natural mode of philosophical expression, as the intensive self-reflection of a subject, and almost all the existentialist philosophers have written autobiographically. A sub-theme running through my study of Rousseau, Mill, and Camus is a common relationship to romanticism that binds together these otherwise disparate thinkers.

I begin a series of essays on philosophical issues in religion by first re-examining "Pascal's Wager, Past and Present" in the seventh essay, proposing that the Wager Argument is illuminating, no longer as an exercise in Christian apologetics, but as a kind of existentialist parable of reflective forms of theistic faith in modern Western culture. In the eighth essay, "Evolution, Theism, and Naturalism," I argue, appealing to the history of affirmative theological responses to evolution (with a special focus on Christian existentialism), that the only serious theological issue with regard to evolution is between theistic and naturalistic versions of evolutionism—not between "biblical creationism" and "godless evolution." In essay nine, "The Faith of a Heretic," I explore the creative contribution of German-American philosopher and Nietzsche scholar Walter Kaufmann as a philosopher of religion and suggest that in his original criticisms of theology and eloquent articulation of a religious skepticism he expressed a profoundly existentialist frame of mind. The tenth essay, "Two Types of Religious and Secular World-Orientation," is a phenomenological analysis of two types of sensibility, being "at home" and "not at home" in the world, which cut across the division between religious and secular ideas and patterns of life and help shed light on the familiar fact that some "believers" seem to have more in common with "unbelievers" than with some of their co-religionists.

The Existentialist Legacy seems to me to contribute distinctively to contemporary philosophical scholarship by showing the continuing applicability of existentialist themes and methods to a variety of issues in philosophy and religion, while at the same time offering internal criticism of the existentialist heritage. The collection also represents for me a bringing together of some of the main issues that have dominated my teaching and research throughout my career.

The book that most readily comes to mind as a similar sort of collection of wide-ranging essays on existentialist philosophy and religion is Walter Kaufmann's *Existentialism, Religion, and Death: Thirteen Essays* (1976). Gabriel Marcel's *Homo Viator* (1951) and *The Philosophy of Existentialism* (1956) were also books of essays exploring both philosophical and religious issues. A more recent example, and someone whose characteristic mode of publication is the essay collection, is Stanley Cavell, whose works encompass both analytic and Continental approaches to philosophy, literature, and film, as in his book *Philosophical Passages: Wittgenstein, Emerson, Austin, Derrida* (1995). I mention these eminent thinkers merely to point out that the "genre" represented by my book has worthy predecessors. Indeed, most of my own previous books have been collections of essays, often deliberately written with a view to incorporation in a book-length study having an overarching theme and approach, and substantially reworked for inclusion in such a study.

Preface

The original versions of the following essays, under different titles, appeared in the following publications: "Existentialism and the Problem of Freedom: Viktor Frankl" in *Journal of Social Philosophy* 13:3, September 1982; "Pascal's Wager, Past and Present" in Don Thompson *et al.*, eds., *Universality and History: Foundations of Core* (Lanham, MD: University Press of America, 2002); "The Faith of a Heretic: Walter Kaufmann" in *American Journal of Theology and Philosophy* 15:2, 1994; and "Two Types of Religious and Secular World-Orientation" in James Woelfel, *The Agnostic Spirit as a Common Motif in Liberal Theology and Liberal Scepticism* (Lewiston, NY: The Edwin Mellen Press, 1990).

Finally, a word about the way I have done citations throughout the book. I have avoided footnotes or endnotes, preferring the simplicity of the "author-date" system: indicating a source cited by the author's surname, the publication year, and the page numbers in parentheses in the text and providing at the end of the book a bibliography of all works cited. Following *Chicago Manual of Style* guidelines, I have made things even simpler by indicating only the year of publication the first time I mention an author and title without further specification, and only the page numbers when it is obvious what author and work I'm quoting from or referring to. My aim has been to distract the reader as little as possible from what I have to say in the essays.

James Woelfel
The University of Kansas
Lawrence, Kansas
August, 2005

Acknowledgments

I want to acknowledge with appreciation a sabbatical leave from the University of Kansas for the fall semester of 2004, which gave me the time I needed to bring the writing and revisions of the book to completion. My intellectual indebtedness extends to more people than I can remember and name who have contributed over many years to the creation and gestation of the themes and ideas in these essays—among them my constant partner in dialogue, Sarah Trulove, good friends and colleagues near and far, generations of my undergraduate and graduate students, and favorite philosophical authors like Albert Camus, Rudolf Bultmann, Viktor Frankl, and William James. None of them, of course, is to blame for whatever errors, misinterpretations, and other infelicities there are in the essays that follow. Finally, a very special word of thanks to Paula Courtney, director of KU's College of Liberal Arts & Sciences Word Processing Center, who transformed my very un-uniform documents into seamless camera-ready copy. Her expertise, efficiency, and graciousness have truly humanized the whole process of preparing the book for publication.

Grateful acknowledgment is made to the following publishers for permission to use quoted material:

From *Lyrical and Critical Essays* by Albert Camus, translated by Ellen Conroy Kennedy, copyright © 1968 by Alfred A. Knopf, a division of Random House, Inc. Copyright © 1967 by Hamish Hamilton Ltd and Alfred A. Knopf, a division of Random House, Inc. Used by permission of Alfred A. Knopf, a division of Random House, Inc.

From *The Black Prince* by Iris Murdoch, copyright © 1973 by Iris Murdoch. Used by permission of Viking Penguin, a division of Penguin Group (USA) Inc.

From *The Story I Tell Myself: A Venture in Existentialist Autobiography* by Hazel Barnes, copyright © 1997 by The University of Chicago Press. Used by permission of the author and the publisher.

– 1 –

The Existentialist Legacy

> ... if you were to ask me, I suppose that I would have to say, if awkwardly, "I am an existentialist." At a time when American philosophy is well on its way to becoming a respectable branch of cognitive science and a mandated prerequisite for law school, I find myself quaintly worrying about the significance of feelings, about who or what I really am and about the kinds of personal responsibilities that don't concern national policy and jurisprudence. In an age when philosophers have finally become professionals instead of street-corner kibitzers, I stubbornly believe that philosophy ought to speak to ordinary, intelligent people about personal worries, reflections, and experiences. It's embarrassing to be so out of style. (Robert Solomon, *From Hegel to Existentialism*, New York: Oxford University Press, 1987, vii)

1. The continuing popularity of existentialism

Existentialism is the only philosophical movement of the past hundred years to have captured the popular imagination, and its popularity has endured. There are of course the romantic associations that existentialism (mostly of the French variety) still conjures up—left-bank Paris cafes, *film noir*, the "theater of the absurd," student protests of the 1960s, and the bracing language of freedom and authenticity. A two-page Microsoft ad several years ago pictured two little girls saying, "'Forget Goldilocks and the Three Bears. . . . C'mon, Dad, tell us about Sartre and existentialism and his belief in the inescapable responsibility of all individuals for their decisions and his relationship with Simone de Beauvoir,' we pleaded as he tucked us in for the night." Comic books have featured a sequel to Samuel Beckett's *Waiting for Godot* (1954) and an "Existendo" game based on Albert Camus' *The Myth of Sisyphus* (1942). A postcard features a "Jean-Paul Sartre Lite" cartoon with the Sartre figure saying, "Being and Nothingness . . . . Go figure it." The Kevin Kline character in the 1980s film *A Fish Called Wanda* read Nietzsche and was a comical stereotype of Nietzsche's "superman." Woody Allen has written essays that are sendups of existentialist texts: for example, his "Notes from the Overfed," a parody of Dostoevsky's *Notes from Underground* (1864). The predictable Woody Allen character in his films is filled with "existential anxiety" about the meaning of life, and in *Annie Hall* is shown reading Ernest Becker's 1973 existentialist-psychoanalytic work *The Denial of Death*. A French film of the 1990s was entitled *The Diary of the Seducer*, and takes not only its title but also the initiating action of the plot from Kierkegaard's most popular work, a section of his book *Either/Or* (1843).

But is the legacy of existentialism anything more, in the early years of the twenty-first century, than an artifact of popular culture—"Existentialism Lite"? The answer, I believe, is an emphatic "Yes," and that is the theme of this essay—a theme that will manifest itself in a variety of ways throughout the book. I teach a course on existentialist thought almost every year. The course always enrolls well, and I am repeatedly struck by existentialism's continuing appeal to students and the philosophical excitement it engenders in them as they read and discuss the existentialist thinkers. I hope in this book to persuade my readers of the enduring appeal and contributions of the existentialist heritage. What that heritage discloses is the serious agenda that lies beneath the surface of the continuing popular images: an agenda that I think of as an *authentic humanism* which needs continuing reaffirmation in our time and in time to come. By that I mean that the existentialist writings profoundly illuminate the common features of how we actually experience and engage with ourselves, one another, and the world. In so doing they remain an abiding critique of all forms of reductionism and objectification—whether advanced in the name of biology, sociology, psychology, or cognitive science—insofar as they claim to be complete and fully coherent accounts of what it is to be human. They pose acutely, for humanists and scientists alike, the problem of doing justice to and reconciling what would seem to be a fundamental incommensurability between the ways we deal with the world as subjects and the ways we understand ourselves and the world theoretically and objectively.

I hasten to add that my generally existentialist approach to matters philosophical (and also theological and literary) is by no means uncritical, as this essay and some of those that follow will show. But my criticisms are a matter of sympathetic discussion and revision of a philosophical perspective that continues to be essential to our efforts to shed some light on the mystery of what it is to be human and a corrective to our persistent need to try to eliminate the mystery by truncation and oversimplification.

2. A brief history of existentialism

The cast of characters. The main sources of the existentialist movement in modern philosophy and literature were two nineteenth-century thinkers: the Danish writer Søren Kierkegaard (1813-1855) and the German philosopher Friedrich Nietzsche (1844-1900). A third important influence was the Russian novelist Fyodor Dostoevsky (1821-1881). In strikingly different ways, all three stand out from the times in which they lived because of their intense preoccupation with, and penetrating insight into, what it is to be a living, individual human subject engaged with the world and other human subjects. It was not until well into the twentieth century, however, that a diverse group of philosophers and writers came to be identified as a new intellectual and cultural movement, loosely grouped together because of their common focus on the character of "lived" human experience. It was the most famous of the existentialists, the Frenchman Jean-Paul Sartre (1905-1980), who actually coined the term "existentialism" in the 1940s, although other philosophers had been using similar terms for years. For example, one influential philosopher associated with existentialism, the German Karl Jaspers (1883-1969), began calling his ideas "existence-philosophy" early in the century, and at the end of the 1930s the French Algerian writer Albert Camus (1913-1960) was referring to various philosophers and writers as the "existentials."

The philosophers and writers we call existentialists were primarily associated with countries on the continent of Europe. In Britain and the United States very different philosophical developments such as logical empiricism and the philosophy of language came to dominate, although as we shall see existentialism has also had a significant influence. Perhaps the earliest of the twentieth-century existentialists was the Spaniard Miguel de Unamuno (1864-1936), a philosopher and novelist. His fellow countryman and younger contemporary José Ortega y Gasset (1883-1955) was a philosopher and social critic. Both were actively involved as republicans in the turbulent Spanish politics of their time. Two Russians, exiles from the Bolshevik Revolution of 1917 and heirs of the tradition of Dostoevsky, are included among the existentialists: the unconventional Orthodox Christian Nikolai Berdyaev (1874-1948) and the Jew Lev Shestov (1866-1938). Germany produced two important philosophers who contributed to the existentialist movement: Karl Jaspers, who was originally a physician and psychiatrist, and Martin Heidegger (1889-1976), a professor who wrote one of the twentieth century's most influential philosophical works, *Being and Time* (1927). Also from Germany were three of the leading religious thinkers of the twentieth century, all of whom have been associated with existentialism: Martin Buber (1878-1965), a Jewish philosopher whose impact on both Jewish and Christian religious thought was profound, and Paul Tillich (1886-1965) and Rudolf Bultmann (1884-1976), two of the major Protestant theologians of the twentieth century. Among the most prominent French intellectuals associated with existentialism were Sartre and Simone de Beauvoir (1908-86), who were both philosophers and widely-read writers of fiction; Maurice Merleau-Ponty (1908-1961), a distinguished academic with a special interest in psychology; and Gabriel Marcel (1889-1973), a Catholic philosopher and playwright. Albert Camus, a French colonial from Algeria and one of the most widely-read authors of the twentieth century, wrote philosophical essays, novels, and plays exploring the human condition.

Existentialism and the arts. Not coincidentally, several of the existentialist philosophers were also writers of novels, short stories, and plays. Imaginative literature has for centuries been an important vehicle for shedding light on what it is concretely to be a human being living in the world, which is precisely the central focus of existentialist philosophies. In addition to the writers mentioned above, other writers known exclusively or mainly for their fiction have been identified as "existentialists"—novelists, poets, and playwrights such as Leo Tolstoy (1828-1910), Franz Kafka (1883-1924), Rainer Maria Rilke (1875-1926), Hermann Hesse (1877-1962), T. S. Eliot (1888-1965), Samuel Beckett (1906-95), Eugene Ionesco (1912-96), Ralph Ellison (1914-94), Joseph Heller (1923-99), and Harold Pinter (1930-).

Existentialism also had an impact on the visual arts in the mid-twentieth century. In 1993 the Tate Gallery (now the Tate Britain) in London mounted an exhibition called *Paris Post War: Art and Existentialism 1945-55*, featuring the art of painters and sculptors closely associated with French existentialism such as Pablo Picasso, Alberto Giacometti, Antonin Artaud, and Jean Dubuffet. Sartre was a good friend and promoter of Giacometti, and wrote essays on his paintings and on his striking sculpture, with its emaciated and elongated human figures.

Existentialism and psychology. A prominent movement in twentieth-century psychology, "existential psychology," was also born out of existentialism. As a comprehensive exploration of human subjectivity, including the nature of consciousness and the role of intentions, feelings, and relationships in human life, existentialist thought clearly had important psychological implications. For some thinkers associated with the movement, building on the psychological insights of Kierkegaard and Nietzsche, those implications were quite explicit. Jaspers was himself a psychiatrist who always placed psychology within the context of wider philosophical issues. Sartre saw himself as developing a new alternative to Freudian psychoanalysis which he called "existential psychoanalysis." Among the existential psychologists were such distinguished psychiatrists as Viktor Frankl (1905-97) in Austria and Rollo May (1909-94) in the United States, and the Canadian cultural anthropologist Ernest Becker (1924-74).

Existentialism and religion. One common misconception about existentialism, due largely to the popular influence of Sartre and Camus, has been that it excludes religious belief of all kinds. According to the long-held popular caricature, and even in the writings of some scholars, the existentialists described human life and the universe as "meaningless" or "absurd" and without God, and their interest in exploring the moods of anxiety and despair was a reflection of what they believed to be our "abandoned" situation as human beings. It should have been clear already from the list of philosophers and writers above that this is not accurate. When we look at the various beliefs about religion held by those who have been associated with existentialism, a wide range of positions is apparent. Among the religious existentialists there have been devout Christians—Protestant, Catholic, and Orthodox—and Jews. Heidegger, nurtured and educated in the Catholic tradition and a convert to Lutheranism, was somewhat elusive about the question of God but insisted that he was not an atheist. Sartre and Beauvoir certainly considered themselves atheists, but Camus was searchingly and poignantly agnostic about religious claims, and even his emphasis on "absurdity" was a carefully-defined way of talking about the human situation vis-à-vis the world and not a declaration of atheism. Kierkegaard and Friedrich Nietzsche, two of the chief nineteenth-century sources of existentialism, are good examples of the religious diversity that has characterized the movement. Kierkegaard was a Protestant Christian who believed that Christian faith was the highest and fullest expression of human subjectivity. Nietzsche, on the other hand, was quite hostile to the Christian religion and believed it to be the great enemy to individual self-knowledge, freedom, creativity, and active engagement with the world.

Impact of the two world wars. Significantly, all the leading figures associated with twentieth-century existentialism lived through World War I (1914-18) and the dramatic social, political, artistic, and intellectual changes it brought about in Europe. Some, like Heidegger, Tillich, and Bultmann, did military service during the war. Others "came of age" as young adults during the 1920s and 1930s, a period fraught with hope, despair, confusion, and upheaval that resulted from the aftermath of the most devastating war the world had known up to that time. All had their thinking profoundly shaped—in some cases decisively—by the war and the post-war developments it produced. Most lived to see yet another global conflagration, World War II, and some of the French existentialists—notably Camus and Merleau-Ponty (and to a lesser degree Sartre)—participated in that war as combatants or members of the Resistance movement. Ideas that were completely "against the stream" when Kierkegaard, Nietzsche, and Dostoevsky set them forth as lonely prophets in the nineteenth century, came to have a striking relevance in a Europe convulsed by two world wars and severe economic depression in between.

Existentialism in America and Britain. For Americans, who were not popularly introduced to existentialism until after 1945, William Barrett's lively and accessible 1958 introduction to existentialism, *Irrational Man*, both announced and epitomized the movement at its high tide as a major intellectual and cultural phenomenon. It was standard for commentators on current philosophical trends in the 1940s, '50s, and '60s to refer to "Continental" existentialism and "Anglo-American" philosophies of language as the two great contemporary "schools of thought"—sharply separated not only by geographical regions but also by their assumptions and methods, and not really speaking to each other.

But while analytic philosophy has been heavily dominant in the U.S., existentialism has had important American precursors and representatives. For example, during the last part of the nineteenth and the early twentieth centuries one of America's most original philosophers, the Pragmatist William James, developed a philosophical outlook he called "radical empiricism": a holistic and richly textured approach to the analysis of human experience that in its emphasis on the immediacy and irreducibility of individual subjectivity bears striking resemblances to those of the existentialists. Also closely related have been those philosophies grouped together under the term "personalism." Personalism in philosophy is predicated on the irreducibility and primacy of the categories that characterize human beings as personal and interpersonal subjects, such as values, choices, and relationships—themes that overlap a great deal with those of existentialism. In the U.S. there was a whole school of thought associated with Boston University, the Boston Personalists, that had a long and continuous tradition beginning in the late nineteenth century and continuing through the twentieth. Its founding figure was Borden Parker Bowne (1847-1910) and perhaps its most influential exponent was Edgar S. Brightman (1884-1953). Its best-known adherent was Martin Luther King, Jr. (1929-68), who earned his doctorate at Boston University in the 1950s and always called his philosophical-theological outlook a personalism.

Then there are the many Americans—philosophers, theologians, writers—who have been directly associated with existentialism through much of the twentieth and into the twenty-first centuries. (The definitive account of the neglected story of American existentialism is George Cotkin's *Existential America*.) As early as the 1930s there were pioneering American scholars of existentialism such as Walter Lowrie and David Swenson, the first translators of Kierkegaard into English. They were closely followed, in the 1940s and 1950s, by interpreters such as William Barrett; Walter Kaufmann, translator and interpreter of Nietzsche and influential commentator on the existentialists; and Hazel Barnes, the English translator of Sartre's *Being and Nothingness* and herself a distinguished and creative contributor to existentialist thought.

If many philosophy departments in the United States were ignoring existentialism during the decades of the 1940s, '50s, and '60s, theological seminaries and departments of religion were definitely not. Since the dominant developments particularly in Protestant theology in the twentieth century were directly influenced by and bound up with existentialist philosophy, American students of religion were significantly influenced by existentialism through such influential figures as Buber, Bultmann, and Tillich, and also American theologians such as Reinhold Niebuhr, H. Richard Niebuhr, and David Roberts. Among prominent American writers who were deeply influenced by existentialist thought were Ralph Ellison, John Updike, and Walker Percy. Today, although the analytic tradition still dominates, the philosophical landscape in the U.S. has become more diverse, with the perspectives and methods of "Continental" philosophy, both existentialist and post-existentialist, widely represented among both faculty and graduate students, and some philosophers who have sought to "build bridges" between the two traditions in their work. I headed this chapter with a quotation from one of America's most distinguished contemporary philosophers, Robert Solomon of the University of Texas, who still calls himself an existentialist and has written very substantially on existentialist themes and philosophers.

In Britain, the home of analytic philosophy, there were also alternative and counter philosophical currents. One of the most popular nonfiction books of the 1950s, on both sides of the Atlantic, was Colin Wilson's *The Outsider* (1956), a philosophical and literary study particularly of the French existentialists. Wilson went on to write novels, plays, and essays on a bewildering number of topics, but he has continued to see himself as standing broadly in the existentialist tradition. Almost alone among British philosophers of the 1950s and 1960s, Iris Murdoch took seriously and published books and essays on existentialism and particularly Sartre. I will have occasion in the third essay to examine her appreciative but critical relationship to existentialism. (She was also a prolific novelist who explored the connections between philosophy and literature.) There was a distinctively twentieth-century Scottish tradition in philosophy and theology that went its own way, very much influenced by developments on the European continent. The thought of its earlier leaders, such as H. R. Mackintosh, John Baillie, Donald Baillie, and Edgar Dickie, was shaped by German philosophers such as Buber and theologians such as Karl Barth, Emil Brunner, Karl Heim, and Rudolf Bultmann. A second generation of Scottish theologians who were explicitly existentialists and wrote books on existentialist thought included John Macquarrie, one of Britain's most distinguished theologians of the second half of the twentieth century and an authority on Heidegger and Bultmann, and Ronald Gregor Smith, the original translator of Buber's *I and Thou*. In philosophy John Macmurray, who preceded A. J. Ayer as Grote Professor of Mind and Logic at University College, London, developed a version of personalism with striking similarities to the analyses of human beings as active subjects in interpersonal relation that we find among the existentialist thinkers.

3. Historical sources and influences

While existentialism is certainly a product of the nineteenth and twentieth centuries, it has, like all significant ideas, deep historical roots. Existentialist themes can be found in writings as old as the biblical story of Job and the conversations of Socrates in Plato's dialogues, as well as in the writings of the Church Father Augustine, the Renaissance humanist Pico della Mirandola, Luther, and Shakespeare. The seventeenth-century mathematician and scientist Blaise Pascal, in his religious writings, was a direct predecessor, showing remarkable resemblances to, and influencing, later existentialists from Kierkegaard to Camus. (In essay seven I will suggest a new existential interpretation of Pascal's famous "Wager" argument.) Coming closer in time to the beginnings of existentialism were the romantic poets, novelists, philosophers, and theologians of the late eighteenth and early nineteenth centuries: writers such as Wordsworth and Shelley in England, Goethe and Schleiermacher in Germany, Madame de Staël and Lamartine in France, and Emerson and Thoreau in America. The romantic emphasis on personal self-expression, individual freedom, and social criticism contributed importantly to the mental climate out of which existentialism emerged. These varied sources can certainly be read as foreshadowing the nineteenth- and twentieth-century existentialists, displaying a common interest in the contingency and fragility of human existence, the primacy of desire and emotions in human life, the limits of reason, the mystery of life's meaning, and the deceit and artificiality—the "inauthenticity"—that often characterizes our lives as human beings. So while issues such as these are central to the subject-matter of existentialism in the nineteenth and twentieth centuries, they have a rich history with ancient roots—and precisely because they are issues bound up with the very meaning of what it is to be human in any age.

The existentialists were also indebted, in a variety of ways, to the two most important shapers of modern European philosophical thought: Kant and Hegel. The critical philosophy of Immanuel Kant (1724-1804) constitutes a modern intellectual watershed. Analyzing the nature, scope, and limits of human knowledge, Kant argued, first, that the human mind actively constructs the data of sense experience into an ordered and intelligible world through categories in the mind itself. Secondly, in its efforts to make sense of things the mind is limited in its theoretical capacity to understanding the world as it appears to the senses, the *phenomenal* world studied by the natural sciences. Thirdly, Kant tried to show that the mind has access to "metaphysical" or *noumenal* realities beyond the phenomenal world—the self in its freedom or capacity for choice, the existence of God, and immortality—only as practical postulates or beliefs that are needed to make sense of our moral life. Beginning with Kierkegaard, the existentialists generally have inherited and carried forward Kant's emphasis on the active role of the mind in shaping the human world, the limitations of reason to the finite or natural sphere, and the practical or "existential" nature of our beliefs about our own freedom and selfhood and whatever realities may transcend the world of the senses and empirical knowledge.

G. W. F. Hegel (1770-1831) built upon Kant's intellectual revolution, but believed Kant had been arbitrary in leaving us with a complete dichotomy between phenomena and noumena. If the human mind actively constructs the meaning of the universe of phenomena through categories within itself, Hegel reasoned, then the mind is the clue to understanding the whole of reality, and indeed all of reality—both nature and culture—is the unfolding manifestation of mind (or spirit, as Hegel typically called it). He created a systematic speculative philosophy that sought to encompass the whole of reality, finite and infinite. In influential works like his *Phenomenology of Spirit* (1807) Hegel argued that the emergence of human consciousness marks a sharp break in the order of nature, the appearance of a being capable of self-awareness and reflection, which "becomes itself" through a dynamic or "dialectical" unfolding or development in time. Kierkegaard appropriated Hegel's characterization of human existence as the becoming of consciousness in time through stages of opposition and resolution (the dialectic) and borrowed some of his terminology. But Kierkegaard vigorously rejected Hegel's subsuming of the individual subject and its concrete existence under an abstract universal human consciousness and world-process, and likewise rejected his assumption that finite reason can encompass all of reality in a rational system. Twentieth-century existentialists such as Sartre and Beauvoir were influenced by Hegel's analysis of the development of human subjectivity and borrowed some of his vocabulary. But along with Kierkegaard, the existentialists unanimously rejected Hegel's abstract subsuming of the individual entirely under the collective human consciousness, applying his ideas instead to the study of individual subjectivity, and they denied the capacity of finite intelligence to comprehend rationally the whole or the infinite.

Standing in the tradition begun by Descartes and revolutionized by Kant, both of whom grounded philosophy in the activity of human consciousness, Edmund Husserl (1859-1938) is a third important figure, as one who contributed influentially to the existentialist movement as an older contemporary rather than a predecessor. If Hegel had laid the foundations, Husserl became the leading twentieth-century figure in the development of what is called *phenomenology*. The phenomenologist tries to develop appropriate methods to describe the active relationship of human consciousness to what appears (the meaning of "phenomena") to it. Central to the project is the characterization of consciousness as *intentional*: it is always directed toward an object, whether something in nature, a person, or an idea. Consciousness furthermore constitutes its objects as meaningful. Husserl himself "bracketed" all questions of the independent reality of consciousness and its objects, in an effort to create a pure "science" of phenomenology using precise methods to analyze universal structures of meaning disclosed through intentionality. Husserl had a direct and fundamental influence on the philosophies of Heidegger, Sartre, and Merleau-Ponty. Each of them deviated, however, from Husserl in believing that their task was to use the methods of phenomenology as a way of illuminating universal characteristics of "lived" human experience. Because of their work phenomenological analysis has been in a

4. Søren Kierkegaard: the "father" of existentialism

Søren Kierkegaard (1813-55) was born and lived almost all of his short life in Copenhagen, the capital and cultural and intellectual center of Denmark. As a student at the University of Copenhagen he lived a "playboy" life until his father's death caused him to devote himself more seriously to his studies, and he ended up earning both bachelor's and master's degrees in theology. The two most important personal influences in his life were his father and the fiancée he never married. His father, a wealthy self-made cloth merchant, was something of an intellectual and a devout but guilt-ridden Christian who passed on to Søren his faith, his love of argument, and his melancholy. After a year's engagement (1840-41) to Regina Olsen, Kierkegaard broke it off, partly because of his fear of injecting gloom into her cheerful life and partly because of his growing conviction that God was calling him to a vocation as a Christian writer-witness that prevented him from leading a normal life. It was the breakup with Regina—whom he loved deeply until his death—that made him a writer. In his early, "aesthetic" writings he translated their love and the marriage he had rejected into universal metaphors of human experience, and he dedicated the whole of his authorship to her.

Between 1843 and his death in 1855, Kierkegaard wrote some eighteen books and a number of shorter pieces. Almost all were directed to his single-minded purpose of "reintroducing Christianity into 'Christendom.'" He confronted a society in which Christianity had been the official religion for centuries (in Denmark, the state-supported Danish Lutheran Church) and was thus taken for granted, with what he believed to be New Testament Christianity in all its stringency. Kierkegaard believed that Christianity's entire focus was on the individual human being in his or her life and relationship to God. In his writings he explored the depths of what it is to be an individual subject in the world and the different ways people choose to live their lives. He attacked every form of thinking—above all the philosophy of the most influential philosopher of his time, Hegel—that ignored the individual person or subsumed the individual under some grand scheme. Most of his earlier writings (1843-46) he called "aesthetic." He wrote them under pseudonyms in order to communicate his message indirectly, to begin with his contemporaries where they were rather than simply throwing the Christian message at them. In the early writings he used a wide array of genres and literary devices, expressing himself with striking originality in novels, fictional journals and letters, poetic essays, and extended aphorisms. Kierkegaard's brilliant explorations of human selfhood, in the service of leading people to Christian faith, laid the foundations of existentialism.

Kierkegaard's philosophical reflections begin where Descartes' end. Whereas Descartes' skeptical doubts finally find an end in the *cogito*—the self as a thinking being, a mind—Kierkegaard suggests that a thinking subject is unable to find rest in thought alone, because a mind is never at rest but is always in the process of change. The object of thought and the existentially thinking subject (the one who is doing the thinking) cannot be made one, says Kierkegaard, in the way Descartes had hoped. Nor can rational thought ever completely escape the human subject. If we involve ourselves in a rational inquiry such as science or philosophy, according to Kierkegaard, then we must be consciously aware of the fact that it is an existing human being who is doing the investigating, and that there is no way finally to escape the human subject and attain complete objectivity. This emphasis on the primacy of the concretely existing human being in his or her subjectivity is forcefully presented and developed by Kierkegaard in his most important philosophical book, *Concluding Unscientific Postscript to the Philosophical Fragments* (1846).

Kierkegaard held that any attempt to reduce human beings to or understand them as wholly rational beings leaves out one important fact of human life: that human beings are finite, temporal beings who are always in the process of becoming something new. Rational inquiries try to systematize, fully explain, and completely capture that changing existence. What such rational ambitions forget, however, according to Kierkegaard, is that rational systems are not a "view from nowhere." Rational understandings of the world and of human beings within it necessarily require human subjects in intersubjective relationship in order to be possible. Since human subjects are temporal, finite, changing beings, those qualities will always be a part of the rational understanding that human beings achieve. Hence, for Kierkegaard, complete and final rational understanding is impossible for human beings.

There is only one kind of being, according to Kierkegaard, who could have such complete and final knowledge. It "is he who is outside of existence yet in existence... it is God." (Kierkegaard [1846] (1992), 119) Since human beings are not God, they can only hope for limited understandings of themselves and the world. We must come to see human life as a persistent striving for truth without any hope of fully achieving that truth. Life is a struggle to achieve the unattainable. Human life is in a constant state of becoming and it cannot be fully or completely systematized or understood. Wonder and mystery will always be a part of human existence.

Furthermore, said Kierkegaard, in their concrete existence and at the deepest level human beings are just as much creatures of passion and will as we are "rational animals." Our lives are largely governed by our feelings, desires, and choices. Humans do indeed uniquely possess the remarkable capacity to reason that has given us language, knowledge, and the other achievements that set us apart from nature. But we must *choose* to use our reason or not, and our desires and feelings direct us to what we choose to reason *about*. The most important questions in life—whether there is a God, how we ought to live, what is the meaning and destiny of our lives—cannot be answered by reason alone, but only by the whole person's seeking and choosing answers with what Kierkegaard called the "passion of the infinite." For Kierkegaard himself the most satisfactory answer was faith in the "Absolute Paradox"—God come among us as a human being in the person of Christ—but he emphasized how repellent to reason such a paradox was and how only through the passion of faith could a person embrace it.

How, then, according to Kierkegaard, is a person to live in light of the facts of our existence as living subjects? Kierkegaard offered an "either/or" answer. A person can *either* "do everything to forget he is existing" and thus become contradictory and comical, because "existence possesses the remarkable quality that an existing person exists whether he wants to or not"; *or* "he can direct all his attention to his existing" (120). Kierkegaard believes that the person who does the latter will come to recognize that human life is a ceaseless process defined by finite individual subjects' desires and choices. To such a person it will be clear that the idea of human existence as a never-ending striving is the only view of life that does not carry with it an inevitable disillusionment. This claim became a common one in existentialist writing, and it is one of the reasons Kierkegaard is considered foundational to any study of existentialism. Life, he attempts to show us, is a constant struggle that requires individual persistence, passion, and conscious choice if it is to have any meaning.

5. Main themes of existentialist thought

With such a large and diverse group of philosophers and writers identified with the movement, existentialism must be seen as a large intellectual "tent" accommodating much variety rather than as a well-defined "school of thought." At the same time, there are good reasons why people have lumped all these thinkers and writers together, common themes to which they give voice in many different ways.

What it is to be a subject. At the very core of existentialism is the recognition that among the things that make up the world, humans (perhaps not exclusively) are characterized by *subjectivity*, the quality of being subjects. Subjectivity is awareness that is *self-awareness*, which means that humans are not only aware of the world around them but are also aware that they are aware—aware of themselves as subjects. Subjectivity is what Sartre calls a *transcendence*: it transcends or "goes beyond" everything else in the world, in the sense that everything other than the subject is what it is *for* a subject. As a subject I am not reducible to or identical with anything that I am aware of. I can distinguish myself as subject not only from things in the world and other people, but even from my own body, my feelings, my thoughts, my past or my future, or my circumstances. All these things can and do become objects for my self-awareness.

As Sartre also emphasized, the fact that as a subject I am an awareness that is distinguishable from everything it is aware of also means that subjectivity is always elusive and unstable. It is an active, interpreting matrix for all that I experience, but is itself non-objectifiable—what Sartre called a "nothingness" in relation to the solid world of objects or "being." Every attempt I make to define myself, to form an image of myself, as a substantial or permanent "I" or "ego" is a form of objectification and thus doomed to failure, because as a subject I always transcend my self-definition at any given time. Hence as subjects we are dynamic, never-finished, ever-changing creatures who define and redefine ourselves as we live out our lives.

The quality of being a subject manifests itself in those fundamental and defining human activities such as existing embedded in a social relationship of interdependence with other persons and the physical environment; within that context, creating, learning, and dwelling in a richly symbolic world of thinking and speaking, gesture and art; experiencing the world through a range of moods and feelings, interpretations and values; remembering, anticipating, and hoping; making choices and projecting goals; examining one's own thoughts, feelings, and choices as a kind of internal observer; and knowing that one will die. Existentialist inquiry focuses on illuminating these aspects of "lived" human experience as *universal characteristics of human subjectivity.*

Let me explain further what I mean by "universal characteristics of subjectivity," and why they consist of the features of human experience I have referred to above. In trying to understand what I am as a human being, what it is to be human, the most fundamental question to ask is: what do I have in common with all other human beings?, because only those things we all have in common will count as universal characteristics. Obviously there is a biological answer: we are all bipedal mammals of the genus *homo* and the species *sapiens*, with a certain evolutionary history and genetic code. That is a necessary but by no means a sufficient account of what we have in common, because as subjects we experience ourselves and live our lives as much more than our biology. So the more interesting and important sense of the question is: what do I have in common with all other human beings *as subjects*, as knowers and actors living out our lives in the world? The tools for reflection are 1) careful introspection and observation of myself and those around me, for which some of the existentialists developed and adapted formal philosophical methods such as phenomenological analysis; together with 2) the study of human beings past and present through history, anthropology, sociology, psychology, literature, and all the other ways we have developed of acquiring knowledge of humans as subjects acting in the world. These two approaches are inseparable as sources of knowledge and bases for criticism and corroboration.

What are we looking for when we try by these methods to find "universal characteristics of subjectivity"? We're looking for those qualities of self-awareness that manifest themselves in all human times and places, from the person who created the first known image of a human being, the Venus of Willendorf statue, 30,000 years ago to the contemporary computer user clicking on to hundreds of different icons that bring the world to her fingertips. In order to do this we have to get behind the mind-boggling cultural and individual diversity among human beings to the common human activities that are manifested in and through such diversity. We have to uncover what we share regardless of genetic individuality, gender, race and ethnicity, religion, nationality, class, education, work, relationships, culture, and historical period. And what we find is that all human beings as subjects are creatures who are self-aware, live interdependently in communities and with the physical world, construct symbolic meanings, pursue values, remember and interpret the past and project the future, make choices and assume responsibilities, dwell in moods, and experience ourselves as finite and living toward death.

I want to pause here to clarify my use of "subjectivity" in connection with the existentialists in order to avoid misunderstanding. "Subjectivity" here means simply the property of being a subject, which includes those qualities I have listed above under self-awareness. By contrast, the term *subjectivism*, with which it might possibly be confused, refers to specific theories which hold that knowledge and values are entirely expressions of the individual subject's perceptions, feelings, and intentions. Human *subjects* may hold a wide variety of theories of what constitutes knowing and valuing, only one of which is *subjectivism*. Similarly, we typically distinguish between the adjectives *subjective* and *objective*. In this essay I am using the term "subjective" as the adjectival form of "subjectivity": that is, as referring to the qualities human beings have as subjects. I'm not using the term in its other senses, as 1) particular to a given individual, entirely personal, as when we speak of a "subjective experience"; 2) existing only within the experiencer's mind, incapable of external verification, as in the case of illusions and hallucinations; or 3) ideas, beliefs, and attitudes that simply express an individual's state of mind without regard for what is actually the case, as when we speak of "subjective opinions." "Objective" can mean 1) having actual existence or actual reality outside the subject's mind, or, as applied to the activity of the mind, 2) setting aside, as much as possible, purely personal considerations in order to attain accurate knowledge or be fair-minded—minimizing the influence of one's own feelings, beliefs, and opinions. Hence one of the ways in which a subject expresses its subjectivity is by trying to be objective!

Two more clarifications on the nature of subjectivity: 1) To say that human beings are subjects is not the same thing as, nor does it entail, the view that mind and body are two separate entities or that we are immortal souls. In speaking of individuals as subjects the existentialists are describing phenomenologically the distinctive and self-defining characteristics of those psychophysical entities we call human beings. It may well be that subjectivity is entirely a function of our existence as living organisms, beginning with birth, or even at some indeterminate point after birth, and ending with death. Some of the religious existentialists, such as Kierkegaard and Marcel, believed that the human subject is also an immortal soul, but as a theological belief that undergirded their philosophical explorations. The nonreligious existentialists, such as Sartre and Camus, described the phenomenon of subjectivity without recourse either to mind/body dualism or to theological beliefs about God and immortality.

2) Nor does focusing on humans in their subjectivity entail any particular view about the similarities and differences between human beings and other animals. It doesn't require that we assert that human subjectivity is unique, or even sharply differentiated from the subjectivity of other highly complex mammals such as our primate cousins, with some of whom we share 98% of our genes, or cetaceans. Clearly, a combination of features of human beings such as living on land, brain size, a long period of infantile dependence, grasping thumbs, bipedality and walking upright, and complex language capability have contributed to our distinctive and dominating culture. But some of those characteristics are shared with other "higher" mammals. The main thing is that we know what hu-

mans are by being them, whereas we can only understand other mammals by observation and very limited forms of communication.

Freedom and responsibility. As subjects we are creatures who because of our subjectivity are always more than the sum of our attempts to define ourselves. At birth we are biologically *homo sapiens* shaped by the species' evolutionary history, with a unique genetic makeup that determines everything from gender to predispositions to certain diseases, socially members of a certain family, and participants in a particular culture. But what we become as an individual will also be shaped by the subjective choices we make within the "givens" of heredity and environment: how we interpret our context and ourselves, what goals we seek, what decisions we make, what values we embrace.

All the existentialists have insisted, in varying degrees, on freedom and its correlate, responsibility or accountability, as essential characteristics of what it is to be human. While heredity and environment *condition* what we are as individuals—in many respects quite heavily and often to an indeterminate degree—they do not completely *determine* our identity. The "givens" of our heredity and environment are always "given" *to* us and *for* us as subjects who are not simply identical with those givens, and what they mean and what we do with them are always matters of interpretation and choice. The scope of freedom may vary considerably among individual persons, from extremely narrow to quite broad, because of the substantial weight and subtle interplay of genetic and social factors in shaping who we are, but as a subjectivity, the existentialists claim, no human being is totally determined. For all the existentialists, human freedom also means that through the interaction of our choices with the people and the world around us we are always directed toward a future that is, to however small a degree, not fully predictable. To the extent that a person chooses freely she is also responsible or accountable for her choices.

The fact that we are shaped to an indeterminately large extent by hereditary and environmental conditions means that we are susceptible to being both hurt and helped by those conditions. To claim that as a subject I am free doesn't mean that I escape the harm of a genetic predisposition to a certain form of cancer or the violence and injustice of living in an oppressive society; nor does it mean that I am not healed and restored by surgery or psychotherapy or by a secure and just political and social context in which I can thrive. But what the attention to freedom as an aspect of subjectivity does mean is that all the conditions that mould and influence me for good and ill are what they are *for me* as a subject who interprets them and decides how to deal with them.

The existentialist argument for freedom and against determinism is an appeal to the phenomenological analysis of subjectivity. It is the character of "lived" self-awareness, as transcending its objects and constituting itself by its choices, that is the existentialists' evidence for a measure of freedom or indeterminacy in human behavior, not metaphysical and scientific arguments about free will and determinism. The latter debate has been going on for centuries and remains unresolved. In the fifth essay I will offer criticisms of what I call the "high" existentialist doctrine of freedom as extreme and incoherent, and suggest an alternative way of speaking that also has roots in the existentialist tradition.

The flight from freedom and responsibility. The other side of the existentialists' emphasis on individual freedom and responsibility has been their illuminating analyses of the many ways in which human beings persistently try to *evade or deny* freedom and responsibility. Kierkegaard set true individuality over against the tendency of individuals to lose themselves in the "crowd" or the "public," and was a powerful critic of the society of his day in his native Denmark. Heidegger talked about *Das Man*, the anonymous or "they"-self of everyday life, which passively conforms to what "they" (the surrounding society) say and do. He describes this state as a "falling away" from what we are as finitely free beings, characterized by the tranquillizing, disintegration, and alienation of the self. Sartre formulated our flight from freedom in the expression "bad faith" (*mauvaise foi*) or self-deception. The realization that we have the capacity for choice and are to that extent responsible for what we make of ourselves fills us with anxiety or anguish (*angoisse*), and we typically flee from our freedom, making deterministic excuses for ourselves by explaining and justifying our choices on the basis of our heredity and environment. Heidegger has given us the general terms in which these issues are discussed: *authenticity* and *inauthenticity*. Authenticity refers to trying as much as possible to live my life in the conscious awareness that I am free and therefore responsible for what I do and make of myself. It is "becoming what I am," since as subjects humans are, to however limited a degree, free. Inauthenticity refers to all the ways in which I try to escape from my freedom—through mindless conformity and conventionality, going along with the crowd, making excuses for myself. It is refusing to become what I am. Achieving authenticity is a lifelong struggle that has to be repeatedly renewed, because of our fear of freedom, our inertia, and our need for social belonging and acceptance. It is a struggle that in many cases, as Beauvoir sensitively recognized, is also to an indeterminately large degree shaped and impeded by oppressive life-circumstances such as poverty, abuse, mental illness, physical or mental disability, discrimination, and political violence and repression.

Morality and moral failure. My presentation of the existentialists on the flight from freedom and responsibility, on "authenticity" and "inauthenticity," is perhaps the appropriate point at which to raise and try to address briefly the questions of morality and its failures in existentialist thought. I have said that one of the universal characteristics of human subjectivity is living our lives in terms of meanings and values—religious, ethical, aesthetic, political, economic, personal—and as inherently choice-making beings appropriating and deciding on the basis of those meanings and values. As the nineteenth-century British poet and cultural critic Matthew Arnold famously observed, morality or "conduct" is "three-fourths of life." Since for the existentialists concrete human living is defined and thoroughly pervaded by values and choices, an emphasis on ethics is central to existentialism. Having said that, I hasten to add that there is not a common "existentialist ethics" to which the various thinkers and writers would subscribe. Authenticity is "good" and inauthenticity is "bad," in the sense that it is better to live consciously in the awareness that as a subject I am responsible for what I do with my life and how I treat other persons than it is to avoid or escape that reality ignorantly through oppressive circumstances or consciously through making excuses for myself. Authenticity would seem to involve the moral values of integrity and honesty as well as self-knowledge—being "true to oneself." But as has often been observed, there doesn't seem to be any contradiction in saying that a person could be quite conscious of and assume full responsibility for acts of indifference and cruelty to others or for a life of crime or conquest. It has often puzzled and disturbed his interpreters that during the 1930s Martin Heidegger apparently believed that being a loyal Nazi was, at least for Germans, the highest expression of living authentically.

What is common to the existentialists is what we might call the "meta-ethical" foundations of ethics in human experience: the universal and essential role of meanings, values, choice, and responsibility in human life. Beyond that there is diversity and disagreement. Some of the thinkers associated with existentialism, notably Nietzsche, Sartre, and Beauvoir, believed that humans freely invent all values; there are no universal moral principles given in the nature of things but only postulates of subjectivity. Others, such as Kierkegaard, Dostoevsky, Marcel, Camus, and Frankl, believed that there are universal moral imperatives either grounded in God or yielded by the human condition, and human beings discover and appropriate (or fail to appropriate) them through their choices. In his early books *Either/Or* and *Fear and Trembling* (1843), Kierkegaard seems to have adopted a concrete, existentialized version of Kant's ethics of categorical moral duties universally known to human beings, as modified and intensified by the higher, "revealed" moral demands of Christ. Martin Buber grounded an ethics of love and justice toward others in his analysis of what he called the "I-Thou" relationship as one of the two fundamental and essential relationships of humans to the world (the other being the "I-It" relationship). Camus, in his post-war writings, worked out a universal ethics arising from the human experience of resistance to and revolt against oppression, which he believed brought to light the values of honesty and lucidity, respect for human life and strict limits on what one individual may do to another, rejection of all forms of moral and political absolutism and authoritarianism, and solidarity with other human beings in their suffering and happiness. In general, we can say that the common existentialist description of human beings in terms of their unique individual subjectivity, together with the inherently social or intersubjective character of human life, would seem to provide at least a foundation for an ethics of respect for and sensitivity to persons and a rejection of all attempts to reduce them to objects.

But of course any approach to ethics has to take into account the persistent failures of human beings in their efforts to be moral. More than that, it has to deal with the appalling record of our inhumanity to one another, at both the "micro" level of interpersonal relations and the "macro" level of society and politics: the many forms of cruelty and destruction we inflict on one another (and on ourselves). Again, those thinkers associated with the existentialist movement have by no means been of one mind on this issue. An interesting question is whether the universal reality of moral failure should be included among the universal characteristics of the subjective human "life-world" that existentialists analyze. I definitely believe it should, and I think it is fair to say that all the philosophers associated with existentialism include in their analyses of lived human experience some account of the aspects of subjectivity that give rise to moral failure, as for example the human tendency to evade responsibility for one's actions that I've highlighted.

The existentialists did not, generally speaking, appeal to scientific knowledge of human nature—which today would be found primarily in evolutionary psychology, cognitive science, genetics, and neuroscience—for the light it can shed on the problematic character of the human situation: for example, the conflict between what cognitive scientist Steven Pinker calls the "moral sense" and deeply rooted aggressive and self-interested tendencies in human nature. Nietzsche did try to explain human perversity psychophysically and deterministically, but in that he was decidedly unexistentialist—indeed, anti-existentialist. Frankl and Sartre incorporated psychoanalytic ideas, but with their firm rejection of any sort of psychobiological determinism (and Sartre's rejection of the idea of the unconscious) neither saw psychoanalytic explanation as ultimately decisive. In fairness to the existentialist failure to incorporate scientific data on moral failure, it must be said that during the existentialist era social-scientific inquiry into human behavior was dominant, with its emphasis on social and cultural environment rather than genetic and evolutionary characteristics as shapers of behavior, and the reigning models saw human beings as infinitely malleable.

When all is said and done, the existentialists were no more or less successful in explaining the chronic difficulties of human relationship, community, and society than anyone else. Sartre probably offered the most thorough and penetrating account, with his theory of the inherent instability of consciousness, manifested in the desire for solidity, the evasion of responsibility through "bad faith," and the inevitable objectifying of other persons; but Sartre's account is in important respects both extreme and insufficient. Camus, acutely aware of his own moral fallibility and failures, was appalled by the suffering humans cause to one another but did not speculate about the reasons. He believed that all one can do is to try actively to alleviate suffering, in one or more of the many ways open to us, and to exhort others to do the same. The Christian existentialists had recourse to the idea of sin, in its proper ontological sense of universal estrangement from God, as an explanation, but of course they imported the idea from their theology into their philosophical considerations. Kierkegaard brilliantly analyzed the Christian doctrine of original sin in psychological terms in his book *The Concept of Anxiety*, bequeathing to the existentialist movement the central importance of anxiety as the mood accompanying the emergence of the awareness and exercise of "possibility" in the individual; but of course hardly any of the later existentialists who adopted and adapted that analysis also accepted the doctrine of original sin. Perhaps the distinctive contribution of existentialist thought generally to the problem of moral failure is to have insisted that it cannot simply be reduced to biological, environmental, and other determining conditions but is in its depths a failure of "spirit"—of the human being as subject.

The limits of reason. Beginning with Kierkegaard's attack on Hegel's system, the existentialists argued that existence cannot be categorized and systematized in any complete and final kind of way. Human subjects (and the universe itself) are inexhaustible in their concrete richness and complexity, and human beings are finite and always in process or "becoming." So no rational system, whether traditional speculative philosophy or modern science, can do more than describe and synthesize a range of aspects of reality, and those who construct such systems deceive themselves if they think they can encompass the whole. Such schemes, which can be quite valuable as illuminating and enriching our knowledge of the world, typically succeed either by treating human beings entirely in terms of objective knowledge or by assuming that reason enables humans to understand the universe from the standpoint of a kind of godlike "view from nowhere." The rejection of all such claims to rational completeness and objectivity was powerfully articulated by Kierkegaard and reaffirmed by his existentialist successors.

We have acquired an enormous amount of knowledge about ourselves and the world through the natural and social sciences—knowledge which, although always open to revision, it would be foolish in the extreme to gainsay. The ideal of objectivity, of dispassionate inquiry, has been essential in the development of human knowledge, as has been the belief in or assumption of causality. The task of understanding the world and ourselves through the methods and the conclusions of objective inquiry—whether in biology or history, anthropology or sociology—is incumbent upon all those who are capable of it, as individuals seeking self-knowledge and citizens of a global community. Indeed, a deficiency generally among the existentialists, beginning with Kierkegaard's insistence on the complete incommensurability between "objective" and "subjective" knowledge, may have been to neglect the importance of scientific knowledge of ourselves precisely as it is taken up into and over time alters our subjective "life-world." It nevertheless remains the case that such knowledge is always open-ended, partial, incomplete, and relative to our finite position in the world.

The will to meaning. The existentialist emphasis on trying to understand what it is to be human in terms of how we actually live our lives has also involved an intense preoccupation with the question of the *meaning of life*. As subjects who construct and interpret what the world is for us, and decide on the values we will affirm and enact, we are inherently meaning-creating beings. As subjects who are born to die and in our finitude suffer all the "changes and chances of this mortal life," we wonder who we are, tiny and fragile beings within a vast cosmos, and why we are here. As social beings, members of societies, we commune and conflict with one another in terms of shared meanings including the myths and mores that undergird and bind together our common lives. As the beings who ask the question of what it is to be, we find answers to the "big questions" in religions, philosophies, political institutions and social ideologies, and artistic creations. In our everyday lives we seek and find "small-scale," personal meanings that we believe will give our lives sense and satisfaction: love and friendship, children and family life, the search for knowledge, work to do, a project or cause to commit ourselves to, avocations and hobbies, or the varied pursuits of pleasure, fame, money, or power.

It was one of the most eminent of the existential psychologists, Viktor Frankl, who developed the theory that because humans are subjects and not simply organisms, what he called the *will to meaning* is existentially more decisive in the living of human life than are the powerful sexual and aggressive instincts that Freud brought to light. Frankl called his psychological theory and therapeutic practice *logotherapy*, from the Greek word *logos*, "word" or "reason," which he interpreted as "meaning." "Logotherapy," he wrote in *Man's Search for Meaning*, "deviates from psychoanalysis insofar as it considers man as a being whose main concern consists in fulfilling a meaning and in actualizing values, rather than in the mere gratification and satisfaction of drives and instincts, the mere reconciliation of the conflicting claims of id, ego and superego, or mere adaptation and adjustment to the society and environment" (Frankl [1959] 1984, 108-109). While acknowledging that there are neuroses that can be explained and helped in terms of the theory and therapy of Freud, Frankl argued that there are many "noögenic neuroses" (from the Greek *nous*, "mind") that arise from needs and conflicts an individual experiences as she struggles with the meaning of her life. A survivor of the horrors of the Nazi concentration camps and author of one of the classic memoirs of life in the camps, Frankl believed that what he experienced there added further confirmation to the logotherapeutic theory he had developed before the war and tested in his clinical experience with patients. He wrote that, after we factor out the role that sheer luck and Nazi malevolence played in whether an inmate lived or died, the factor that enabled some to survive while others perished was not physical constitution or general health but whether or not persons retained something that gave meaning to their life—a loved one to be reunited with, a project to be resumed and finished (which was Frankl's own case), the memory of creating or enjoying beauty in the arts, or a God to serve.

In writing about the question of the meaning of life in the large sense of a worldview or a total perspective on reality, the existentialists characteristically insisted that all our beliefs about the ultimate nature of reality and the human place and purpose in it are culturally-shaped commitments and conjectures in the face of the limitations and uncertainty of our knowledge. We are a part trying to think the whole, finite creatures trying to think the infinite, a becoming trying to think Being. If knowledge is, as philosophers commonly say, "justified true belief," then the problem with all attempts at knowledge of the whole is that they can never be adequately justified: for thoughtful people, reasons for their ultimate beliefs about things are necessary but never sufficient. Whether we are theists or atheists, Christians or Marxists, Buddhists or Hindus, idealists or materialists, all expressions of our "ultimate concern," as Tillich called it, are acts of faith, matters of trust or commitment in the face of the possibility of doubt and error. Kierkegaard called commitment to the Christian vision of reality a "leap," but he also tried to show that all our ways of interpreting the whole are expressions of personal choice. (He did not, I think, sufficiently recognize that they are also expressions of cultural and historical context.) Sartre presented some arguments for atheism, but it is clear that for him commitment to human freedom through political engagement was his version of "faith." Camus saw that all ultimate concerns are fundamental choices about how to understand and live one's life, and he chose, as he says, to "live with what I know": his human need for meaning confronting and revolting against the silence of the world rather than resolving the question of meaning through a religious commitment.

But as with the closely-connected issue of the limits of reason, the existentialists—and I have in mind here specifically the religious existentialists—were, it seems to me, too quick to gloss over serious and well-established philosophical discussion of religious truth-claims pro and con; either simply assuming the truth of, say, Christianity or implying that all choices of ultimate concerns are equal and equally arbitrary. An existentialist emphasis on the limits of finite reason and the importance of choice in trying to make sense of the whole need not excuse the reflective person from the obligation to think through as fully as possible her ultimate commitments. If reasons are never sufficient, they are nevertheless surely necessary.

Human nature. Now that we've looked at some of the central themes and issues in existentialist thought and literature, I want to say a word about existentialism and the problem of human nature. I do so because Sartre provocatively denied that there is a universal human nature, and that denial became part of the popular understanding of existentialism. The problem is that Sartre's position on the issue was extreme (as it was on the problem of freedom), not fully consistent or coherent, and rested on a kind of linguistic sleight-of-hand. Because of his insistence that as subjects human beings entirely shape their lives by their free choices of action and interpretation, he was eager to deny all of the many traditional theological and philosophical views that there is a universal, fixed human nature or "essence." He went on, however, to speak of a universal human "condition," consisting of the combination of the physical and social circumstances or "givens" all humans share, together with each individual's freedom to appropriate and shape those circumstances. Sartre's denial and redefinition of human nature were by no means general among the existentialists, his contemporary and friend Camus being a notable example of one who insisted that there is a human nature. In the final analysis the dispute Sartre created was a fruitless one. In the preceding sections I have been describing universal characteristics of humans as subjects, to which we must add and into which we must incorporate what we know of our biological and social nature. There is simply no contradiction in saying that a foundational and defining aspect of human nature is an individualized subjectivity that is the creative matrix of all our knowledge, relationships, and values and the source of our capacity for novelty and change.

6. Misunderstandings and caricatures of existentialism

Sartre's denial of human nature provides a segue into some remarks about misinterpretations and misrepresentations of existentialism. I'm referring to general characterizations, not to debate over specific texts and issues. I will discuss this theme at length in essay three, "Existentialist (Mis)Interpretation: Iris Murdoch," so here I will simply and briefly summarize. In the early decades of existentialist influence after World War II, a certain model of what existentialism "is" came to dominate philosophical and literary presentation and discussion of existentialist thought, which in the hands of the media became the basis of the popular images of existentialism some of which I mentioned early in this essay:

solipsistic individualism, godlessness and meaninglessness, pessimism, radical freedom and arbitrary assertion of will, moral relativism and antinomianism. The source of almost all the misunderstanding can be simply stated: the identification of "existentialism" with "Sartrianism."

But even as Sartre was shaping the definition and image of existentialism, the idea of an existentialist "tradition" or movement was developing among participants in and scholars of the movement. Sartre himself had been deeply influenced by Kierkegaard, Husserl, and Heidegger. Those philosophers and writers I identified in section 2 came to be seen as predecessors or participants in a broad and varied movement called "existentialism." Certainly by the end of the 1950s and the decade of the 1960s there was a large and diverse group of philosophers and writers identified as existentialists.

But if existentialism is to be identified in terms of a wide range of authors who sound common themes but in very diverse ways and with differences of emphasis and disagreements, then it cannot also be reducible to the philosophy of Sartre. He is instead one representative of a much wider tradition. Yet the confusion and inconsistency persisted among many interpreters of existentialism for decades, including distinguished philosophers such as Iris Murdoch.

7. The "Kierkegaardian model": a definition of existentialism

I distinguish between those writers who commonly explored the themes first adumbrated by Pascal and articulated by Kierkegaard, and those who were major contributors to existentialist theory and method but in one way or another had different overall aims. The former I regard as "existentialists" proper, while the latter were intimately associated with the existentialist movement as influences and interlocutors but in one way or another don't reflect the Kierkegaardian tradition. Those who philosophized according to what I call the "Kierkegaardian model" 1) focused their attention, as Kierkegaard had, on *human* existence rather than trying to develop speculative worldviews or "philosophies of everything," 2) specifically engaged in analyzing those common characteristics of individual "lived" subjectivity or self-awareness that I presented in the previous section, and 3) typically adopted a more informal, literary, personal, and engaged style of reflection and presentation from that of the academic philosophical treatise. Among the philosophers who chiefly represent the Kierkegaardian model were Unamuno, Shestov, Buber, Marcel, Sartre, Beauvoir, and Camus. All are "existentialists" in what I propose is a readily identifiable and (I hope) reasonably uncontroversial sense.

The approach I'm taking here is not the usual one among interpreters of existentialism, and needs further explanation. The standard approach is an inclusive one—not in the sense of trying to "cover" everyone who is generally associated with the existentialist movement, but in the sense of treating "equally," as it were, a wide range of philosophers with quite different agendas and ways of doing philosophy. There is Nietzsche, for example, considered along with Kierkegaard one of the two major sources of existentialism, whose style of writing philosophy is "existential" but whose philosophical content is often sharply at odds with characteristically existentialist themes and emphases. Then there are philosophers such as Jaspers, Heidegger, and Tillich, all of whom were professors in the German tradition and most of whose writings are thoroughly academic treatises and represent attempts at a systematic and comprehensive philosophy. And in Section 3 I briefly discussed Husserl, whose substantial influence on an existentialist like Sartre was matched only by his adamant rejection of all attempts to "existentialize" his "pure science" of phenomenology.

Further confusing the would-be student of existentialism is the fact that certain of the leading figures always associated with the movement—notably Heidegger and Camus—famously denied that they were existentialists. Heidegger's denial was a way of dissociating himself specifically from Sartre's "humanism," the latter's focus on and approach to analyzing human subjectivity. By contrast, Heidegger saw his own thought as a general inquiry into the meaning of "being," for which the analysis of human existence was the necessary foundation but not the goal of the enterprise. Camus's denial is a bit complicated. Suffice it to say that in the 1930s and early 1940s, as in his book *The Myth of Sisyphus*, he separated himself from thinkers and writers he called the "existentials" on the basis of an inaccurate and eccentric characterization of what they were doing, and from the 1940s on he was mainly concerned to distance himself from Sartre, with whom he was closely identified in the public mind. Unlike Heidegger, however, Camus stands squarely in the Kierkegaardian tradition and hence was clearly an existentialist despite his protestations.

What I'm frankly doing, then, is proposing to define existentialism stipulatively on the basis of what I've called the Kierkegaardian model. I do so partly in order to resolve the "identity problems" I have mentioned by introducing a clearer and more coherent way to characterize the movement. But I offer it mainly because I believe such a definition most nearly captures the "essence" or "spirit" of existentialism: what is at the core of its concerns and methods. Kierkegaard established that spirit by writing as an engaged individual to other individuals, not as a member of the professoriate; by communicating through a variety of literary genres and thought-experiments rather than through the formal philosophical treatise; by focusing all his attention on the question of what it is to be an individual subject in the world, with others, and before God; by emphasizing the defining importance of interiority and choice to being human and the many ways we try to escape from both; and by rejecting as a form of self-deception all speculative systems that presume rationally to think the whole of reality.

When we read texts such as Unamuno's *Tragic Sense of Life* (1912), Buber's *I and Thou* (1923), Shestov's *Athens and Jerusalem* (1938), Marcel's *Being and Having* (1949), Camus's *The Myth of Sisyphus* (1942), Sartre's *Anti-Semite and Jew* (1946), and Beauvoir's *The Ethics of Ambiguity* (1947), we are directly in touch with the tradition that emanates from Kierkegaard. All these works, whether long or short, are literary, essayistic, and engaged with the problem of what it is to be human whether generally or in terms of specific moral, social, and religious issues. In each of them the person of the author—the "I" who is writing—manifests itself, often quite directly. I have pointed out the close association of existentialist thought with literature, and we see something similar but more purely "literary" in the works of philosophical fiction writers such as Dostoevsky, Tolstoy, and Kafka. However, given the fact that the philosophers I have listed were without exception "literary" in the way they wrote philosophy and most were also writers of fiction, we must see the distinction between the "philosophical" and the "literary" existentialists as somewhat blurry and arbitrary. To be sure, among the philosophers I listed at the beginning of this paragraph are those who wrote "big books" of existentialist philosophy: notably Sartre's *Being and Nothingness* (1943) and Marcel's *The Mystery of Being* (1950). Beauvoir, for her part, produced an exhaustive study of the condition of women in *The Second Sex* (1949). But even at their most technical, these works are characterized by an informality of organization and treatment of topics, with sections of technical philosophical exposition interspersed or juxtaposed with descriptions of concrete and often personal situations. And all, of course, are dedicated from beginning to end to illuminating the human situation as it is lived by subjects like themselves.

–2–
Existentialism Today

Textbooks and anthologies on existentialism continue to be published in abundance, while scholarly studies of Kierkegaard, Nietzsche, Heidegger, Sartre, and Beauvoir continue to appear regularly. Recent works often attempt to take a fresh look at these thinkers by interpreting them in the light of those developments called "postmodernism." When all is said and done, however, scholarly interest in existentialism survives at the beginning of the twenty-first century in an intellectual context that in recent years has tended to ignore or reject what I consider to be the chief and enduring insights of the existentialist philosophers and writers. It is a context defined by very different sorts of developments in the natural sciences and in the humanities.

1. **Recent science and "human nature"**
When they study human beings, the natural sciences, given their presuppositions and methods, seek not only general but objective knowledge of human nature and behavior: the empirical knowledge gained through hypotheses rigorously and repeatedly confirmed according to accepted scientific protocols of observation and experiment. That is entirely as it should be, and we have gained a wealth of essential knowledge of what we are as human beings from the sciences. But since human beings are subjects who define and dwell in a life-world that is the context of all knowledge and the other values, they must additionally be understood with presuppositions and methods appropriate to humanistic inquiry—methods that are different from those of the sciences. In the introductory essay I argued that the existentialist tradition has played a dominant role in modern thought in pioneering and developing such presuppositions and methods.

The past twenty-five years or so have seen dramatic advances in knowledge among the sciences of human nature and behavior, involving the creation of new subfields. Genetics, evolutionary biology, sociobiology and evolutionary psychology, cognitive science, and neuroscience are lively areas of research which together are providing an ever-expanding scientific "picture" of what it is to be human—from the Human Genome Project to brain research to psycholinguistics.

These advances, especially as presented and interpreted by the media, often seem to the informed public and to humanist intellectuals and scholars alike to be new versions of the old tendencies of the natural sciences to be *deterministic* and *reductionistic*. The kind of determinism people have in mind is not simply the general assumption that all events have causes that are in principle explainable (which has played a central role in the history of science), but more specifically what they see as the inference that the physical and mental makeup and life history of the individual human being are completely "programmed" or "hardwired" by genes, evolutionary history, and brain structure and function. There are various meanings of "reductionism," but in the present context I mean by it the tendency to regard the perspectives of scientific knowledge of human nature and behavior as not merely indispensable but as entirely sufficient explanations of what we are and do. From the standpoint of existentialist analyses of "lived" human experience, determinism and reductionism as applied to human beings are intellectually truncated and unwarrantedly generalized. These assumptions abstract from and objectify human nature and behavior, ignoring the fact that all knowledge of ourselves is knowledge *for* concrete subjects who transcend that knowledge and make decisions about how to interpret and act upon it.

Closely related to the fear of determinism and reductionism in the "new" sciences of human nature is the perception of where they seem to come down in the "nature-nurture" controversy, the long-standing debate over whether human beings are primarily shaped and defined by "nature" or by "experience"—by their biological nature or by their social environment. To the lay observer it often looks as though the new sciences think they have resolved the controversy firmly on the side of "nature": genetic composition, brain structure, and evolutionary history account for everything. If it were true, this would be a complete reversal of the dominance throughout the twentieth century of the view that human behavior is very largely if not almost entirely shaped by "nurture," by the social environment, and the minimizing of genetic and other biological causes. The social and behavioral sciences—chiefly anthropology, sociology, and various schools of psychology—articulated what became a widespread belief that human beings are infinitely malleable. Environmental causation and explanation have for decades undergirded our thinking and practice regarding everything from child-rearing and education to crime and delinquency and the legal system. Mixed in with it have been our intuitive and traditional assumptions about free will. We have seen, in an existentialist like Sartre (and, as we shall see, Frankl), the view that human beings are radically free—so much so that Sartre denied that there is a human nature. So it often looks to the scientific "outsider" as though recent scientific research on understanding human beings threatens to undermine the role of both society and freedom. An important and emotionally-charged fear is that the newer emphasis on biological causation undermines our moral and social commitments to human rights and gender and racial equality.

A careful reading of some of the major books and articles written for the educated layperson by recent scientists of human nature and serious science journalists suggests that the fears of determinism, reductionism, and "naturism" are somewhat exaggerated or inaccurate. There is no better example than the noted cognitive scientist Steven Pinker's 2002 book *The Blank Slate: The Modern Denial of Human Nature*. A very broadly educated reader and an excellent writer, Pinker has produced a kind of comprehensive summary of research in genetics, evolutionary biology and psychology, neuroscience, and cognitive science, as applied to a range of theoretical and practical issues from the problem of human nature and morality to gender, politics, and violence. He specifically addresses—by and large successfully—the worries and misunderstandings about determinism, reductionism, and the replacement of social by biological explanations.

Pinker's big book is a kind of virtuoso performance, marked by a dazzling display of knowledge over several fields and a wide range of issues and by literary flair, wit, and contemporaneity. *The Blank Slate* is a sustained and well-documented attack on the "nurturism" that has dominated our thinking for a very long time: the assumption that human beings are to be defined and explained almost entirely in terms of nurture—of the influence of culture and society. This is the model of the human mind as a *tabula rasa*—a "blank slate" (literally a "scraped tablet")—written upon by experience, an idea famously associated with the father of British Empiricism, John Locke, in the seventeenth century.

Pinker argues that what I'm calling "nurturism," the "blank slate" theory, has so completely triumphed that scientists like himself who suggest that "nature," our biological nature or heredity, also plays an essential role in defining what we are, are attacked as "extremists." Pinker describes his purpose in writing the book:

> This book is about the moral, emotional, and political colorings of the concept of human nature in modern life. . . . I am not, as many people assume, countering an extreme "nurture" position with an extreme "nature" position, with the truth lying somewhere in between. In some cases, an extreme environmentalist explanation is correct: which language you speak is an obvious example, and differences among races and ethnic groups in test scores may be another. In other cases, such as certain inherited neurological disorders, an extreme hereditarian explanation is correct. In most cases the correct explanation will invoke a complex interaction between heredity and environment: culture is crucial, but culture could not exist without mental faculties that allow humans to create and learn culture to begin with. My goal in this book is not to argue that genes are everything and culture is nothing—no one believes that—but to explore why the extreme position (that culture is everything) is so often seen as moderate, and the moderate position is seen as extreme (viii-ix).

He insists that recognizing the influence of our biological nature "does not . . . require one to abandon feminism, or to accept current levels of inequality or violence, or to treat morality as a fiction" (ix), and throughout the book he engages in substantial discussion of those topics and others. Pinker is concerned to show that the extreme emphasis on "nurture" and the neglect or denial of "nature" has seriously distorted our knowledge of human behavior and resulted in policies and practices that are ill-informed and wrong-headed.

I can't emphasize sufficiently how important and valuable I think Pinker's book is. Although some of his conclusions are by no means uncontroversial among his scientific peers, for the scientific lay person he has provided a clear and comprehensive synthesis of the current state of scientific knowledge of human nature and behavior. It is knowledge that humanists—and indeed everyone concerned with knowledge of ourselves and its applications to moral, social, and political problems—need to incorporate as fully as possible. Pinker clearly makes the case against "nurturism" and for the recognition of the importance of "nature" in human behavior; and he is sensitive to the subtleties of the nature/nurture interaction in shaping what we are. Just as clearly, he argues persuasively that on a number of contemporary issues we have been led by our irrational fear of the implications of taking seriously our biological nature into policies and practices that are profoundly mistaken.

To provide an even somewhat adequate summary of Pinker's very rich book, however, is beyond the scope and purpose of this essay. I want instead to focus critically on his notion of "human nature" as an important example of the limitations of the natural-science approach to understanding human beings—limitations that even an expansive and humanistic scientist like Pinker doesn't fully acknowledge. Having introduced the "nature"/"nurture" controversy, in which "nature" refers to the role of our biology in shaping what we are, Pinker goes on to identify "nature" so defined with "human nature." But this is both misleading and mistaken. "Human nature" has historically been used to refer to all those qualities that give humans the character of humanness. That includes both "nature" and "nurture"—both our biological and our social-cultural characteristics. It also includes, the existentialists would insist, the individual subjectivity which mediates and interprets all the rest and constitutes the actual human life-world, uniquely to each person but universally within the framework of characteristics or "horizons" of lived subjectivity such as the pursuit of meanings and the exercise of choice.

The problem is not with saying that our biological nature *grounds and sustains* our social and subjective existence. Anyone who doesn't want to introduce theological considerations can agree to that obvious and reasonable thesis. The problem is rather with *reducing* the idea of human nature to its biological dimensions. Having based his whole book on the "nature"/"nurture" debate, Pinker needlessly confuses the issue by identifying only the "nature" side with the general and historically-freighted term "human nature." He has every right, as a cognitive scientist, to focus on the genetic and evolutionary foundations of human behavior, and to that extent he is richly illuminating. But he "loads the dice" in a reductionistic way by defining human nature as its biological basis. It makes his defense of appeals to "nurture," as in the passage I quoted above, simply puzzling. If there are aspects of human behavior generally that require explanation in terms of the social environment, then surely "nurture" is an integral element in constituting human nature. Again, no one should wish to deny that our social behavior has its roots in and interacts with our biological nature. The point is that human social and cultural existence introduces a level of explanation that is not reducible to biological inheritance and dispositions. As we have seen, Pinker grants this methodologically and functionally, and he even goes on to reply plausibly to the charge of reductionism; but he insists on a definition of "human nature" that reduces what humans "really are" to their biology.

Pinker argues for what he calls the "computational theory of mind": the theory that "mental life can be explained in terms of information, computation, and feedback."

> Beliefs and memories are collections of information—like facts in a database, but residing in patterns of activity and structure in the brain. Thinking and planning are systematic transformations of these patterns, like the operation of a computer program. Wanting and trying are feedback loops, like the principle behind a thermostat (32)....

Here Pinker summarizes the "new" sciences' refutation of the idea that the human mind is either a "blank slate" or, as Gilbert Ryle famously characterized Descartes' theory of mind, a "ghost in the machine." On this view human mental activities are complex but not mysterious, nor do they require the postulating of some sort of purely mental entity or activity (mind, soul) that supervenes on the physical. The sciences investigating human nature and behavior can now explain mental activities as various sorts of physical (brain) operations. Again, this account of mental activities is not objectionable as far as it goes. The natural sciences seek physical explanations for natural phenomena, including the human organism, and are guided by the principle of parsimony (no more causes or forces should be assumed than are necessary to explain the facts).

But having adopted a "computational" theory of mind and listed some of the remarkable accomplishments in the field of artificial intelligence, Pinker nevertheless rejects the "computer" model of the human mind:

> None of this is to say that the brain works like a digital computer, that artificial intelligence will ever duplicate the human mind, or that computers are *conscious in the sense of having first-person subjective experience*. But it does suggest that reasoning, intelligence, imagination, and creativity are forms of information processing, a well-understood physical process (34; italics added).

Here, and occasionally elsewhere in *The Blank Slate*, Pinker refers to "first-person subjective experience"—individual subjectivity—but doesn't pursue further any implications of the phenomenon of subjectivity beyond its general basis in the human brain and biology. Nor indeed is he obliged to, working within the parameters of scientific explanation. But the omission of a phenomenological account of the life-world in favor of physical and environmental causal theories once again points up the limitations of Pinker's scientific approach and his reduction of the idea of human nature to the biological. He assumes or "brackets," without really examining as a level of human reality in its own right, the individual subjective matrix of his own scientific inquiry along with his entire personal, concrete existence with its many interests and choices and relationships other than science. In a similar manner he discusses the biological foundations of the human "moral sense"—and quite illuminatingly and valuably—while taking for granted as a norm the modern liberal moral consensus (equality, democracy, human rights, tolerance) that requires justifications that significantly transcend the biological and can't even be fully accounted for at the level of the social.

Early in *The Blank Slate*, in arguing against the "nurturist" assumption that humans are a "blank slate," Pinker writes, "A great divide between mind and matter has always seemed natural because behavior appears to be a different kind of trigger than other physical events. Ordinary events have *causes*, it seems, but human behavior has *reasons*" (31-2). Pinker appears to be using the common philosophical distinction between causes and reasons as an example of why we persist in talking about mind as something distinct and fundamentally different from body. Whether he himself accepts, or indeed understands, the distinction between causes and reasons as a broader and essential principle of explanation of human activities is unclear. By contrast, Pinker's older colleague, sociobiologist E. O. Wilson, is quite unambiguous in rejecting—or ignoring—the distinction.

Wilson's 1998 book *Consilience: The Unity of Knowledge* is a truly magisterial presentation of scientific reductionism. More grandly ambitious and much less subtle than Pinker's book, it is a sophisticated and superbly written attempt to formulate a comprehensive, unifying vision of knowledge and to propose the methods for achieving it, by a distinguished (if controversial) American scientist the breadth of whose humanistic learning is as impressive as his scientific learning. The model for both the vision and the methods is the natural sciences. Wilson ranges over topics from the nature of science to art, religion, and ethics. Appropriately reminding his readers of the constructive and fallible character of scientific knowledge, Wilson has nevertheless articulated an end-of-century manifesto that quite explicitly revives and carries forward a certain Enlightenment vision of the rational unity of all knowledge under the aegis of science.

Yet at the heart of Wilson's vision is a failure to observe the most fundamental categorial distinction between causes and reasons. Wilson defines consilience as the unity of "causal explanation[s]" (13), and his accounts of the physical bases of mind, culture, art, ethics, and religion are an illuminating if often conjectural contribution to our knowledge from the standpoint of evolutionary biology and genetics. What he does not seem to see is that explanation in terms of physical causes is *logically irrelevant* to what counts as explanation over a very substantial portion and variety of human discourse—including, for example, ethics, politics, art, religion, and philosophy. He commits what philosophers call a "category mistake," applying one sort of explanation (causes) to issues that require a completely different sort of explanation (reasons appropriate to the discourse under consideration). It is only by such logical confusion that Wilson's reductionism works.

For example, in the chapter on "The Natural Sciences," Wilson argues that we can solve the problem of what constitutes objective knowledge by discovering what brain processes produce it!

> The canonical definition of objective scientific knowledge ... is not a philosophical problem. ... It is an empirical question that can be answered only by

a continuing probe of the physical basis of the thought process itself. . . . If the exact biological processes of concept formation can be defined, we might devise superior methods of inquiry into both the brain and the world outside it. As a consequence we could expect to tighten the connectedness between the events and laws of nature and the physical basis of human thought processes. Might it be possible then to take the final step and devise an unassailable definition of objective truth (70)?

Wilson answers his own question by saying that perhaps it is not possible but that we should make every effort to try to do it. The reasoning in this remarkable passage is entirely circular, and its circularity points to the confusion in it between causes and reasons. Wilson begins with an understanding of objective knowledge derived from philosophical discussion, not from examination of brain processes, and argues that it is on the basis of empirical investigation of the brain processes that produce objective knowledge thus defined that we will be able to construct a foolproof definition of objective knowledge! What his remarks make clear, contrary to his intentions, is that the question of objective knowledge is *precisely* a "philosophical problem" and *not* a matter of brain research. It is a problem involving consideration of issues such as the relationship between language and world, the justification of assertions, the determination of what counts as evidence, theory formation, and the like. These are properly reasons and not causes. Brain research may produce illuminating data on the physical bases of various mental processes, but it literally has nothing to do with how to deal with the question of what counts as objective knowledge.

In a fascinating chapter on "The Mind," Wilson does the same thing with mental activities, "explaining" consciousness, selfhood, emotion, and ratiocination as functions of brain activity while ignoring not only social context but also the existential phenomenon of individual subjectivity with its self-transcending paradoxes and vocabulary. The fact that there is a deep incommensurability, a yawning and puzzling gap, between the ways in which human beings as subjects concretely experience and reflect on the world and their lives, and their objective description in terms of evolutionary and genetic biology and brain research, is not a problem of which Wilson seems aware. As with Pinker, but more obviously, it's not that Wilson as a scientist is obliged to "explain" the subjective life-world—which in any case and necessarily eludes the objectifying methods of science—but that he, a concretely-existing subject, assumes that there is nothing "there" to be explained or taken notice of; that evolutionary, genetic, and neurological explanation is not only necessary but sufficient.

When he deals with the arts, ethics, and religion, Wilson similarly reduces everything to biological-evolutionary causes. For example: ". . . even the greatest works of art might be understood fundamentally with knowledge of the biologically evolved epigenetic rules that guided them" (233). That the whole realm of aesthetic judgments might be characterized by considerations having nothing whatever to do with biological causes and not in need of such causal explanation—considerations such as composition, balance, harmony, sensibility, and taste—seems simply to escape Wilson's purview.

According to Wilson, then, all those issues that are the very stuff of our lives as humans (including scientists) will find definitive answers in the indefinite expansion of scientific knowledge: the meanings of our lives, our values and exercise of choice, our ethics, religion, and art—and of course at bottom our subjectivity itself.

In his wise, witty, and unsettling 1983 book *Lost in the Cosmos: The Last Self-Help Book*, the American novelist Walker Percy—who graduated from Columbia University Medical School before becoming a writer—entitled a chapter "The Exempted Self: How Scientists Don't Have to Take Account of Themselves and Other Selves in their Science and Some Difficulties that Arise when they have to" (159-166). A major theme in the book is the "reentry" problems of modern selves that are involved in self-transcending activities such as the sciences and literature and the arts. He cites a true and dramatic example of a scientist with "reentry" problems:

> The divorced wife of an astronomer at the Mount Wilson Observatory accused her husband of "angelism-bestialism." He was so absorbed in his work, the search for the quasar with the greatest red shift, that when he came home to his pleasant subdivision house, he seemed to take his pleasure like a god descending from Olympus into the world of mortals, ate heartily, had frequent intercourse with his wife, watched TV, read Mickey Spillane, and said not a word to wife or children (116).

Obviously Percy's story is not a generalization about scientists—whose personal lives undoubtedly range as widely as the lives of humanists or anyone else, from very conventional to very eccentric—but rather, using an extreme case, a provocative reminder of what I have been calling the incommensurability between human existence as lived and concretely understood by individual subjects and objective knowledge of human nature and behavior. (Percy, by the way, was deeply influenced by existentialism, notably the work of Kierkegaard, and I would nominate his book *Lost in the Cosmos* for a place in the existentialist "canon.")

2. Postmodernism and the dissolution of the subject

From the side of the humanities, especially but by no means exclusively in literary studies, we have seen the emergence of viewpoints and methods that are broadly lumped together as "postmodernism." There are widely varied and not always compatible definitions of postmodernism, some broader and some narrower, and hence a certain arbitrariness about "defining" the term. I find it most useful to characterize postmodernism broadly in terms of modern intellectual history, which provides a comprehensive framework in which to place both existentialism and more recent trends.

We can understand *post*-modernism by understanding not only modernism but also *pre*-modernism. We can use the term *premodern* to characterize the traditional and typically religious worldviews that dominated before the seventeenth- and eighteenth-century European Enlightenment. Premodern forms of thought located the foundations of human life in an absolute God or Ultimate Reality revealed in timeless scriptures and in objective natural laws discoverable by universal reason.

Modernism, those outlooks created by the Enlightenment and the various workings out of its legacy down to the 1960s or so, celebrate the individual human subject in its unity and autonomy as the foundation of meanings and values. Since modernist thought is based on the experiencing subject and its relation to the world rather than God, in some of its versions it espouses relativistic approaches to knowledge and values—but relative always to the individual subject or consciousness that is the matrix of all experience. Modernism has expressed itself in religious as well as non-religious forms, and religiously it is represented by the post-Kantian abandonment of metaphysical arguments for faith in favor of practical or existential appeals. The existentialists belong to the modernist tradition, and are also among its most trenchant internal critics.

I recognize that "modernism" also has a more narrowly defined meaning to designate a twentieth-century literary movement. Literary modernism encompassed the period roughly from 1900 through the 1940s, and included such major twentieth-century writers as Marcel Proust, Thomas Mann, Ezra Pound, T. S. Eliot, Wallace Stevens, James Joyce, Virginia Woolf, D. H. Lawrence, and Franz Kafka. As the names especially of Eliot and Kafka suggest, those existentialists who were writers belong to the tradition of literary modernism, and Nietzsche and Dostoevsky were important influences on the tradition. As Ricardo Quinones argues in his book *Mapping Literary Modernism* (1985), the literary modernists, like modernists in the visual arts, saw themselves as living in a time of crisis in Western civilization (the cataclysm of World War I played an important but not all-decisive contributing role), and represented a conscious break with the past in terms of sensibility, relationship to history, themes, and styles. But they also recognizably carried forward the wider modernist emphasis on the individual subject and her relationship to the world as knower and actor.

Postmodernism as a development in humanistic learning was chiefly inspired by the writings of Frenchmen Jacques Derrida and Michel Foucault, and postmodernists generally regard Nietzsche as the "prophet" and forebear of their views. Postmodernism began to transform French literary. philosophical, and psychological studies in the 1960s and 1970s, but soon found its most receptive audience in the United States, particularly among scholars and teachers of literature. A leading American philosopher, Richard Rorty, is an influential contemporary voice of postmodernism. Derrida is specifically credited with the approach to literary and philosophical texts called "deconstruction," an idea he adopted and adapted from Heidegger's original and comprehensive re-reading of the history of Western philosophy. (Heidegger called his approach the *Destruktion* of philosophy, by which he meant only the "destruction" of the standard ways of interpreting the tradition regarding the question of being in favor of a new interpretation.) Deconstruction is based on the idea that language always means more and even other than we think it does in speaking or writing it, and the deconstructionist engages in close reading of texts with a view to illuminating those inevitable points at which the writer loses control of the process, creates incoherence and even contradiction despite herself, and generates meanings that are opposed to and escape the immediate reference of the text itself—what Derrida called "différance" (a combination of "difference" and "deferral").

Generalizing about and critically appraising postmodernism is a hazardous enterprise. When Derrida died in October of 2004, the obituaries in both Europe and the U.S. were sharply divided between critical praise and outright hostility. Was Derrida (who refused to use the term "postmodern") a profoundly creative reinterpreter of the critical heritage of the Enlightenment, illuminating old texts in startlingly fresh ways, or was he a "destroyer" of that heritage, gleefully and unintelligibly undermining all claims to truth and knowledge? In characterizing postmodernism I will refrain from identifying the views I present with those of Derrida (and also those of Foucault). They represent instead generalizations based upon what it seems to me postmodernism has come to mean among many of its practitioners and its detractors particularly in the U.S. As one who has sought over the years sympathetically to read and learn from authors who are considered "postmodern" but with little success and much frustration, I confess freely that I continue to consider myself a "chastened modernist" and a critic of the assumptions that appear to me to be expressed or implied by the postmodernist movement. I do so as an inheritor of an existentialist approach to things, and with the aim of showing its divergence from and problems with postmodernism.

While the postmodern frame of mind manifests itself in a variety of ways, it centers in the view that "reality" is nothing other than the ever-changing play of human social and linguistic constructions. This is a viewpoint often called *perspectivism*, which has its roots in Nietzsche's thought: all knowing and valuing arises out of the many cultural and social contexts of meaning in which all human existence takes place, and we can never step outside of perspectives and look at them "objectively" or in relation to some independently-existing reality of which they purport to give us knowledge. An important postmodern metaphor has been that everything (not just the written word but also nature, people, and institutions) is "text," a product of human interpretation that has no intrinsic, essential, or stable meaning but is itself subject to endless interpretation and reinterpretation. This is as much the case with scientific knowledge as it is with literature or art. Very importantly from the standpoint of our study of existentialism, postmodern thought even dissolves or "deconstructs" the human subject into an ever-shifting "text," or to put it another way, into an ensemble of social relations and interpretations. Just as we no longer need to be concerned about the "author" behind a literary or philosophical or historical text, who is herself a construction or text, so with the idea of the unified subject generally.

Another way of looking at postmodernism is to describe it as the destruction of what are called "grand narratives"—what Foucault called "totalizing discourses." Grand narratives (also called "metanarratives") are the "big stories" which both premodernist and modernist worldviews took for granted: those great myths and ideas believed to be universal paradigms of reality and human life. Christianity and Buddhism, Platonism and Stoicism, rationalism and empiricism, Marxism and liberal individualism are a few of the metanarratives that have provided a framework of cosmic meaning and guided people's lives (and some of them of course still do). Postmodernism claims to undermine all grand narratives, since like everything else they are entirely constructions of the human imagination none of which has any claim to refer to the way things "really" are. In the postmodernist world there are only "micronarratives": guiding stories for this group or individual for this particular time and place.

To put it in familiar and traditional terms, postmodernism is characterized by a pervasive skepticism and relativism—what I think of as a general dissolving of claims to objective knowledge, reality, and value. Within this general framework a special focus is that since everything is social construction, human social existence is thoroughly *ideological*—permeated by beliefs about gender, sexuality, race and ethnicity, and class and manifesting often-hidden manipulations of power that profoundly mould the ways societies and individuals deal with one another. Postmodern thinking has had an important influence on gender, ethnic, and cultural studies, where it has contributed to what is called a "hermeneutics of suspicion," an approach to interpreting texts which examines all claims as social-specific, shaped by ideologies of gender, race, and class, and expressive of very unequal power relations. Moral, political, aesthetic, and religious values, as well as intellectual inquiry, are seen as thoroughly shaped by culture-, gender-, race-, and class-specific forces. The unified and transcending subject of modernism is dissolved into these social contexts and relations.

Postmodern thinkers and writers have provocatively raised a number of important issues and illuminated others. Like Nietzsche in the late nineteenth century, they valuably hold up to critical scrutiny our late-twentieth-century "idols": our taken-for-granted assumptions, inherited from the Enlightenment, about the objectivity of reason and the universality of our dominant moral, social, and political values as defined by the modern white, patriarchal Western world. Postmodern influence has been especially effective in exposing the often hidden role of social ideologies, as discussed above. For example, once we have learned from feminist literary criticism, we can no longer read works of literature without being aware of the gender-related "subtexts" running through them. The case is similar with issues of race and class.

The problem is that postmodernists typically insist on taking these valuable questionings and insights to extremes. They generalize them into an outlook, a point of view, that is intellectually untenable and enmesh themselves in paradoxes. At a basic level, the assertion that there are no universal truths, only perspectives, is caught up in what is called the "self-referential fallacy": the assertion itself is put forward as a universally true statement and therefore as transcending any particular perspective. Within that general framework, the particular statements that comprise the setting forth of postmodern theories seem clearly to be intended as universally true and worthy of acceptance. If they are not, then why should we take them seriously as theories and either accept or challenge them? In the realm of moral values, we have the contradiction that postmodernists often combine a complete moral relativism with a passionate commitment to certain values as better than others. They are typically egalitarians, feminists, and multiculturalists, and vigorous opponents of the traditionalist values of social conservatives. They often protest against certain practices of other cultures, such as genital mutilation of millions of girls in some African and Middle Eastern societies, on the basis of moral values that they seem to regard as trans-cultural in scope. Dissolvers of the human subject into an endlessly re-inscribed "text" or a nexus of social relations, individual postmodern thinkers normally carry on a rich inner life, assume continuity between their past, present, and future self, and decide and act as though they were an autonomous individual. They affirm individual rights, and celebrate the uniqueness and irreplaceability of other individuals they care deeply about.

Speaking from a Sartrian perspective, Hazel Barnes, looking back over intellectual developments after Sartre and the existentialists in her 1997 autobiography *The Story I Tell Myself*, nicely exemplifies an existentialist critical response to postmodernism:

> ... I do not go along with the notion, current today, that no individual subject exists within us, that our psychic core is only a set of fragmented structures imposed on us by our social environment.... I do not hold that what we call the self is the product of discourse, a linguistic convention, a reflecting pool of otherness.... I think Sartre is right in claiming that a free, prepersonal consciousness forms a self (or ego) by imposing a unity on its own experiences and reactions to them, past and present (xvii).

And again:

> ... as a Sartrean I was dismayed by the overall tendency of Deconstruction to depersonalize, to reduce the person to modes of discourse, to view individuals as only reflections of the input of others. Nor could I accept the idea ... that we are "spoken by language," its servants rather than its creators and users. And ... I—like many others—resisted the notion that since in interpreting literature absolute truth is unobtainable in most instances, the only alternative is a relativity that would put all meanings on the same level (178).

With their intense focus on the individual subject and "lived" human existence, the existentialists, it might be argued, should have recognized and emphasized the profound role that gender, sexuality, race, and ethnicity play in shaping our individual and social identities. But in their general lack of attention to these issues the existentialists were far from unique or even unusual. The concept of ideology and the analysis of *class* differences, pioneered by Marxism, were well established during the existentialist era. But until the dramatic and comprehensive impact of the most recent phases of the movements for black, women's, and gay liberation beginning in the 1950s and '60s there was little attention paid in "mainstream" thought and literature to anything but the political and legal aspects of gender and race discrimination and the struggle to overcome it.

Given that general obliviousness and the limitations of outlook it produced, what is striking is the prominence of social and ideological criticism among the existentialist philosophers and writers. It has its foundations in the nineteenth-century precursors: for example, in Kierkegaard's attacks on the role of the press in creating that modern anonymity, the "public"; in Nietzsche's sustained exposure of the roots of the ideologies by which the modern West lives; and in Dostoevsky's satirical commentaries on the incompatibility between utopian socialist schemes and human nature.

Twentieth-century existentialism produced a significant body of social and ideological criticism. I will mention only a few especially prominent examples out of many more. Ortega's influential book *The Revolt of the Masses* (1930) was a penetrating analysis of the phenomenon of "mass man" produced by modern industrialization and bureaucratization. The Second World War produced important existentialist commentaries on the issues it urgently raised. Among them were Jaspers' *The Question of German Guilt* (1946) and *The Future of Mankind* (1958), the latter a study of the impact and implications of the development of atomic weapons. Sartre's *Anti-Semite and Jew* (1946) is widely considered one of the most illuminating studies of the ideology of antisemitism ever written and is a direct "practical" application of his philosophical analysis of human existence. Beauvoir's exhaustive study of women, *The Second Sex* (1949), is the pioneering classic of "second wave" feminism, in which she builds on her work in existentialist ethics and employs the influential idea of "otherness" to describe the historic situation of women. We will have occasion to examine Beauvoir's ideas in more detail in essay four.

3. Conclusion

From an existentialist point of view the natural and social sciences have contributed immeasurably and invaluably to our knowledge of who we are as human beings, and so likewise the insights of recent cultural and ideological criticism. It is their claims to all-sufficiency as explanations that must be rejected. Their explanations are inevitably abstractions from or particular perspectives on a richly complex concrete reality centered in a subjectivity that always eludes objectification and reduction, because it is the living matrix which is the transcending source and recipient of all explanation. Because of this, an existentialist outlook further suspects that those who hold such reductionistic or relativizing views are engaged in a form of self-deception. The existentialist observes that no one holding such views lives her life as if they were entirely true and adequate. There is a kind of "cognitive dissonance" between what she says she believes about human beings and how she conducts herself as a living subject who is involved with the world and other persons in terms of all sorts of choices, feelings, and values that appeal for their validation to completely different criteria and considerations from those contained in the theory she holds. One might say that as concrete individuals people don't really believe in the complete adequacy of such theories; they only think they do, and manage to do so by bracketing out or, as Percy put it, "exempting" their own and others' status as individual subjects. A major strength of existentialism is precisely the ways in which it illuminates this inescapable and, in the final analysis, decisive character of what it is to be human.

As we've seen, the existentialist philosophers certainly allowed for a significant and indeterminate degree of social and biological conditioning as the "facticity" or set of givens that in fact largely shape the individual person and provide the limits and context of her freedom. There are also clearly connections between the existentialists' thoroughly dynamic and concrete analysis of the self as imbedded in the world and always in process and the recent fashions in the humanities. But the existentialists rejected epistemological and social relativism as surely as they rejected genetic and evolutionary reductionism. They assumed that "in, with, and under" our diversity, humans share not only a common biological species-inheritance but also generalizable social structures, both of which are manifest in human communication, knowledge, and values. While the "world" is always and inescapably a human-constructed world, it exists independently of us and is so constituted as to render some interpretations of it more accurate and adequate than others. To this the scientist, unlike the postmodernist, will heartily agree. But very centrally, the existentialists went on to affirm the unity and transcendence of individual human subjectivity, and devoted themselves to illuminating universal characteristics or structures of subjectivity which each individual uniquely manifests—phenomena that the sciences of the human can illuminate only by rendering them in objective terms and thereby missing or reducing the very heart of humans' lived reality.

– 3 –

Existentialist (Mis)Interpretation: Iris Murdoch

Almost alone among British philosophers of the middle decades of the twentieth century, Iris Murdoch engaged seriously with existentialist philosophy and literature throughout her career. Her first book was *Sartre: Romantic Rationalist* (1953), almost twenty years later she published a long literary essay on "Existentialists and Mystics" (1970), and in one of her last philosophical works, *Metaphysics as a Guide to Morals* (1992), she devoted serious attention to such thinkers as Kierkegaard, Sartre, Heidegger, and Martin Buber. It's by no means coincidental to her interest in existentialism that Iris Murdoch was also one of Britain's most distinguished novelists, producing some twenty-six novels over a forty-year period and winning the Man Booker Prize in 1978. Additionally, she authored or co-authored five plays, three of them adaptations of her novels.

In this essay I want to examine critically Murdoch's essays on existentialism in the collection *Existentialists and Mystics*: *Writings on Philosophy and Literature* (1997). What I hope to show is that, although in some respects treating her subject with great discernment, she simply identified "existentialism" with Sartre's early philosophy while inconsistently and confusingly including as existentialists philosophers and writers—notably Albert Camus and Gabriel Marcel—whose views contrasted sharply with those of Sartre. The point of this exercise is that Murdoch, whose knowledge of existentialist philosophy and literature was substantial and critically sympathetic, exemplifies a chronic misunderstanding and misrepresentation on the part of many interpreters of the existentialist movement, from scholars to popularizers. The problem lies in the incoherence of identifying "existentialism"with ideas that are peculiar to Sartre, while at the same time including among the existentialists philosophers and writers whose ideas are often dramatically different from and even opposed to those of Sartre.

In her recent Introduction to the Penguin Classics edition of Murdoch's novel *The Black Prince*, Martha Nussbaum has called her "a major moral philosopher" (Murdoch [1973] 2003, x). As a moral philosopher she was quite original, going her own way independently of the reigning analytic approach in British moral philosophy. Influenced by the thought of the French philosopher and mystic Simone Weil, Murdoch worked out a "virtue ethics" that was a modern version of Platonism. My focus, however, is not on Murdoch's own constructive philosophy, but on how she characterized and analyzed existentialism. Nor will I discuss Murdoch as a writer except very briefly at the end of the essay and in the context of her relationship to the existentialists. In Murdoch's writings on the existentialists her own philosophical perspective and also her literary predilections certainly manifest themselves, but they are not the primary object of my inquiry.

I'll begin by describing in greater detail the general problem I've introduced and then go on to examine Murdoch's essays on existentialism. In the early days of existentialist influence following World War II, a certain model of what existentialism "is" came to dominate philosophical and literary presentation and discussion of existentialist thought and then to be exaggerated further in popular culture. Existentialism was identified with a solipsistic individualism, a view of the world as "absurd" (in the sense of lacking any overall meaning whether transcendent or immanent), and an understanding of individual consciousness as the totally free and arbitrary creator of all meanings and values, with its corollary that the individual person is entirely self-creating and completely responsible for what she makes of herself. The source of this characterization can be simply stated: the identification of "existentialism" with "Sartrianism," or more precisely with the standard interpretations of Sartre's early philosophy—the philosophy articulated the most comprehensively and influentially in *Being and Nothingness* (1943). (By 1950 Sartre was in the process of substantially modifying his original existentialism in the direction of an "existentialized Marxism," but that is not the Sartre who was seen as defining "existentialism.") Sartre was a giant of the movement, and through the originality and dramatic quality of his thought, the sheer range and quantity of his philosophical, literary, and political writings, and his colorful and controversial life and left-wing politics made a larger and more dramatic impact on both the scholarly and the educated popular mind than anyone else. Having himself coined the term "existentialism," Sartre in a real sense also defined the movement for many.

But even as Sartre was shaping the definition and image of existentialism, the idea of an existentialist "tradition" or movement was developing among participants in and scholars of the movement. Sartre himself had been substantially influenced by Kierkegaard and Heidegger, and was a close friend and partner in dialogue of three other prominent figures identified with the movement—Beauvoir, Camus, and Merleau-Ponty. During the 1950s a number of philosophers and writers came to be seen as predecessors or participants in a broad and varied movement called "existentialism." As we saw in the first essay on "The Existentialist Legacy," the list included, among others, Kierkegaard, Nietzsche, and Dostoevsky in the nineteenth century and, in the twentieth, Unamuno and Ortega, Berdyaev and Shestov, Jaspers and Heidegger, Buber, Bultmann, and Tillich, Marcel and Merleau-Ponty, and Beauvoir and Camus. Kierkegaard and Nietzsche experimented with various literary genres; Dostoevsky wrote "philosophical novels" rather than formal philosophy; Sartre, Beauvoir, and Camus were as well known for their literary as for their philosophical writings; and Unamuno and Marcel were also writers of fiction and drama. Other novelists and playwrights also came early on to be included as representatives of the movement, among them Kafka, Eliot, Rilke, Hesse, Hemingway, and Beckett.

In the 1950s anthologies of existentialist philosophers and writers began to appear, the editors of which selected widely or narrowly among the "likely suspects" but always with a substantial degree of overlap. Walter Kaufmann's *Existentialism from Dostoevsky to Sartre* appeared in 1956, with excerpts from eight existentialist authors. In his 1958 book *Irrational Man*, which introduced many Americans to existentialism, William Barrett named a long and diverse list of philosophers and writers as belonging to "existentialism." The recognition of the existentialist movement as encompassing a large and varied group of philosophers and writers has continued to the present day, as seen for example in the recent publication of the second edition of Robert Solomon's much-used anthology *Existentialism* (Solomon 2005), which currently contains selections from twenty-eight authors ranging from Kierkegaard to Arthur Miller. (Barrett and Kaufmann, by the way, are still in print.)

The point of this brief history is that we can't have it both ways: If existentialism comprises a wide range of authors who sound common themes but in very diverse ways and with differences of emphasis and outright disagreements, then it cannot also be reducible to the philosophy of Sartre. He becomes instead one representative (certainly an important and influential one) of a much broader, richer tradition. As we saw in "The Existentialist Legacy," some of the existentialists were religious and others non-religious. The former spoke of human experience as containing intimations of an unfathomable ontological mystery, the latter of humans as alone in and solely responsible for a world without ultimate meaning. All the existentialists recognized and analyzed the inherent sociality as well as the individuality of human beings, but some focused on the problematic aspects of the relationship of the "I" to the "other," while others explored the "I-Thou" relationship as the profoundest disclosure of the human situation. While all emphasized the human capacity for choice, and its defining role in human life, their assessments of the scope of human freedom varied. Some insisted on the radical power of individual choice or will, while others were more attentive to human ambiguity, the capacity to receive, and the role of "grace" in life. Correspondingly, some accentuated our ability to shape the world through imposing meaning on it, while others stressed the extent to which we are at the mercy of chance and circumstance in a world that is in a metaphysical sense opaque to our efforts to understand it. Some saw moral values as arbitrary inventions of human subjects, others as universal principles arising from common features of human experience or grounded in God. The point of this brief sketch is that there are substantial differences of emphasis and interpretation among the existentialists.

So what *do* the existentialists have in common, such that they have been identified as a movement called "existentialism"? We have seen that they share a concern to explore and illuminate common features of the concrete human "life-world"—how we as individual subjects experience ourselves, one another, and our physical environment—by contrast with objective theoretical accounts of human nature and behavior such as we find, for example, in evolutionary biology and psychology, genetics, neuroscience, or cognitive science. In a variety of ways the existentialists articulate what can broadly (and in the case of certain of the existentialists, explicitly and formally) be called a phenomenology of human experience. The existentialists point to what would seem to be a basic gap or incommensurability between the ways we concretely understand and live our lives as subjects and the ways we understand ourselves and the world theoretically and objectively.

For the existentialists, priority must be given to the subjective pole of this dialectic because, as Kierkegaard humorously observed, "[human] existence possesses the remarkable quality that an existing person exists [as a subject] whether he wants to or not." (Kierkegaard [1846] 1992, 120) Even the person who tries conscientiously to incorporate into her understanding and decisions the best objective knowledge available does so as a unique subject negotiating a specific and complex network of relationships to others and to the world, not as a member of a class of organisms displaying certain characteristics and behaviors. So, for example, I don't fall in love or stay in love with someone of the opposite sex out of a desire to contribute to the gene pool; my efforts to reason soundly and communicate clearly have nothing to do with attending to synapses in my brain; and the knowledge that my prehistoric ancestors may have engaged in constant warfare yields no moral imperatives to help me in my deliberations and actions regarding the reduction of violence among people today.

Let me remind the reader of some of the "lived" commonalities that the existentialists explore. For human beings as subjects the "world" is most fundamentally, at an existential level, an environment organized and interpreted in terms of human concerns, of human meanings and values, not space filled with physical objects. Existentially, time is experienced concretely and primarily as a present emerging from the "no more" of the past and opening into the "not yet" of the future, not the temporal units measured by clocks and calendars. My human "being-in-the-world" is also intrinsically a "being-with" other subjects, whether the "others" of my affinity group or alien "others," and adopting attitudes and actions with regard to this "given" intersubjectivity is one of the foundational realities and burdens of human existence. Further, human beings as individual subjects, whether strongly or only dimly aware of their individuality, are constant choice-makers whose choices contribute in a defining sense to the ways in which they interpret the world and "become" as persons—a responsibility that individuals characteristically and in "bad faith" try to hide from themselves. The facts of being-with-others, choice, and "bad faith" mean that ethics is a dominant and inescapable aspect of human life. Humans are "in" the world through moods—happiness, sadness, boredom, fear, anxiety—which are present whether in intense or attenuated form in all our transactions with the world and one another. And human subjects are aware that they are finite and will die, and that awareness (however suppressed or rationalized away) plays a profound role in the shaping of human life. The differences among the existentialists have to do mainly with what aspects of human experience they emphasize as most important and disclosive, which also can involve disagreements about particular phenomenological analyses. Those differences of emphasis are in turn related to their ontological predilections, which I will illustrate shortly.

Now (at last!) to Iris Murdoch on existentialism, as she articulated her interpretation especially in some of the essays collected in *Existentialists and Mystics*. Her earliest presentations were two short BBC Third Programme radio talks in 1950,

"The Novelist as Metaphysician" and "The Existentialist Hero." As the titles suggest, her talks were about what she called the "existentialist novel," and she focused specifically on the novels of Sartre, Beauvoir, and Camus. In "The Novelist as Metaphysician," Murdoch calls attention to the close connection between existentialist philosophy and literature: "The existentialists have generalized and given a philosophical form to something which, piecemeal, most of us can recognize in the crises of our own lives, and which some novelists have been at pains to display" (104).

Then Murdoch goes on to observe that "the existentialists" emphasize "that real value is a function of a free act of valuing, not an objective quality of the world. . . " (106). The view here attributed to "the existentialists" is really that of Sartre, and in this case we can reasonably include Beauvoir and, with appropriate qualifications, the early Camus of *The Myth of Sisyphus* (1942). By the late 1940s, however, Camus had developed, in sharp contrast to Sartre, an affirmation of universal values grounded in an idea of human nature. He articulated this fictionally in *The Plague* (1947) and in his major philosophical work *The Rebel* (1951). Even before and during World War II Camus and Sartre were very different sorts of thinkers and writers. After they became friends and both were well-known, however, their ideas were routinely lumped together and Camus's typically subsumed under and interpreted in the light of Sartre's. Even in *Sisyphus*, while at that time regarding values as human inventions, Camus explicitly denied any interest in the whole question of "free will"and would certainly not have followed Sartre in his equation of individual consciousness with a radical freedom. In the years immediately following the war it was increasingly clear that the two were moving in opposing directions, so that continuing to pair them either as philosophers or as writers should have become increasingly untenable (but often did not). In "The Existentialist Hero" Murdoch describes the hero of the "existentialist novel" in this way:

> The existentialist tells us that we are free and that the meaning of the universe depends on us—but he also admits that we enter into a situation which is already partly formed. We must both engage in some consistent course of action, and keep on remembering that nothing guarantees that we are right. The temper required here is heroic. . . . Rieux [the physician-narrator of *The Plague*] is perhaps the perfect instance of the existentialist hero. He is a person with no illusions and no certainties. He does his job and he loves his fellows and serves them as far as he can. . . . Rieux is a Christian *manqué* (113-114).

What is interesting here is that, having begun with a Sartrian characterization of "the existentialist," and having just discussed Mathieu, the "hero" of Sartre's series of novels *Roads to Freedom*, Murdoch turns to Camus's Dr. Rieux as "the perfect instance of the existentialist hero." In his absorbing and perceptive study *Camus and Sartre: The Story of a Friendship and the Quarrel that Ended It*, Ronald Aronson, contrasting Camus's *The Plague* with Sartre's fiction up to about 1950, observes:

> From Orestes in *The Flies*, who leaves Argos after avenging his father, to Garcin in *No Exit*, the pacifist editor who heads for the border when the going gets tough, to Mathieu in the first two volumes of *Roads to Freedom*, who is painfully adrift in an uncommitted freedom, Sartre's characters feel unreal to themselves, or unable to act, or uncommitted, or swallowed up by necessity. Or they act in bad faith and through dramatic gesture (Aronson 2004, 96).

Aronson might well have also included Roquentin, the protagonist of Sartre's first novel, *Nausea*, as yet another Sartrian "hero" who is paralyzed into inactivity. So the "existentialist hero" as defined in Sartrian terms is to be found not in Sartre's but in Camus's fiction. All the main characters in *The Plague*, by the way—Rieux, Tarrou, Father Paneloux—certainly reflect on their actions and engage in metaphysical debates, but none of them shows any interest in the problem of freedom in Sartre's sense of the term.

So from the outset Murdoch, by defining "existentialism" as "Sartrianism" and subsuming Camus under that definition, muddies the waters—and thus far she is dealing only with the three secular French existentialists who were frequently being grouped and discussed together. I should add here that by this time (1950) Beauvoir, while firmly insisting on her philosophical dependence on Sartre, had already begun moving subtly in an independent direction and disagreeing with Sartre—notably on the problem of freedom—as in her 1947 book *The Ethics of Ambiguity* and in her most influential work *The Second Sex* in 1949. Only in the past couple of decades has Beauvoir come to be properly appreciated as a creative philosopher in her own right and not simply "Sartre warmed over." (We will examine some of Beauvoir's differences from Sartre in the next essay.) In the case of Camus, however, it should have been clear from early on to the discerning reader—and certainly by the late 1940s—that he and Sartre were strikingly different in their emphases, their methods, and their conclusions.

But now, in "The Existentialist Hero," Murdoch goes on to widen the "existentialist" circle dramatically, thereby simply deepening the confusion:

> In . . . [the novels of Sartre, Beauvoir, and Camus] there is ambiguity but there is no mystery. And this alone would condemn them in the eyes . . . of *a rival existentialist*, Gabriel Marcel. This fact alone, that there is no mystery, would falsify their claim to be true pictures of the situation of man (115; italics added).

Marcel, a theistic existentialist and convert to Catholicism, explored the subjective character of human experience and the fragile and fragmentary nature of our human grasp of reality, and sharply criticized Sartre's phenomenology of consciousness and his aggressively atheistic portrayal of the human condition. As it happens, in the early 1950s Murdoch was quite familiar with and interested in Marcel's writings, and one of the essays included in *Existentialists and Mystics* is her review of the first volume of Marcel's 1949-50 Gifford Lectures, *The Mystery of Being*, in the journal *University* in 1951.

Murdoch clearly appreciated Marcel's thought. The quotation in the preceding paragraph should be seen as expressing a concern of her own as well as of Marcel. In her review of *The Mystery of Being*, entitled "The Image of Mind," Murdoch summarizes Marcel's approach to philosophy:

> Mental activity, experience, is a constantly renewed *reflection*, in the course of which the facts and circumstances of my life become the facts and circumstances of *my* life by being appropriated or interiorized by me.... In the course of this reflection there is demanded of me a certain sensibility or respect for an *otherness* to which I find myself related, the varying nature of which Marcel attempts to conjure up for us by such terms as "mystery," "presence," "essence." This otherness is felt, in the last analysis, as being connected with a "supra-empirical" source....

Murdoch goes on to highlight "his use of special concepts such as mystery, availability [*disponibilité*, a central Marcelian idea], participation" (126). "His genius," she comments, "lies in the revelatory power of the concepts which he coins to describe aspects of our experience which we will agree with him in finding important... (129). "Indeed," she asserts, "the whole of his argument raises the question which our philosophizing has not yet satisfactorily answered: what *is* a description of experience?" Murdoch follows these remarks with a criticism of then-current British analytic philosophy of mind as a "hygienic and dehydrated analysis of mental concepts." Her main criticism of Marcel, whose philosophical writings are for the most part not technical treatises but quasi-personal reflections, is for a deficiency at the opposite end of the philosophical spectrum: he is "excessively obscure and imprecise.... impressionistic." (127) (This was and has remained a standard objection to the existentialists generally.)

It should be apparent even from this brief account that the answer Marcel gives to the question "What is a description of experience?"—his phenomenology of the life of the human subject—is very different from Sartre's. And in the last part of the review Murdoch explicitly contrasts the two in partly biographical terms:

> Sartre represents... a defiant rationalism, a spiritual *tabula rasa*.... Sartre lives in a café and eschews intimate bonds. *L'Etre et le néant* [*Being and Nothingness*] is dominated by the image of consciousness as a perpetual escape from solidification. Marcel on the other hand values intimacy and family relations; his favourite images are of continuity, participation, merging. He values respect for natural bonds, for the inherited, for the mysterious and fruitful links with being, which our deracinate civilization seems to threaten (129).

Murdoch's images contrasting "living in a café" with "intimacy and family relations" come directly from Marcel's critical essay on Sartre, "Existence and Human Freedom" (1946), published in English in the volume *The Philosophy of Existentialism* (Marcel 1956).

The essay, in which Marcel analyzes the main ideas in *Being and Nothingness*, is a very illuminating short introduction to the profound differences between the two

French existentialists. Approaching his subject with the respect and graciousness for which he was well known (he also knew Sartre personally), Marcel combines thoughtful appreciation with vigorous philosophical and moral criticism. At point after point he finds in Sartre's phenomenological analysis of human experience a valuable insight taken to an extreme and assumed to be the sole truth about the phenomenon being examined: "... it is possible to start from a profoundly true and just observation and, by pushing it to its limit, to arrive at a conception of human life and sensibility which is not only false, but odiously offensive and degrading" (67). Three important examples of this distortion, according to Marcel, are Sartre's analyses of 1) human relationships, 2) the freedom of consciousness, and 3) values— also main themes of Murdoch's characterization of "existentialism."

1) Sartre, beginning his analysis with individual consciousness, interprets our human "being-with" one another as a tension in which each subject inevitably renders other subjects, and is in turn rendered by them, as an object. Human relations are a struggle in which I try to escape the objectifying "gaze" of the other and preserve my sovereign freedom, while also desiring to appropriate the other as if she were an object for me. Those relationships we call "love" exhibit the struggle the most intensely. Thus human relationships are, in a broad sense, inherently sado-masochistic, and genuine communion or community between persons—being able to say "we" instead of "I" in a qualitative rather a merely quantitative sense—is impossible except as an exercise in "bad faith." Marcel observes that "Sartre's analysis of love is conducted in such a way that it is bound to arrive at a wholly negative conception. The aim of love is to appropriate the will of another . . . in order to acquire absolute value in the eyes of the beloved. . . ." (Marcel 1956, 74). By contrast, the possibility and the reality, however imperfect and incomplete, of authentic communion—of genuine giving and receiving, caring and sharing—between and among persons is at the very heart of Marcel's phenomenology of experience.

2) For Sartre, the individual consciousness, in its primary and pre-reflective state, is freedom: a perpetual spontaneity within the density of being that asserts itself as a "negativizing" (*néantisation*) and is undetermined by anything else, while at the same time being "nothing" other than this activity of awareness of everything else. As consciousness I am "not" (meaning that I distinguish myself from) the things I am aware of: the physical world, other persons, my own body, even my thoughts and feelings and my past and future. Since as consciousness I freely and continually construct and reconstruct both my world and myself through my choices and actions, I am entirely responsible for my life. Sartre, with his flair for the dramatic, calls this condition being "condemned to be free."

Marcel lodges various criticisms against Sartre's extreme analysis of freedom. His chief concern is to point out that, just as Sartre has no place for love as genuine altruism and openness to another, so he has no place for grace as part of human experience but only for an autonomy and responsibility so absolute and unrelieved that everyone is indeed "condemned." By "grace" Marcel refers broadly to all those aspects of human experience that are "given" or "gifted" to us apart from our striving and willing, although of course for him as a theist they have their ultimate source in divine grace. Again, Marcel considers Sartre's analysis a severely distorted and unbalanced phenomenology of human experience. "I do not believe that in the whole history of human thought, grace, even in its most secularized forms, has ever been denied with such audacity or such impudence" (79). For Sartre, he goes on to say, "to receive is incompatible with being free; indeed, a being who is free is bound to deny to himself that he has received anything" (82).

3) According to Sartre, my individual consciousness as freedom is the sole foundation of values, and as such nothing outside of myself can justify me in adopting one value or another. Values are entirely invented or created by us, and Sartre sometimes uses artistic creation as a model for understanding how moral values are to be understood as well. Marcel notes that Sartre has indicated that the third of his series of novels *Roads to Freedom* (*Death in the Soul*, 1949) will be devoted to praising the heroes of the World War II Resistance in France. "Now I ask you," Marcel rhetorically queries,

> in the name of what principle, having first denied the existence of values or at least of their objective basis, can he [Sartre] establish any appreciable difference between those utterly misguided but undoubtedly courageous men who joined voluntarily the [pro-Nazi] Anti-Bolshevik Legion, on the one hand, and the heroes of the Resistance movement, on the other? I can see no way of establishing this difference without admitting . . . that values are real (87).

Interestingly, Camus also affords a striking contrast with Sartre on the issue of the morality of the Resistance. In a series of four "Letters to a German Friend" (available in English in the volume *Resistance, Rebellion, and Death*, 1960) that Camus wrote in 1944 as editor of the Resistance newspaper *Combat*, he was struggling with precisely this problem: On the basis of the moral subjectivism and relativism of *The Myth of Sisyphus*, he could not justify his choice to resist the Nazis as morally preferable to his (fictional) "German friend's" choice to join the Nazis. Here we see Camus beginning to explore an idea of human nature and universal moral values which by the end of the war and the immediate post-war years he had developed into a philosophical, moral, and political outlook that put him sharply at odds with Sartre. For his part, Marcel concludes his critique of Sartre on values by observing that "if I examine myself honestly and without reference to any preconceived body of ideas, I find that I do not 'choose' my values at all, but that I *recognise* them and then posit my actions in accordance or in contradiction with these values, not, however, without being painfully aware of this contradiction" (87-88).

I've lingered over Marcel's criticisms of Sartre in order to illustrate, using a philosopher and writer whom Murdoch called a "rival existentialist" and whose work she knew well, that the differences among those authors who even in 1950 were being called "existentialists" could be significant. Marcel is a perfect example because his analysis and assessment of human experience were at crucial points fundamentally opposed to those of Sartre. What also emerges from the contrast between Marcel and Sartre is something I mentioned earlier in my thumbnail sketch of common themes of the existentialists: the differences among the existentialists in their descriptions of our experience as subjects seem clearly to be influenced by their ontological assumptions or predispositions. Marcel finds in Sartre an "aggressive atheism," a gratuitous and militant closing of all doors of human experience to the possibility of transcendence and mystery, and as we have seen even to love and grace as authentic human experiences, that seriously truncates and distorts his account of human experience. Marcel suggests that Sartre seems to have made this choice early in life (which Sartre later seems to confirm in his 1963 autobiography of his early years, *Words*) and, with his passion for extremes of every sort, was determined to "run it out" consistently and relentlessly to the end. As his language implies in the passages I've quoted, Marcel the serious moralist found important aspects of Sartre's thinking not only wrong but offensive. As a theist, albeit one with considerable sympathy toward those who can no longer believe, Marcel highlighted those aspects of individual and interpersonal experience—our making ourselves available to one another in love, our experiences of interdependence and grace, our recognition of commonly binding moral values and obligations—that provide the existential bases out of which arise interpretations of the "mystery of being" in terms of God. (It's interesting, in this connection, that in her review Murdoch faults Marcel for failing to make fully explicit this ontology that underlies his phenomenological analysis [Murdoch 1997, 128].)

Murdoch's essay "The Existentialist Political Myth" was originally published in 1952 in *Socratic Digest*. It is a creative attempt, during the early years of the Cold War, to find in some of the ideas of "the existentialists" a not-clearly-formulated but hopeful challenge to explore a third, middle way between capitalism and communism. Again defining existentialism in terms of Sartre, Murdoch sees in the emphasis on individual consciousness as the source of values and in the "pure moment" of individual choice a rebuke to both sides:

> The pure moment is something which is poised between the dead conventions of capitalist society on the one hand and the rigid dogma of the Communist Party bureaucrat on the other. There is something typically existentialist about this position (140).

Murdoch finds in "the existentialists" no answer to the question of how to "think morally about politics," but rather "an expression of a passionate and sincere desire to keep to the middle way, to preserve the values of an innocent and vital individualism in a world which seems to menace them from both sides" (144-5).

In keeping with my aim in this essay, what interests me primarily about "The Existentialist Political Myth" is less Murdoch's thesis than her depiction of existentialism. References to Marcel appear here and there in the essay. Early on she includes both Sartre and Marcel in a fair generalization about existentialist method:

> It is ... in this sort of semi-psychological description and analysis that existentialist writings are at their most brilliant and illuminating. The new concepts which they invent (such as Sartre's *etre-pour-autui*, Gabriel Marcel's *fidelité*) draw a line round important aspects of experience, naming what has not been named before. (133)

Interestingly, Murdoch echoes Marcel in going on to characterize individual human consciousness as interpreted by Sartre as "non-historical, non-social, and non-determined.... solipsistic..." (134). But then, continuing to describe Sartre's view of the world, she writes:

> Man is an emptiness poised between two inaccessible totalities. The world of objects is impenetrable, the world of intelligible being is unattainable, even contradictory. This rather bitter view of objective reality as "fallen" is a persistent feature of *existentialist thinking*... (136; italics added).

Having included Marcel earlier, Murdoch now lapses once again into generalizing as "existentialist thinking" ideas held only by Sartre. Marcel would have entirely rejected this summary as describing his views. For him humans are not an "emptiness," nor is knowledge of the world "inaccessible." While as a Christian Marcel certainly regarded the world as in some sense "fallen," he would not have regarded this as a "bitter" condition but as an estrangement in and through which is fragmentarily disclosed a mysterious unity in which all things dwell.

Up to this point I've deliberately avoided raising the issue of whether Murdoch's characterization even of Sartre's early ideas is entirely accurate. My theme is her confusing presentation of "existentialism" as "Sartrianism" while including among the existentialists thinkers such as Camus and Marcel, and I haven't wanted to complicate things even further—nor do I want to prolong this essay indefinitely. But here I pause to insert into the discussion the observation that some of Murdoch's interpretations of and generalizations about Sartre, as well as about existentialism generally, are careless and contestable. Every adjective in her description of Sartre's phenomenology of consciousness as "non-historical, non-social, ... [and] solipsistic" would be disputed as at least one-sided if not inaccurate by many Sartre scholars, as would her summary, in the indented quotation above, of Sartre's interpretation of human knowledge of the world. One such corrective to some of the standard characterizations of Sartre's early philosophy is the writings of Hazel Barnes, his foremost American translator, interpreter, and by-no-means-uncritical "disciple"—notably her books *Humanistic Existentialism* (1959) and *An Existentialist Ethics* (1967), and most recently her defense of a Sartrian perspective and response to his and her critics in her 1997 autobiography *The Story I Tell Myself: A Venture in Existentialist Autobiography*. It seems to me that Murdoch's (and also Marcel's) assessments of the philosophy of *Being and Nothingness*, like those of many others who represent the "standard interpretation," certainly can adduce textual support and describe definite *tendencies* in Sartre's early thought, but whether they are entirely balanced and accurate is open to question and resolvable only by a close analysis that lies outside the scope of this essay.

I will, however, address myself to one of Murdoch's characterizations of existentialism in "The Existentialist Political Myth" as a good example of the sort of sweeping and inaccurate generalizations in which she was all too wont to indulge (perhaps an occupational hazard for a very prolific and imaginative author who wrote constantly). The generalization in question was not peculiar to Murdoch but was an aspect of standard interpretation of the existentialists, although her version of it is extreme and almost caricatural:

> The trend of [existentialist] thought is anti-rational, anti-scientific, anti-technical. The world of clear-cut rational distinctions, of techniques and positions and institutions and rights is unreal. This is the echo which we hear in the writings of thinkers as apparently far apart as . . . Camus . . . [and] Marcel (136).

These statements follow immediately upon a discussion of Roquentin, the fictionalized Sartre of *Nausea*, and we have seen abundant evidence that Sartre is Murdoch's model of existentialism, so there can be no doubt that they are also intended to include Sartre. Since she subtitled her early book on Sartre "romantic rationalist," and in one of the earlier essays we've examined referred to Sartre's "defiant rationalism," her describing "the existentialists" as "anti-rational" is at minimum very puzzling. All the existentialists—and some certainly more than Sartre—were critical of rational*ism*, scient*ism*, and the modern tendency of humans (or, more accurately, of educated elites) to let their understanding of the world and of themselves be dominated by the presuppositions and methods of the sciences and by their technological applications. Marcel devoted a good deal of attention to the theme that "man is at the mercy of his technics," and it was a major preoccupation of Heidegger, as in his essay "The Question Concerning Technology" (Heidegger [1962] 1977). But critiquing these peculiarly modern idolatries is by no means the same thing as opposing reason, science, and technology themselves. When Murdoch goes on to say that for the existentialists rational distinctions, techniques, institutions, and rights are "unreal," she seems to narrow her identification of existentialism with Sartre even farther to the character Roquentin, despite almost a decade of Sartre's thoroughgoing political engagement as a committed writer and also increasingly as an activist, not to mention his consistent acceptance and affirmation of the importance of reason and scientific knowledge. Nor does her statement accurately describe any of the other existentialists, including the two she names, Marcel and Camus.

Having mentioned Sartre's political engagement, I want to note that Murdoch's suggestion that the existentialists could represent a moral and political "middle way" between Soviet-style communism and Western capitalism in the early Cold War era had been actively pursued by both Camus and Sartre for several years. Camus and Sartre were always men of the Left, but by the end of the war Camus was becoming actively anti-communist. He spoke out increasingly against Stalinist atrocities, the French Communist Party's rationalizations and dogmatism, and the politics of violence that had pervaded the communist revolution and state. In *The Rebel*, published a year before Murdoch's essay, Camus articulated his position comprehensively. He found in the historical phenomenon of human revolt against oppression, from the slave against the master to the many protests against divine and human injustices, a fundamental affirmation of human life and solidarity and a creative source of values. But he went on to argue that revolt that moves beyond the limited aim of righting specific wrongs and restoring the possibility of human dignity and happiness in the here-and-now into full-scale revolution is a betrayal of precisely those values that revolt brings to light. Camus attacked both Marxist ideology and practicing communism, and on historical grounds rejected the major modern European revolutions as having inevitably fallen into absolutist ideological dogma and the willingness to adopt any means, including violence on a large scale, to achieve the abstract end of a future utopia. No apologist for capitalism, he advocated social democracy and active nonviolent reforms over a range of issues from working conditions to human rights, and was a strong supporter of trade unions and other affinity groups struggling for justice.

As for Sartre, it's noteworthy that in 1952, the very year Murdoch's essay appeared, he underwent—or, more accurately, completed—his "conversion" from left-wing critic of communism seeking a socialist "third way" to committed supporter of and apologist for communism and active advocate of violence as a legitimate and necessary tactic of the oppressed. Famously declaring his commitment to "hate the bourgeoisie" until the day he died, Sartre had come to the conclusion that there could be no middle course between capitalism and communism. One must choose sides, and the only side committed to the oppressed and capable of evoking their loyalty was the communists. Not surprisingly, it was the publication of Camus's *The Rebel* in 1951 that brought about the definitive break between the two old friends and fully revealed just how far apart they were philosophically, ethically, and politically. I should add that after several years of suppressing his criticisms of communism, Sartre re-emerged in 1956 as a powerful internal critic of communism, the leading exponent of a revised and humanized Marxism (articulated the most fully in his *Critique of Dialectical Reason*), and a tenacious champion of people of the Third World struggling to free themselves from the legacy of colonialism.

The final Murdoch essay I want to discuss is a much later one, "Existentialists and Mystics," published in 1970 in a volume of *Essays & Poems Presented to Lord David Cecil*. The essay is a broad and imaginative study of the twentieth-century European and American novel in which Murdoch traces its roots in and differences from the nineteenth-century novel and, writing at a time of rapid cultural and technological change, offers a forecast regarding the future of the novel. I will confine my remarks, however, to her characterization of what she calls the "existentialist novel" and contrasts with the "mystical novel."

Murdoch calls the novel "that great sensitive mirror, or screen, or field of forces" that continues to be "one of the most articulate expressions of the dilemmas of its age." She intends, she says, "to use the fairly recent history of the novel as an instrument of diagnosis" (221). To this end she introduces two types of recent novel, acknowledging the inherent limitations of what she calls a "ramshackle classification" and the possibility that many novels may fall under both types or neither. Beginning with a brief summary of the two types, Murdoch says that the "existentialist novel" presents freedom and virtue as "the assertion of will," while the "mystical novel" portrays freedom and virtue as flowing from "understanding, or obedience to the Good" (223).

In introducing the two types of novel, Murdoch says parenthetically, "I use the word 'existentialist' in a broad atmospheric sense" (223). A little further on she introduces a more general term, "voluntarism," and briefly uses it interchangeably with "existentialism." By speaking of existentialism in terms of "atmosphere" and subsuming it under the broader category "voluntarism," she appears at first glance to protect herself against the sorts of criticisms to which, as we've seen, her early essays were open. Here Murdoch seems to be saying, "I'm going to identify a prominent type of contemporary novel, which I'll call 'existentialist' because of certain general associations that will be familiar to the reader; but we can just as well call it 'voluntarist' if you prefer." What is of interest, of course, is to see how she fills in the content of the type of novel she calls "existentialist" or "voluntarist."

Murdoch begins by calling the existentialist novel "the natural heir and outcome of Western nineteenth-century thought" and more specifically as "the child of the Romantic movement." She elaborates on these connections as follows:

> Existentialism, or, to use an even more general term, voluntarism, philosophy which emphasizes and values will-power, is of course an offspring of the thought of Immanuel Kant. It is also a natural mode of being of the capitalist era. It is attractive, and indeed to most of us still natural, because it suggests individualism, self-reliance, private conscience, and what we ordinarily think of as political freedom, in that important sense where freedom means not doing what is right but doing what is desired (223-4).

Murdoch goes on to specify that the existentialist novel is the quintessential expression of "the anxious modern consciousness."

Here, then, is the "typical" existentialist novel, with its protagonist the "existentialist hero":

> We know this novel and its hero well. The story of the lonely brave man, defiant without optimism, proud without pretension, always an exposer of shams, whose mode of being is a deep criticism of society. He is an adventurer. He is godless. He does not suffer from guilt. He thinks of himself as free. He may have faults, he may be self-assertive or even violent, but he has sincerity and courage, and for this we forgive him.

We saw a similar sort of portrayal in her early essay "The Existentialist Hero." Murdoch goes on to describe the will of the existentialist hero as an "adventurous instrument" that is "separate from the rest of his being and uncontaminated. He *might* do anything" (225). This characterization of will reminds us of Murdoch's use of the idea of the "pure moment" of decision in her essay on existentialism and politics. In the present essay she follows this characterization of will with a somewhat eccentric sample list of novelists—not with titles of specific novels—who write existentialist novels: D. H. Lawrence, Hemingway, Camus, Sartre, and Kingsley Amis.

Not only individual self-assertion but "godlessness" is for Murdoch essential to the existentialist hero. Again looking at the existentialist novel as the natural further development of nineteenth-century themes, she describes it as "the first and immediate expression of a consciousness without God," as heir to the nineteenth century's "Luciferian pride in the individual and in the achievements of science." The existentialist hero, Murdoch says, tries to be "cheerfully godless," and even the "famous gloom" associated with existentialism is "a mode of satisfaction" (226).

By contrast, the mystical novel represents "second thoughts" about the modern condition, reflecting "the uneasy suspicion that perhaps after all man is not God."

> As we readily recognize and sympathise with the hero of willpower, so we can also recognize and sympathise with the mystical hero. He too is a man in tension, but here the tension is not between will and nature, but between nature and God. This is the man who has given up traditional religion but is still haunted by a sense of the reality and unity of some sort of spiritual world (226-7).

Anxiety characterizes both types of hero, but whereas the existentialist hero is struggling "to impose or assert or find himself," the mystical hero seeks "to discipline or purge or diminish himself." The pitfall of the former is egoism, of the latter masochism. The existentialist hero is a twentieth-century version of "romantic man," the mystical hero of the "man of faith" (227). As with the existentialist novel, Murdoch provides only a bare list of examples of writers who can be said to write mystical novels: Graham Greene, Patrick White, Saul Bellow, Muriel Spark, and William Golding.

Keeping in mind the latitude Murdoch desired in using the term "existentialism" very broadly in "Existentialists and Mystics," I've thus far confined myself simply to exposition. But I trust that my presentation has shown that she has once again defined "existentialism" in quintessentially Sartrian terms. The "existentialist hero" is the individual alone in a world without God who anxiously recognizes that he must create his life and affect the world through acts of pure freedom of will, and has the courage despite his limitations to do it.

Murdoch's favorite non-Sartrian existentialist, Gabriel Marcel, would seem clearly to belong among the "mystical" writers, although his "heroes" are less heroic than in Murdoch's characterization of the type. In 1950 Marcel gave a lecture about his plays at the Institut Français in London entitled, significantly, "The Drama of the Soul in Exile." He describes the soul in exile as "the soul who has become a stranger to itself, who can no longer understand itself, who has lost its way.... most of my heroes are unaware of what they are and of their own worth...." (Marcel

1965, 16). Acting out of their spiritual exile, Marcel says, his characters in their uncertainty don't understand their own intentions and behavior. He speaks of

> the kind of fatality which a human being can carry in himself and constantly discharge upon others, even when his intentions are above reproach. We are infinitely more than we are aware of wishing to be and sometimes, strange to say, the apparently most conscious and clear-headed are, in fact, most ignorant of their inner selves (21).

The dramatist's task, he says, is "to make apparent, and even intelligible, *qua* mystery, that inscrutable something which each of us carries within himself"; philosophically stated, the purpose of drama is "to awaken or re-awaken in us the consciousness of the infinite which is concealed in the particular" (27). In these words of "rival existentialist" Gabriel Marcel we are, again, very far from the Sartrian model of existentialism.

One of the striking things about Marcel's characterization of his purpose as a writer and of the "souls in exile" who are his characters is that to a remarkable degree it also describes the outlook and characters in Iris Murdoch's novels. In terms of her own typology, Murdoch's affinities are certainly with the "mystical novelists," as I think she would have readily agreed. Her Platonism permeates her narratives, both in the form of explicit reflection and through her portrayal of people who are ignorantly, blindly, and often destructively propelled by the struggle between their natural egoism and a desire for a transcendent Good, and who sometimes very fragmentarily glimpse the object of their desire through romantic love, friendship, art, and religion. We know from Murdoch's philosophical writings that Bradley Pearson, the narrator-protagonist of *The Black Prince*, looking back on his having fallen desperately in love with a much younger woman, speaks for the author when he reflects: "The human soul craves for the eternal of which, apart from certain mysteries of religion, only love and art can give a glimpse (202)."

On her own terms, Murdoch was not an "existentialist" writer, but in the wider sense of "existentialism" that embraces a range of generalized descriptions of "lived" human experience she can be seen as an illuminating contributor. Indeed, the combination of her philosophical orientation and interests (ethics, aesthetics, religion) and the depth of her psychological insight makes Murdoch's novels a particularly rich source of existentialist "wisdom." Again, Bradley Pearson can provide us with a tiny sampling. He sounds a central existentialist theme when he reflects: "There is thus an eternal discrepancy between the self-knowledge which we gain by observing ourselves objectively and the self-awareness which we have of ourselves subjectively: a discrepancy which probably makes it impossible for us ever to arrive at the truth" (181). Bradley goes on to try to capture the difficulty in characterizing both the unity and the evanescence of consciousness as experienced by the individual subject.

In fact the problem remains unclarified because no philosopher and hardly any novelist has ever managed to explain what that weird stuff, human consciousness, is really made of. Body, external objects, darty memories, warm fantasies, other minds, guilt, fear, hesitation, lies, glees, doles, breathtaking pains, a thousand things which words can only fumble at, coexist, many fused together in a single unit of consciousnesss (182).

But in her philosophical reflections on existentialism Murdoch remained to the end captive to a particular and narrow image of existentialism that she had learned from her early study of Sartre. Despite the fact that from early on she also read, among others, Marcel, Kierkegaard, Nietzsche, Heidegger, and Buber—all of whom received significant attention in her 1992 book *Metaphysics as a Guide to Morals*— when she generalized about "existentialism" as a philosophical or literary phenomenon she always reverted to a somewhat stereotypical Sartrianism.

In an important 1969 essay, "On 'God' and 'Good,'" in which Murdoch was surveying the contemporary philosophical scene for its possibilities as a resource in developing an adequate moral philosophy, she prefers "existentialism" to analytic philosophy because "it at least professes and tries to be a philosophy one could live by" (46). But then she immediately goes on to find "existentialism" lacking as the basis for a moral philosophy: it is "still Cartesian and egocentric," with "an unrealistic conception of will" and having "no adequate conception of original sin." (46) For "existentialism," she says, "an authentic mode of existence is . . . attainable by intelligence and force of will" (47). "The existentialist picture of choice" she characterizes as "unrealistic, over-optimistic, romantic" (53), because of its fixation on the "pure" will or moment and its discontinuity with the person's past. It hardly needs pointing out by now that Camus, Marcel, Kierkegaard, Buber, and Heidegger would not have recognized themselves in this description.

Murdoch's repeated denials that she was an existentialist make sense in the light of what we've seen to be her persistent identification of existentialism with a certain picture of Sartre's early philosophy. In his recent biography *Iris Murdoch As I Knew Her*, A. N. Wilson, the novelist, biographer, and long-time friend of Murdoch, brushes aside her denials and states flatly (and, at first blush, hopefully) that "IM was an existentialist, and her best novels are all profoundly existentialist" (Wilson 2004, 137). Unfortunately, Wilson is maddeningly offhanded and somewhat dilettantish about ideas, and his succeeding remarks about existentialism can only be described as confused. In moments of clarity, however, and when speaking directly of Murdoch's relationship to existentialism, he reveals what he means by insisting on her "existentialism." While characterizing her philosophical essays as "anti-existentialist," he writes that "all her early novels are in the broadest sense existentialist: that is to say, her characters seem to be making quite arbitrary choices about their lives without any clear sense of a code outside themselves" (150). He goes on to say that "the moments of decision in her books . . . are existential moments, dependent not upon some change in outward facts or circumstances, but upon changes in their own will or perception" (151).

Wilson seems to have taken over Murdoch's own reduction of existentialism to a certain interpretation of the Sartrian emphasis on the "pure" and arbitrary exertion of individual will. I've suggested that there is a much wider, richer, and more adequate sense in which Murdoch might be called an "existentialist" novelist; but my chief aim has been to describe and critically examine her long and active engagement, as an important philosopher and writer in her own right, with existentialist philosophy and literature. I realize that by focusing only on that engagement I may seem to have cast only in a negative light a philosopher and writer whom I generally admire. However, by highlighting the limitations and inconsistencies of an otherwise learned and imaginative discussion of the movement, I've tried to shed light on a problem that has been endemic to the interpretation of existentialism.

–4–

Existentialism and Feminism: Simone de Beauvoir and Mary Daly

Existentialism would seem to be a "natural" as a philosophical foundation or resource for feminist thought, and the wide and substantial influence of Beauvoir's *The Second Sex* on the emergence of "second wave" feminism placed an existentialist perspective in the mainstream of modern feminist theory. The existentialists' focus on and detailed attention to concrete human experience provides a context and methods for exploring women's "life-world," so foundational to the feminist enterprise. The existentialist emphasis on the freedom or possibility of the individual person as subject has contributed to the feminist recognition that being a woman is not a fixed "destiny" but a dynamic "situation" that can be changed through personal, social, and institutional choices. Existentialism's varied descriptions of the individual subject as always existing relationally or intersubjectively have provided a resource for feminist explorations of the central importance of relationship in women's experience and self-understanding. The existentialists' criticisms of the sufficiency of abstractive, objective, theoretical modes of thinking about human beings and the world have been congenial to feminists who have also seen in the intellectual dominance of such modes aspects of patriarchalism.

In her 1985 book *Feminist Theory: The Intellectual Traditions of American Feminism*, Josephine Donovan included a chapter on existentialist versions of feminist theory that discussed briefly the formative generation of feminist existentialists who came to prominence as scholars and teachers in the 1960s and 1970s (117-140). Among those she discussed were philosophers Simone de Beauvoir and Sandra Bartky and theologians Kathryn Rabuzzi, Letty Russell, Rosemary Ruether, and Mary Daly. (A serious omission among philosophers was Hazel Barnes, who like Beauvoir was both a creative Sartrian and a feminist.) Donovan found in Sartre's phenomenological ontology the philosophical basis of existentialist feminism, in particular his analysis of the freedom of consciousness with regard to both external objects and its own self-image, the distinction between "bad faith" and authenticity, and the phenomenon of both individual and collective "otherness." She interpreted feminist existentialist theologians in terms of Buber's contrast between "I-Thou" and "I-It" as the subject's two primary ways of relating to the world, other persons, and God. The feminist theologians, she wrote, "reject objectified, reified forms of relationship and abstract hypostasized images of the deity; instead, they urge that one see God as an experience of Being in the midst of life, as a Thou" (127). I will return to a consideration of the ideas of two of these "pioneering" existentialist feminist philosophers and theologians, Simone de Beauvoir and Mary Daly, because they laid the foundations and set the agenda for further development in both areas.

1. Feminist interpretation of male philosophers: the case of Kierkegaard

First, however, I want to examine the issue of feminist interpretation of important male philosophers in the Western tradition. In 1994 Nancy Tuana published a volume of essays she edited entitled *Feminist Interpretations of Plato* and published by Penn State University Press. That became the first of an ongoing series of such volumes on philosophers ranging from Plato and Aristotle through Descartes, Kant, and Hegel to Foucault and Derrida. Among the philosophers considered are three major figures associated with the existentialist tradition: Kierkegaard, Nietzsche, and Sartre. The series also includes some women philosophers: Mary Wollstonecraft, Beauvoir, Hannah Arendt, and Ayn Rand.

I want to look briefly at one volume in the series, *Feminist Interpretations of Søren Kierkegaard*, edited by Céline Léon and Sylvia Walsh, as a case study of the possibilities and the hazards of feminist rethinking of the male "greats" of the philosophical tradition. Feminist re-examination of influential male thinkers and writers of the past is absolutely necessary, bringing fresh questions to and illuminating new possibilities in old texts; and the editors and publisher of the "feminist interpretations" series are to be commended for encouraging and exhibiting this sort of scholarship. The pitfalls of such reinterpretation are perhaps also obvious. Among them are anachronistically imposing contemporary questions and assumptions upon past thinkers, trying to differentiate among remarks referring to actual women and those directed to "women of the age" or to woman as symbol, and attempting to salvage a hidden core of at least proto-feminist reality under the patriarchal appearances—whether in the ideas or in the man himself. All these pitfalls dot the landscape in the Léon and Walsh volume on Kierkegaard, along with some very illuminating interpretation of Kierkegaard.

My own view is that feminist reinterpretation of male philosophers such as Kierkegaard and the others discussed in the series should focus strictly on their philosophical (and, in Kierkegaard's case, theological) vision, insights, and arguments to see whether or not they contain fruitful possibilities for feminist thought. Interpreters should forget about trying to rehabilitate the man himself and his remarks, ranging from ambiguous to misogynistic, about women. The former seems to me a fruitful and exciting enterprise; the latter a dubious expenditure of energy and intelligence.

On the first page of their Introduction, Léon and Walsh pose what they see as the challenge Kierkegaard presents to feminist reinterpretation:

> ... his attitude toward women, the feminine, and the rapports between men and women is at best ambiguous. On the one hand, he insists on an ultimate and fundamental equality of the sexes before God—even, in some instances, the

greater perfection of woman—and singles out the feminine as the paradigm of religious existence. On the other hand, insofar as his entire production is bestrewn with stereotyped, degrading, and patriarchal remarks about women, a positive reading of his views appears highly problematic for feminism (2).

This is a good example of what I mean by the pitfalls, the problematic aspects, of feminist reinterpretation of "dead white male" thinkers. We find here a concern with Kierkegaard's attitude toward and statements about women that I find unfruitful. Like many other male religious thinkers before and after him, he affirmed the equality of the sexes before God—and of course with no intention of letting that disturb their fundamental *in*equality in society. Another standard way of interpreting gender "equality," which typically accompanied the theological affirmation, was to interpret the sexes as "complementary"—as "separate but equal," each with its own appropriate nature and roles in life. Kierkegaard held this view, and famously Rousseau, but so did almost all male philosophers historically, including those who like Rousseau and Kierkegaard were in other respects quite revolutionary in their thinking. We also find in the passage from Léon and Walsh's Introduction the observation that sometimes in his writings Kierkegaard actually regards women as the "superior" sex spiritually and morally, and the "feminine" as the paradigm of religious existence, since authentic faith in God is a matter of receptivity and surrender. But again, Kierkegaard's "elevation" of woman can be seen as a religious version of the nineteenth-century sentimentalization of ("proper" upper- and middle-class) women, "putting them on a pedestal" as nobler beings and guardians of morals. As with gender equality before God and complementarity, this left all the essentialist assumptions and social disabilities in place.

The editors divide the contributors into three groups. The first group—Wanda Warren Berry, Birgit Bertung, Julia Watkin, and Robert Perkins—defend Kierkegaard against the charge of misogyny by emphasizing the distancing he achieves through writing under pseudonyms and his ironic and dialectical reasoning. They also argue that he challenges men and women alike to the task of self-discovery. The second group—Céline Léon and Sylviane Agacinski—are postmodern critics of Kierkegaard who argue that by insisting on sexual differences conceived from the vantage point even of a flawed and ambiguous masculinity, Kierkegaard traps women on the "lower" side of the traditional gender polarities of culture/nature, active/passive, conscious/unconscious, and soul/body, in effect defining women in such a way as to leave them without a "self" to discover. The third group, which the editors call representatives of the "classical tradition of feminism"—including Mark L. Taylor, Sylvia Walsh, Leslie A. Howe, Jane Duran, and (again) Wanda Warren Berry—take seriously the tensions among the pseudonyms and between pseudonyms and author, and the generally negative elements in Kierkegaard's discussion of women, but emphasize instead the positive role of the feminine in his philosophical outlook as exemplifying qualities that both women and men ought to strive to embody.

As might be expected from my remarks about what I think are fruitful and unfruitful feminist approaches to interpreting male philosophers, I find two essays in the third group that discuss the value of Kierkegaard's thought for feminist theory to be the most valuable. Both see in Kierkegaard's critique and renewal of philosophy an important resource for the feminist philosophical emphases on subjectivity, wholeness, and concreteness and on the theoretical critique of traditional masculinist ideas of objectivity. In "The Kierkegaardian Feminist," Jane Duran explores the implications in terms of his three "stages on life's way" or modes of reflective existence—the aesthetic, the ethical, and the religious. She writes:

> Failing to meet an individual in his or her specificity appears to be conceptually foreign to Kierkegaard, and for good reason. His philosophical thinking asks us to come to grips with our own lives, and to think about, as he might phrase it, the bungling in which we are enmeshed. . . . The feminist, motivated by current work that encourages us to think of ethical and/or religious theorizing in new terms, can have few better friends than Kierkegaard (263) . . . .

Sylvia Walsh, in "Subjectivity Versus Objectivity: Kierkegaard's *Postscript* and Feminist Epistemology," sounds a similar theme by examining the contrast between subjective and objective approaches to the problem of truth advanced by the pseudonymous author of Kierkegaard's *Concluding Unscientific Postscript*, Johannes Climacus. Arguing that the idea of a subjective relationship to existentially important truth is not "subjectivism," Walsh concludes that "Kierkegaard's *Concluding Unscientific Postscript*, often ignored by the philosophical community because of its emphasis on subjectivity, deserves a sympathetic as well as critical re-reading by feminist epistemologists. They may find some viewpoints in it to reject, but also much to support and advance their own attempts to rethink and reformulate the concepts of objectivity and subjectivity in the context of the present age" (280).

Kierkegaard's writings, belatedly "discovered" by the wider European intellectual world long after his death, of course provided the chief inspiration and foundation for the existentialist movement, and *Concluding Unscientific Postscript* is one of the three or four most influential Kierkegaard texts. That part of the "philosophical community" consisting of the existentialists has clearly not "ignored" but on the contrary built upon Kierkegaard's exploration of individual subjectivity and the incommensurability between subjective and objective accounts of what it is to be human. When commentators like Duran and Walsh find in Kierkegaard important resources for feminist philosophy, it needs to be added that the existentialist tradition generally has been and continues to be an important resource. Indeed, existentialism should be one of the richest and most congenial philosophical contributors to feminist thought.

What I have said about feminist approaches to Kierkegaard seems to me to provide a model for dealing with all the male existentialists. Efforts to "rescue" their attitudes toward and remarks about women are a waste of time. As the Duran and Walsh essays exemplify, attention should be focused entirely on their philosophical perspective, insights, and arguments and how they might be critically and creatively appropriated. Beauvoir did this with Hegel, Nietzsche, and Sartre in *The Second Sex*. Critical analysis of the male existentialists' phenomenologies of human experience may also show masculinist biases in what has been emphasized and what neglected. For example, Sartre has been criticized by some feminist interpreters for what they see as his sharply distinguishing consciousness from bodiliness and the physical, privileging the former as surely as did Plato or Descartes. They would say that this is a defective account of individual subjectivity-in-context compared to that of, say, Merleau-Ponty. It can also be seen as weighted on the side of making male experience normative, since males have historically and ideologically been identified with consciousness and females with bodiliness. By contrast, two Sartrian feminist philosophers, Beauvoir and Barnes, both defended and creatively extended Sartre on this issue. (While Barnes duly recognized and documented Sartre's sexism, she also argued for the cogency of his analysis of human existence as a "bodily subjectivity" in her essay "Sartre and Feminism" in *Feminist Interpretations of Jean-Paul Sartre* [Murphy 1999].)

Mention of Beauvoir brings me to what I propose to do in the remainder of this essay. Returning to the overview by Josephine Donovan that I presented at the beginning of the essay, I want to survey the pioneering work of two of the major figures who pioneered existentialist versions of feminist philosophy and theology. I will begin with Beauvoir as the "mother" of existentialist feminism in philosophy, who stands in the mainstream liberal feminist tradition. Then I will briefly examine the formative thought of one of the most prominent existentialist theologians, Mary Daly, one of the leading spokeswomen for a radical separatist feminism.

2. **Existentialist feminist philosophy: Simone de Beauvoir**

Beauvoir (1908-86) was one of the most distinguished women of letters of twentieth-century France. A novelist, essayist, political activist, and one of the best-known of the existentialists, she was also a "founding mother" of the contemporary feminist movement. Beauvoir was born in Paris and had a conventional middle-class upbringing. Her mother was a devout Roman Catholic and her father was an agnostic who strongly encouraged her early desire to become a writer and get a good education. Beauvoir studied philosophy at the Sorbonne, where she met a fellow student named Jean-Paul Sartre. The two became lovers and partners in a common intellectual enterprise, while insisting on their individual freedom including the pursuit of other relationships. They remained committed friends until Sartre's death in 1980.

Following her graduation from the Sorbonne, Beauvoir taught philosophy in various *lycées* (college preparatory high schools). She began writing fiction in the 1930s but did not publish anything until *She Came to Stay* (French title

L'Invitée), one of several novels dealing fictionally with her relationship to Sartre. Among her best-known novels are *The Blood of Others* (1945), a story about a young man who must choose between political commitment and private responsibilities in the period just before World War II, and *The Mandarins* (1954), a fictional portrayal of herself, Sartre, Camus, and their circle of French intellectuals and activists. Following World War II, Beauvoir, together with Sartre and others, founded the journal *Les Temps Modernes* (Modern Times), which became an influential forum for left-wing political and social thought, philosophical reflection, and literary and artistic criticism.

Following the end of the war Beauvoir traveled and lectured in the United States. In 1947 Beauvoir published *The Ethics of Ambiguity* (*Pour une morale de l'ambiguité*), a short but important philosophical essay which we will consider in detail below. It was followed in 1949 by her most famous and influential book, *The Second Sex* (*Le Deuxieme Sexe*), which we will likewise examine more fully. Although she had been one of the best philosophy students at the Sorbonne (she and Sartre received the two highest marks on their comprehensive examinations) and had taught philosophy, Beauvoir always considered herself a writer and engaged intellectual rather than a professional philosopher. Sartre was likewise a writer and activist intellectual, but he also produced comprehensive and technical philosophical treatises, notably *Being and Nothingness* and *The Critique of Dialectical Reason*, in which he developed a highly original and systematic philosophical outlook. Beauvoir generally preferred to articulate philosophical ideas in fictional form, writing "novels of ideas" or "philosophical novels," and believing that Sartre had sufficiently provided the philosophical foundation upon which she built. *The Ethics of Ambiguity* is the "purest" expression of Beauvoir's philosophical outlook, while *The Second Sex* is a broadly humanistic book—a rich tapestry woven from philosophy, history, anthropology, psychology, and literary analysis.

When the contemporary revival of the women's movement began in the 1960s, feminists recognized that Beauvoir was one of its pioneers, and *The Second Sex* has long been a feminist classic alongside earlier works such as Mary Wollstonecraft's *Vindication of the Rights of Woman* (1793). When the contemporary French women's movement began in 1970, Beauvoir, by then sixty-two, was prominently involved, and co-founded a feminist journal, *Nouvelles Questions Féministes* (New Feminist Questions). During her fifties and sixties she also devoted herself to writing four volumes of her autobiography: *Memoirs of a Dutiful Daughter* (*Mémoires d'une jeune fille rangée*) (1958), *The Prime of Life* (*La Force de l'âge*) (1960), *Force of Circumstance* (*La Force des choses*) (1963), and *All Said and Done* (*Tout compte fait*) (1972).

A year after Sartre's death Beauvoir published a moving memoir of the last ten years of his life entitled *Adieux: A Farewell to Sartre* (*La Cérémonie des adieux*) (1981). By then her own health was in decline, and she died in 1986. There was a large public funeral in Paris and an outpouring of expressions of respect and affection worldwide. Beauvoir is buried together with Sartre in the Montparnasse Cemetery in Paris.

The philosophical foundations of *The Second Sex* are to be found in Sartre's philosophy as explicated in *Being and Nothingness*—as critically revised and creatively expanded, however, by Beauvoir in *The Ethics of Ambiguity*. This short book (197 pages in the French edition) is the first serious attempt to develop a theory of ethics on the basis of a Sartrian existentialism. In it Beauvoir clearly builds on the philosophy of *Being and Nothingness*, but just as clearly revises it at crucial points, developing a more positive interpretation of the human situation and a normative ethics. *The Ethics of Ambiguity* is not a detailed, systematic work of philosophy, but an original, insightful, well-written, and occasionally inspiring book. It has been neglected until comparatively recently, partly because of the widespread (and now refuted) assumption that Beauvoir was simply rehashing Sartre and partly because in later years Beauvoir herself dismissed it as "frivolous," "insignificant," and "not worthy of attention" (Beauvoir 1963, 75).

In order to appreciate Beauvoir's originality in *The Ethics of Ambiguity* we have to review briefly its ontological foundations in Sartre's phenomenology of human consciousness as expounded in *Being and Nothingness*. Consciousness (subjectivity, self-awareness) is an original spontaneity (being-for-itself) appearing in the density of the world (being-in-itself). It manifests itself as a negation or lack of being (a "nothingness"): everything else is an object for consciousness, which is never what it is conscious of although it is nothing else than consciousness of objects. Since consciousness is never itself an object, it cannot be determined by anything other than itself, and therefore it can also be described as freedom. Every human being is a mixture of consciousness and facticity (bodiliness, heredity, environment), but as consciousness she creates herself from moment to moment by freely choosing how she will interpret and live her life in the world. As free she is entirely responsible for everything she is and becomes. This is what Sartre means by the phrase "existence precedes essence" and by describing humans as "condemned to be free." Even the inchoate realization of one's freedom fills a person with anguish, and to a very large degree each of us tries in a multitude of ways to evade, escape from, and deny the fact that we're inescapably free.

The problem for Beauvoir, early on in Sartre's working out of his philosophy, was his insistence that everyone, qua consciousness, is "equally" free no matter what their circumstances. In 1940 they had a number of discussions, with Beauvoir posing the examples of a woman in a harem and a slave. Sartre insisted that even though their factical situations are extremely constrained, they are still "free" to adopt an attitude toward or interpretation of their situation, and even to take action—to commit suicide or perhaps to try to escape. Beauvoir found this position unsatisfactory as a basis for consideration of the whole realm of ethics and politics. What sense, for example, does it make to speak of oppressor and oppressed, to distinguish among people in terms of their rights and opportunities, to plead extenuating circumstances? For some time, however, Sartre remained adamant.

Sartre devoted only the last two pages of his 675-page book *Being and Nothingness* to raising the question of the ethical implications of his ontology, and ended by promising a future book on ethics. He never delivered on that promise. After making various attempts at working out an ethics in the late '40s and 50's, he later abandoned the effort entirely when he embraced a form of Marxism. In his popular, much-anthologized 1946 lecture "Existentialism is a Humanism," Sartre makes a preliminary attempt at sketching in the outlines of an ethics. He describes all moral values as free inventions, choices, of human subjectivity; but he is also concerned to locate a universal dimension of morality in the very nature of consciousness. Sartre suggests an ethics based upon the fact that individual subjectivity is a freedom, and exists only within a context of intersubjectivity, the presence of other free subjects: "the intimate discovery of myself [as a freedom] is at the same time the revelation of the other as a freedom which confronts mine, and which cannot think or will without doing so either for or against me" (Sartre 1946, 361). Sartre builds here on his phenomenology of being-for-others and being-with-others. Drawing on Kant's approach to ethics in terms of a universal categorical imperative, Sartre proposes that "freedom, in respect of concrete circumstances, can have no other end and aim but itself; and when once a man has seen that values depend upon himself, ... he can will only one thing, and that is freedom as the foundation of all values" (365-366). But freedom provides only the most abstract basis for moral values, not a guide to specific choices and actions. We can make moral judgments about people, but only when they are clearly acting in "bad faith" or self-deception, seeking "to hide from themselves the wholly voluntary nature of their existence and its complete freedom" (366).

By the time she wrote *The Ethics of Ambiguity* Beauvoir had been working on an existentialist moral theory for several years. While she began, like Sartre, with the freedom of individual subjectivity in its intersubjective context, she went on to distinguish clearly between freedom as a universal fact of human existence and freedom as moral choice. The freedom of subjectivity as an original, universal spontaneity characterizing all human beings is an ontological fact. (Even at this level Beauvoir puts a "positive spin" on Sartre's analysis of consciousness, referring to consciousness as a "lack of being"that "disclose[s] being," a "positive existence" [Beauvoir 1947, 12-13].) The exercise of *moral* freedom, however, is "willing [one's] freedom": consciously accepting one's subjectivity as free and therefore responsible for one's choices. There are human beings who for a variety of reasons—above all, living in oppressive conditions—are unaware of themselves as free, and to that extent are not responsible for their choices.

One of the striking things Beauvoir does as foundational to working out a moral philosophy is articulating an existentialist theory of moral development.

The child, she writes, is not aware of itself as a subject in the full sense of the term, living in an unfathomably "given" world completely under the control of adults and their values but doing so playfully and without responsibility. Adolescence is the time when the individual must begin to "assume his subjectivity" (39). But assuming the burden of one's freedom is a difficult and ceaseless struggle, and the adult life of human beings is dominated by nostalgia for childhood, for a time before real self-awareness when values were imposed by others and one played without accountability. This is Beauvoir's developmental account of "bad faith" among adults: the many and ingenious ways in which they mask and deny their freedom and responsibility as subjects.

Furthermore, there are whole groups or categories of persons who are kept in a state of childlikeness by others through mystification and ignorance. Beauvoir writes:

> There are beings whose life slips by in an infantile world because, having been kept in a state of servitude and ignorance, they have no means of breaking the ceiling which is stretched over their heads. Like the child, they can exercise their freedom, but only within this universe which has been set up before them, without them. This is the case . . . of slaves who have not raised themselves to the consciousness of their slavery. . . . This is also the situation of women in many civilizations; they can only submit to the laws, the gods, the customs, and the truths created by the males (37).

Slaves and women, and exploited people generally, are simply not equally free with their oppressors so long as they lack even the self-awareness and the opportunity to question the elaborate rationalizations of their oppression by those in power over them.

Coming to genuine knowledge of one's situation is the key to Beauvoir's distinction between the ontological status of being a free subject and the actual ability to exercise moral freedom. Once the slave or the woman is aware of her real situation, then she is without excuse. Her complicity in her oppression is revealed, and she is obliged to resist it for the sake of her own and others' freedom. In *Narrative of the Life of Frederick Douglass, An American Slave*, Douglass describes the dramatic moment when, physically resisting his "slave-breaker" master Covey and ending the cycle of brutal whippings, he "resolved that, however long I might remain a slave in form, the day had passed forever when I could be a slave in fact" (Douglass [1845] 1989, 74). Nora Helmer, in Henrik Ibsen's powerful play *A Doll's House*, awakens to her real situation as her husband Torvald's petted and utterly dependent "doll-wife," announcing to him that "I shall never get to know myself—I shall never learn to face reality—unless I stand alone. So I can't stay with you any longer" (Ibsen [1879] 1995, 1098). The play ends "shockingly" with a clear-headed, resolute Nora accepting both her freedom and the responsibility it entails and leaving house, husband, and children.

Beauvoir uses the Heideggerian term *authenticity* straightforwardly as a moral category. I achieve authenticity to the extent that I consciously recognize my freedom and accept full responsibility for my life and its projects, which as we've seen is not possible for all human beings in all circumstances. The striving for authenticity is also a continual *self-surpassing*: the moral goals I seek in each concrete set of circumstances are not absolutes, but ends that I reach and from which I then reach out to other ends.

Further, and centrally, my exercise of freedom as a conscious choice to be moral, and the moral goals I seek, are inevitably social and not simply individual, since I don't exist as an individual subject in isolation but only in a world of other subjects who like me are, *qua* subjects, a freedom. Ethics, then, requires the full recognition that human reality is social as well as individual. Every individual's freedom is limited by that of others, and none of us can be fully free when others are oppressed. Thus my discovery and exercise of my freedom as a moral being entails adopting the enlargement of the freedom of all individual human beings as my universal moral ideal (the good), and engaging myself in actions concretely directed to that end. Being-for-others and being-with-others—the realm of human relationships, community, and conflict—are deeply problematic in *Being and Nothingness*, but foundational and positively interpreted in *The Ethics of Ambiguity*.

Notice that at this point we have in Beauvoir's moral theory three senses of "freedom," one ontological and two moral:

1) Ontological or factual: the universal spontaneity of human consciousness or subjectivity
2) Moral (a): my choice to recognize (or indeed not to recognize) that as a human being I'm free and thus responsible for my life
3) Moral (b): my adoption of individual freedom as the highest moral good, and my active commitment to projects that I believe will concretely assist in the liberation of others

Freedom is the universal ontological reality of human subjectivity and thus the foundation of moral freedom. But moral freedom is specifically the reality that each person, having been brought to the possibility of moral self-awareness, creates herself through choices for which she is responsible. Assuming one's freedom as a moral agent takes place in a world of intersubjectivity and interdependence, and thus entails the positing of the individual freedom of all as the *summum bonum*. But social awareness in turn involves the recognition of the social reality of oppression: some humans are freer than others, and at the expense of others. "It is this interdependence," Beauvoir writes,

> which explains why oppression is possible and why it is hateful. . . . my freedom, in order to fulfill itself, requires that it emerge into an open future: it is other men who open the future to me, it is they who, setting up the world of tomorrow, define my future; but if, instead of allowing me to participate in this constructive movement, they oblige me to consume my transcendence in vain,

... then they are cutting me off from the future, they are changing me into a thing (82).

The moral subject's task is to "disclose the world with the purpose of further disclosure and by the same movement [to] try to free men, by means of whom the world takes on meaning" (74). Later Beauvoir writes that "to be free is not to have the power to do anything you like; it is to be able to surpass the given toward an open future; the existence of others as a freedom defines my situation and is even the condition of my own freedom" (91). We have here a thoroughly social concept of freedom and ethics, the goal of which however is to maximize the freedom of "the individual as such."

Freedom as active social commitment means, within the specific and concrete circumstances in which every moral agent finds herself, liberating the oppressed—changing the facticity, the human and material conditions, that stifle people's opportunity to exercise their freedom in the world. This involves striving for goals familiar to us from the democratic and socialist traditions: individual rights and opportunities, fair distribution of economic goods, equal justice before the law, a meaningful voice in political decisions affecting one's society.

In the last part of *The Ethics of Ambiguity* Beauvoir discusses more concretely the challenges of pursuing the moral goal of individual freedom for all. She argues that liberation of the oppressed requires revolt against existing conditions, which can include a wide spectrum of activities such as consciousness-raising, creating community within and among affinity groups, organizing, demonstrating, civil disobedience, strikes and boycotts, political revolution, and armed insurrection. Beauvoir thoughtfully discusses the acute moral dilemma of violence as a means of revolt—having to kill some people in order to liberate others. Physical violence, she writes, is the extreme expression of "the paradox that no action can be generated for man without its being immediately generated against men" (99). Violence is justified "only if it opens concrete possibilities to the freedom which I am trying to save" (137)—but what does that mean in a wide variety of specific circumstances?

Beauvoir always sees revolt as efforts to change the present into a better future without sacrificing what concrete goods exist in the present to an abstract future. Genuine revolt is always for the sake of the possibility of everyday happiness for real people. Writing of French colonial oppression of the native Arab population of Algeria after a visit there, she writes that "there were children who played and laughed; and their smile exposed the lie of their oppressors: it was an appeal and a promise; it projected a future before the child" (102). A committed socialist, and, with Sartre, sympathetic to Marxism, Beauvoir is nevertheless very critical of collectivist ideologies, and affirms democracy and personal values and relationships: "A collectivist conception of man does not concede a valid existence to such sentiments as love, tenderness, and friendship; the abstract identity of individuals merely authorizes a comradeship between them by means of which each one is likened to each of the others" (108). This world of concrete individual existence and the values associated with human relationship are "what democratic societies understand" (106). Interestingly, in *The Ethics of Ambiguity* Beauvoir sounds much closer in her moral and political philosophy to Camus than she does to Sartre. (We have had occasion to contrast Camus and Sartre on these issues in essay three.)

In a moving and eloquent passage toward the end of *The Ethics of Ambiguity*, Beauvoir sums up her existentialist moral theory in terms which, in their warm and unabashed affirmation of ordinary human life, stand in stark contrast to Sartre's preoccupation in *Being and Nothingness* with the "negativizing" activity of consciousness, the near-impossibility of authenticity or "sincerity," and the sadomasochistic character of human relationships:

> ... it must not be forgotten that there is a concrete bond between freedom and existence; to will man free is to will there to be being, it is to will the disclosure of being in the joy of existence; in order for the idea of liberation to have a concrete meaning, the joy of existence must be asserted in each one, at every instant; the movement toward freedom assumes its real, flesh and blood figure in the world by thickening into pleasure, into happiness. If the satisfaction of an old man drinking a glass of wine counts for nothing, then production and wealth are only hollow myths; they have meaning only if they are capable of being retrieved in individual and living joy. The saving of time and the conquest of leisure have no meaning if we are not moved by the laugh of a child at play. If we do not love life on our own account and through others, it is futile to seek to justify it in any way (136).

In *The Ethics of Ambiguity* Beauvoir presents the outlines of a moral theory and ranges generally over its concrete applications. In her next book, published two years later, she applies the theory specifically to the oppression and liberation of women. Having been strongly encouraged by Sartre to write a book on women, in 1949 Beauvoir published *The Second Sex*, a thoroughly researched, remarkably comprehensive study of the subordination of women: its origins, its history, the mythologies surrounding it, the portrayals of women in literature, the plight of contemporary women, and how women can liberate themselves from their condition as the subordinate "Other" to men. In the Introduction Beauvoir describes her philosophical perspective as an "existentialist ethics," which as we've seen she worked out in *The Ethics of Ambiguity*.

Women have clearly been oppressed by a male-dominated world; but to the extent that they have become aware of their situation they have been complicit in their oppression, and they have the power to revolt against existing conditions— to change things and (together with changed men) work toward a world of gender equality. The global feminist movement is one of the major modern revolutions working toward the highest good of realizing individual freedom for all.

Along with the many characteristics they have in common as human beings, there are clearly genetically-based differences between females and males in aspects of their anatomy and physiology including the fact that women bear children while men do not, their experience of their bodies and sexuality, and their socialization. But Beauvoir's point is that there is no "eternal feminine" or essence of womanhood, just as there is no "eternal masculine" or essence of manhood. The historical condition of women, like that of men, is a situation, not a destiny. As conscious subjects women are autonomous beings like men. Human rights and opportunities cannot be determined by sex differences. Writing only a short time after women had been granted the right to vote in France (1945), Beauvoir believed that political rights, such as the right to vote, were not enough for women to become truly equal and free in their rights and opportunities. Only with economic independence could women begin to attain full liberation.

In her Introduction, Beauvoir uses the category of the "Other" to describe a universal characteristic of human consciousness in intergroup relations. Her discussion of "Otherness" has been widely appropriated, not only by later feminists but also by advocates for the liberation of minority groups. Beauvoir analyzes "Otherness" as it applies especially to women in a world defined by men, but she also applies it to other groups defined by a dominant group as the Other—specifically to Jews as defined by non-Jews and blacks as defined by whites. She writes, "The category of the *Other* is as primordial as consciousness itself" (xxii) This dualistic way of thinking—in which one group sets itself up as the One, the Subject, the normative humans, over against the Other, the Object, the aliens—belongs to the very nature of consciousness, although according to Beauvoir it was not originally applied to the division of the sexes.

Beauvoir also describes Otherness as a reciprocal phenomenon: members of the group that has defined itself as dominant over an Other may find themselves in situations (for example, traveling in another country) where they are in turn rendered an Other by another dominant group. For reasons that she elaborates throughout the book, she sees this reciprocity of mutual objectification as not having existed historically between men and women; that is, women have not been able to define men as Other as men have women. The main reason has been the inherent interdependence of men and women and their common identity and loyalty as members of various racial, ethnic, national, and religious groups.

The dominant group and the Other group typically stand in the relationship of oppressor and oppressed. "Oppress" is from the Latin word *oppressare*, which means "to press down." Pressing others down can take all forms, from mild to severe, from discrimination to annihilation. In situations of oppression the dominant group defines the Others, and the Others come to see themselves through the oppressor's eyes, in the oppressor's terms. This is what Martin Luther King, Jr., for example, had in mind when he used to talk about the feeling of "nobodiness" among black Americans, and what feminists saw expressed in many women's definition of themselves entirely in terms of serving the needs of husband and children. The relationship of the dominant group to the Other is expressed in control, subordination, and devaluation. It is also articulated in elaborate mythologies and ideologies of oppression, which include stereotyping and other sorts of distortion. That women are "daughters of Eve," gullible, dependent, and more inclined to sin; that blacks are an accursed race or have smaller cranial capacity than whites; that Jews are rejected by God and involved in a world conspiracy—these are a few potent samples of the old and tenacious myths and ideologies of Otherness.

Beauvoir makes valuable distinctions among the different forms of Otherness. The treatment of minority groups as Others in a society in which the majority is different is entirely a matter of historical and geographical circumstances. In the United States, blacks are a minority among a white majority; in much of Africa the situation is the reverse. In the U.S., as in many countries, Jews are a minority among a largely Christian population; in Israel the situation is reversed. The substantial but minority population of people of African descent in the U.S. is a contingency of history, specifically of the European slave trade that began in the sixteenth century and the economic and social circumstances surrounding the settling of North America. The Jewish population in America resulted from the dispersion of Jews among other countries that began with the Babylonian Exile in the sixth century B.C.E., and involves the phenomena of historic anti-Semitism and America's reputation as a haven for immigrants.

But two groups treated as Other have not been minorities: the proletariat and women. Not all societies, however, have had a proletariat in Marx's sense of the term—that is, "the class of modern wage-labourers who, having no means of production of their own, are reduced to selling their labour-power in order to live" (Marx [1848]1999, 65). The existence of a large exploited working class is the creation of specific historical and economic circumstances: industrialization and the dominance of capitalism. But the Otherness of women, says Beauvoir, is unique: it is not a result of historical events or circumstances. Women have always been subordinate to men, the result of women's immurement in a uniquely biological "immanence" through bearing and nursing children.

Beauvoir notes that unlike other groups treated as Other, women have not historically said "We"—expressed their solidarity as women—and have not been an organized movement until quite recently. Basic to the unique problem of women's Otherness is not only childbearing and nurture but also the complete interdependence of men and women, an interdependence in which men have been in the dominant, privileged, "transcendent" position in relation both to women and to the world at large. But there is also a unique form of reciprocity, in that the two sexes need each other. Beauvoir goes on to say that historically there has also been complicity or cooperation on the part of women in their oppression; it has had certain advantages for them along with the disadvantages, although the advantages are purchased at the cost of bad faith. This is an important theme of *The Second Sex*.

Beauvoir draws on important male writers of the Western tradition—among them Aristotle, Augustine, and Thomas Aquinas—in describing the ways in which men have negatively interpreted women. (She also points out notable exceptions—male champions of women's equality, among them Poulain de la

Barre, the Marquis de Condorcet, and John Stuart Mill.) Central to male interpretations of women has been the idea that the two sexes are different in their essential natures, and the related idea that they stand in a complementary relationship to each other. According to this standard view, which continues to manifest itself in popular attitudes, men and women behave differently because they have different essential natures, not because of biological and social contingencies. Despite a wide range of behaviors within each sex and behaviors common to both sexes, this traditional view sees women's "natural" or "normal" character and roles as complementary to male characteristics and roles also seen as "natural," generating the standard female/male dipolarities: nature/culture, passive/active, emotional/rational, domestic/public, internal/external, follower/leader, life-giver/risk-taker, nurturer/achiever, and the like.

Central to these traditional male views of women is the idea that males are the normative humans and females are in various ways deficient and in need of "completion"—physically, mentally, emotionally, socially. On the basis of her existentialist philosophical perspective, Beauvoir seriously criticizes and rejects these views, without denying or ignoring genuine differences between the sexes, on the basis of the fact that the defining feature of all human beings is to be a free subject or consciousness: ". . . what peculiarly signalizes the situation of woman is that she—a free and autonomous being like all human creatures—nevertheless finds herself living in a world where men compel her to assume the status of the Other. . . . The drama of woman lies in this conflict between the fundamental aspirations of every subject . . . and the compulsions of a situation in which she is the inessential" (xxxv).

3. Feminist existentialist theology: Mary Daly

Mary Daly is unquestionably the pre-eminent neo-pagan feminist and, along with Rosemary Radford Ruether, a "presiding genius"of American feminist theology. Among secular feminists, and outside the United States, Daly has long been the best-known feminist religious thinker. In her relentless global exposure of the oppression of women past and present, and her efforts to articulate a new women's culture with a new language, she has been at the forefront of radical separatist feminism. As a pioneering feminist theorist she provides a sharp contrast to Beauvoir, who stands squarely within the "mainstream" liberal feminist tradition.

Mary Daly was born in 1928 in Schenectady, New York, into an Irish-American Catholic family. Educated in Catholic schools, she went on to study theology and philosophy. She earned three doctorates: one in religious studies at St. Mary's College in Indiana and two at the University of Fribourg in Switzerland—one in theology and one in philosophy. While in Fribourg Daly got to observe some of the proceedings of the Second Vatican Council, which like many liberal-minded Catholics she initially welcomed with optimism for the church's future.

In 1966 Daly returned to the U.S. as an assistant professor at Jesuit-run Boston College. Her 35-year career there was a stormy one. When her first book, *The Church and the Second Sex*, which examined and criticized misogyny in the Catholic Church, was published in 1968, the administration at Boston College informed her that she would not be reappointed to the faculty. Daly's students—at that time the college had only male students—launched a series of protests on her behalf. She was not only reinstated but promoted to the rank of associate professor with tenure. In the mid-1970s, after Boston College had become coeducational, she began restricting her women's studies classes to women. She continued to offer other classes to interested men, but she argued that having any men in a class on women's issues completely changed the dynamics because men tend to dominate, women tend to let them, and she wanted the female students to feel completely free to speak honestly and explore ideas. Daly had continued this policy through the years, despite periodic objections, but in 1998 two male students attended one of her all-women classes deliberately to challenge the policy. Besides being male, neither had the right prerequisites for the class; one was backed by a right-wing think tank called the Center for Individual Rights. Boston College officials mandated that Daly open her women's studies classes to men. Instead she took a leave of absence, the college forced her to retire, CIR threatened to sue the college for discrimination, and she sued the college for breach of tenure. They reached a confidential monetary settlement in 2001, and Daly officially retired.

Daly came out publicly as a lesbian early in the 1970s, and incorporated her sexual orientation into her ontological reimagining of the universe in female terms. Parallel to her lack of interest in male support for feminism and in "men's liberation" has been her general indifference to gay liberation, which she regards as male-dominated. Daly has also stood entirely aloof from other leading feminist religious thinkers and from the feminist scholars who are active in the American Academy of Religion. While all the other feminist theologians have felt that they must deal with her, she has felt no need of reciprocity. Daly's writings, copiously footnoted, display a substantial and wide-ranging knowledge of historic and recent feminist literature on the one hand and of the Christian theological tradition on the other; but we look in vain for so much as a mention of any Jewish or Christian feminists. Daly reveres the long tradition of what she calls "Foresisters," including figures like Susan B. Anthony and Virginia Woolf, but apart from certain contemporary neo-pagan religious feminists like Nelle Morton and Susan Griffin they are very largely secular figures. Daly's "loud silence" about Christian and Jewish feminism in part reflects her conviction that those religious traditions are inherently patriarchal and thus unredeemable.

In her first feminist book, *The Church and the Second Sex* (1968), written out of the creative theological ferment and hope unleashed by the Second Vatican Council, Daly took a reformist position, sharply calling the Catholic Church to account for its historic subordination and marginalization of women. Her appropriation of Beauvoir and *The Second Sex* can be seen not only in the title, but also in chapter one, which is a useful bringing together and discussion of Beauvoir's scattered remarks on the role of religion and specifically of Catholic Christianity in the oppression of women (53-73). Becoming increasingly radicalized during the period following *The Church and the Second Sex,* Daly in 1975 wrote a new "Feminist Postchristian Introduction" to a new printing of the book, in which she repudiated her earlier position and referred to the author as if she were another person (15-51). For a second reprinting in 1985 she added a new "Archaic Afterwords" in which she in turn commented on the 1975 Introduction.

Daly the radical post-Christian feminist first emerged in her 1973 book *Beyond God the Father: Toward a Philosophy of Women's Liberation.* It was the first in what became a series of books that progressively developed a new ontological vision and a new language in which to express it. *Beyond God the Father* is a highly creative critique of Christian misogyny. Organized like a systematic theology according to the traditional doctrinal topics, the book "liberates"Christian doctrines by transposing them into fully universal and woman-affirming interpretations of the world. In all her radical-feminist writings Daly insists that ontology—a philosophical account of the basic structures of being—is essential as a foundation for a truly whole feminist reinterpretation and for creative, world-changing activity. As a philosophical theologian, Daly has consistently incorporated an understanding of the divine into her ontological reflections.

In her 1998 book *Quintessence: A Radical Elemental Feminist Manifesto,* Daly looks back over the books she has written. She writes of *Beyond God the Father* that its "organic, unifying theme is that the movement for women's liberation is an ontological movement propelled and fired by existential Courage. Such profound Courage to Be is the key to the revelatory power of the Feminist revolution." (15) Daly's thought in *Beyond God the Father* was deeply indebted to the existentialist philosophical theologian Paul Tillich, especially his book *The Courage to Be* (1952), and her critical appropriation and radicalization of Tillich's thought has continued to inform all her later books. Central to her use of Tillich are his ideas of existential courage and of God.

In *The Courage to Be* Tillich had defined courage as fundamentally an ontological category, "the universal and essential self-affirmation of one's being. The courage to be," he wrote, "is the ethical act in which man affirms his own being in spite of those elements of his existence which conflict with his essential self-affirmation." (3) The courage to be is self-affirmation in spite of and as overcoming those elements of our existence that threaten it, which Tillich designates ontologically by the term "nonbeing." Nonbeing refers to all those aspects of our finitude that limit, impede, and destroy us, summarized by Tillich under the three headings of fate and death, guilt and condemnation, and emptiness and meaninglessness. As subjects, humans experience the many-sided threat of nonbeing through the mood of *existential anxiety,* which is a universal and normal "given" of human existence (and to be distinguished from abnormal or pathological anxiety). The human courage to be is self-affirmation that takes anxiety and the threat of nonbeing into itself and overcomes them.

Tillich argues that existential courage must be understood ontologically as rooted in being-itself or the "ground and power of Being in everything that has being." "The courage which takes this threefold anxiety into itself must be rooted in a power of being that is greater than the power of oneself and the power of one's world." (155) The courage to be of human beings is a correlate and manifestation of the "courage to be" of being-itself, which ceaselessly overcomes the threat of nonbeing. Being-itself or the ground and power of being is God, but understood not as a divine being but as "the God above the God of theism." All the theistic (and other) images of the divine are symbols pointing beyond themselves to being-itself or the ultimate structure and dynamic of reality that manifests itself in everything that is. Tillich speaks of the fullest expression of existential courage as "absolute faith," an individual's acceptance that she is "accepted by"—grounded eternally in—the ultimate power of being-itself. This acceptance is available to the non-believer, skeptic, or atheist as well as to the religious believer, since it is an experience that transcends all particular religious symbols.

Central to Daly's appropriation of Tillich is her creative reworking of his analyses of existential courage and of the idea of God as ways of affirming and empowering the being of women. As she writes in *Beyond God the Father*:

> The becoming who we really are requires existential courage to confront the experience of nothingness. . . . at this point in history women are in a unique sense called to be the bearers of existential courage in society. . . . This confrontation [by women] with the anxiety of nonbeing is revelatory, making possible the relativization of structures that are seen as human products and therefore not absolute and ultimate. . . . Courage to be is the key to the revelatory power of the feminist revolution. (23-24)

In discussing the idea of God, Daly finds in Tillich's characterization of God as being-itself or the "ground and power of being" a religious ontology which not only transcends both gender and anthropomorphism but also grounds the empowerment of human beings through existential courage by which the threat of nonbeing is overcome and human potentialities are actualized. God as being-itself is, according to Daly, God as dynamic intransitive Verb rather than static noun. "Be-ing," as she calls ultimate reality throughout her books, transcends and judges the many gods in whose names women have been oppressed.

With the publication of *Gyn/Ecology: The Metaethics of Radical Feminism* in 1978, Daly struck out in a more independent and singular direction in developing a feminist worldview. Here she first exhibits her now-familiar preoccupation with etymological word play and the creation of a revolutionary female language. Although the result can be initially exasperating to read, one is drawn into an enormously imaginative linguistic enterprise that redefines and reinvigorates old words and invents new ones. *Gyn/Ecology* is mostly a devastating chronicle of historic and contemporary atrocities against women, including Indian *suttee*, Chinese footbinding, European witchburning, and modern American gynecological medicine and psychotherapy. In the latter part of the book Daly begins to show how, through existential courage, women can, in community with one another, liberate the "wild Goddess" who is the dynamic power of Be-ing in their true Selves. Daly draws substantially on ancient legends of goddesses, and deconstructs or "a-mazes," as she would put it, their patriarchal interpretations. What she is calling for is a feminist revolution of withdrawal of support from and refusal of oppression by a male-dominated world.

In Daly's next book, *Pure Lust: Elemental Feminist Philosophy* (1984), she "pulls all the stops out." It is an imaginative tour de force that is nevertheless—and by now predictably—replete with learned sources. Here Daly charts a pilgrimage for "Nag-Gnostic Nags" through three realms of "spheres": a) Archespheres, in which women courageously "shrink the alienating archetypes drawn by drones and dangled by flashers to fix/frame women in amnesic oblivion"; b) Pyrospheres, where with "ontological Passion" women begin a new naming of virtues and vices, purifying themselves of "the vestiges of demonic domestication"; and c) Metamorphospheres, where women explore the three Stages of Grace: "Be-Longing, Be-Friending, and Be-Witching" (31-32).

Characteristically, Daly buries in a long footnote in *Pure Lust* an important account of how her view of "Be-ing" or ultimate reality has developed. She describes how she has moved from the symbol "God" as Verb to the metaphor "Goddess" as Verb. She has also moved from speaking in the singular of "power of Be-ing" to the plural form "powers of Be-ing," which she believes gives more adequate emphasis to the "multiple aspects of transcendence." This raises the perennial philosophical problem of the one and the many, which Daly takes quite seriously. She remarks that some feminists speak of Goddesses and seem to espouse a metaphysical pluralism. Daly herself, displaying again the continuity of her ontological approach with that of Tillich, argues for an ultimate unity manifesting itself in multiplicity: "It would be foolish to speak of 'Be-ings.' But women can and do speak of different Powers and manifestations of Be-ing, which are sometimes imaged as Goddesses"(423).

In 1992 Daly published a detailed personal and intellectual autobiography, *Outercourse: The Be-Dazzling Voyage*. There she provides an account of Tillich's influence and her criticisms of him and his work. Daly audited Tillich's lectures at Harvard during the late 1950s. She describes her interest in his ideas but her mixed feelings about him as a person and presence: "He had charisma of astonishing power, but I had felt distanced from it rather than attracted. All the same, his books had been increasingly helpful to me over the years since that time, in the sixties and early seventies." As late as 1972, when she was working on *Beyond God the Father*, Daly spoke of her "ambivalence" toward Tillich, whom she calls in *Outercourse* "the patriarch with useful ideas" (148).

Daly acknowledges that her idea of existential courage came initially from *The Courage to Be*, but she soon critically revised the idea in the service of developing a feminist ontology and ethics. In 1971 she published an article in *The Christian Century* entitled "The Courage to See." Here, she says, she began to put existential courage into another context, "the omnipresent sexual caste system of patriarchy, and applied it to the struggle to see through basic/base assumptions of sexual hierarchy in theology and in popular culture. So the concept of existential courage was radically transformed" (136). Daly became critical of Tillich for his detachment from the concrete struggle against oppression, and included him among those men who "prefer not to see."

Daly's 1998 book *Quintessence* is her most recent major publication. Like her previous books beginning with *Gyn/Ecology*, *Quintessence* is a remarkable work of a dazzling but also deeply learned imagination, building very consciously and systematically on the earlier works but pushing the boundaries of feminist metaphorical and metaphysical possibilities even farther. Daly describes *Quintessence* as the third volume of a trilogy, of which the first two are *Gyn/Ecology* and *Pure Lust*.

The title page announces that this is the 50th anniversary republication of *Quintessence* in 2048 BE (Biophilic Era). There is a Preface by a woman named Anonyma ("Annie") living in 2048 on "Lost and Found Continent," and each chapter is followed by commentary by Anonyma and conversation with Daly, who "transtemporally" travels back and forth between 1998 and 2048. In this way Daly envisions a utopian but not impossible future for women, to inspire existential courage and hope for the success of the feminist revolution. The book thus alternates between the particularly prominent forms of women's oppression in the 1990s—among them the resurgence of Christian and Islamic fundamentalisms asserting the superiority and dominance of men, the systematic rape of tens of thousands of Muslim women in Bosnia by Serbian forces, and the relentless ongoing despoliation and poisoning of the environment—and the way the world might look in 2048 following the implosion of patriarchy and the recovery of a "biophilic" (life-loving) world of courageous women. Such an approach dramatically draws the contrast between the way the world is and the way it might be as envisioned imaginatively by a radical feminist with a richly developed worldview which is poetically as well as philosophically realized.

Daly employs the word "quintessence" as a historical/metaphorical term to symbolize a fundamental, dynamic aspect of Be-ing, just as is the term Goddess:

> In Pythagorean mysticism, *Quintessence* is Spirit that fills the universe and gives it life and vitality. In ancient and medieval philosophy, *Quintessence* Names the fifth and last or highest essence, above fire, air, water, and earth, and permeates all nature. When I use this Word—*Quintessence*—it Names the unifying Living Presence that is at the core of the Integrity and Elemental connectedness of the Universe and that is the Source of our power to Realize a true Future—an Archaic Future (11).

In speaking of an "archaic" future Daly is referring to a central distinction in her philosophy: between the dominant patriarchal *foreground* and the "elemental," archaic *background* rooted historically and recovered transtemporally in the experience of "Wild Women" in every generation. The archaic is "deep time" and "deep structure": both the primordial historical origins and the fundamental ontological reality that ground women's true being. This is Daly's version of the philosophical problem of appearance and reality, and it plays a vital role in her existentialist feminist ontology and ethics. Women struggling courageously against historic and contemporary oppression and asserting their freedom and humanity are affirming their grounding in or "elemental harmony" with the fullness of Be-ing, including their ecological unity with all of nature, and are united in a vast transtemporal sisterhood past, present, and future. Underneath the all-too-real appearances of a male-dominated world there has always been the most fundamental and authentic reality, Be-ing itself manifesting itself dynamically as Quintessence, which grounds and empowers women and manifests itself again and again historically, breaking through and unmasking the cruel and unnatural illusions of "phallocracy." The condition of women worldwide is a *diaspora*: women's "exile, scattering, and enforced migration of consciousness" (38), cutting them off from a deep and conscious realization of their unity and grounding in the background. Daly's whole purpose is to call women to a full and awakened recognition of that unity and grounding.

The ability of women to realize and affirm in the midst of the world their rootedness and oneness in the eternal background that is Be-ing is of course existential courage—which Daly also calls "ontological courage" and the "courage to create," and describes as the courage to "push back the foreground, the nonbeing pompously parading as Be-ing" (89). Daly's ontological distinction between foreground and background seems to me to be the most powerful expression of her feminist vision, and it is intended clearly to function not only as a true account of reality but also as an ontological foundation for empowering women with existential courage—with the courage to say, "I am"(27). That creative courage is the gift of the Goddess, "a Metapatriarchal Metaphor for the Be-ing in which we live, love, create, and are. The impotent jealousy of 'the gods' is not able to stop Be-ing. When we truly know this, Radical Elemental Feminists are free to Act with Contagious Courage" (95-96).

4. Beauvoir and Daly: existentialist feminist alternatives

I have described Beauvoir as a liberal mainstream feminist and Daly as a radical separatist feminist. What is striking is that these two profoundly different thinkers both stand within the existentialist movement, significantly influenced by, but creatively criticizing and departing from, two important male figures in existentialist thought, one a philosopher and one a theologian.

It is easy to state the obvious: Beauvoir describes the familiar world in which women's and men's lives and destinies are bound up together and they exist together in various sorts of relationships to one another that historically and down to the present day have been characterized by an inequality of power and freedom that heavily favors men. She certainly recognizes inherent gender differences, but she affirms that males and females are equally characterized as human subjects by freedom and reason. She envisions a world that is just as gender-mixed but in which women and men will be truly equal as autonomous beings and the institutions and ideologies of societies will express and reinforce equal human rights and opportunities regardless of gender. Most women, and a not insignificant number of men, can recognize themselves and their "other" in Beauvoir's description of how things have been, how they are, and how they might be between the sexes.

By contrast, I think that to read Daly is for most women, and not only for most men, to enter a world that seems strange and strangely described, very difficult to understand and relate to. Daly has created a radically alternative vision of the world and invented a new, lyrical and visionary language in which to describe it. It is a world of women, in relation to which even benign and woman-identified men are inevitably part of the patriarchal "foreground." Where men are no longer controlling and destroying, they are simply irrelevant. Daly's attitude has always been that men who want to be more sensitive to and affirmative of women will just have to look to themselves and work things out for themselves; saving the lives of women and the earth to which they are deeply connected is a more than full-time job. Authentic human community, so far as Daly can see, can only be the community of "wild" or "radical elemental" women asserting their being and trying to reveal and realize Be-ing over against and in the midst of the madness of a phallocratic world. It is hard to draw any other conclusion from Daly's ontology than that she sees women as different from men not only in terms of certain genetic, anatomical, and physiological characteristics but in an essential, ontological way.

But it would be a serious mistake, I think, to see Beauvoir and Daly in mutually exclusive terms. It must not be forgotten that when Beauvoir published *The Second Sex* in 1949 its message was absolutely radical—scandalous and outrageous, in the eyes of many women as well as men. She spoke frankly of women's sexuality, of lesbianism, of traditional marriage and homemaking as a kind of serfdom for women, of the need for women's complete economic independence and relief from the traditional burdens of child care and housekeeping. What's more, Beauvoir's message is of course still radical and her vision of real equality unfulfilled—despite all the gains made in equal rights and opportunities for women in Europe and the U.S. since 1949. Furthermore, Beauvoir was unsparing in her depiction of the historic oppression of women and of the lot of women in her own time. She likewise brilliantly exposed the elaborate rationalizations of women's subordination in religious and social mythologies and their enforcement by political, economic, and social institutions. As a passionate and learned unmasking of and a relentless attack on every aspect of the oppression of women, Beauvoir's *The Second Sex* remains powerful, and seems even more so when we realize what a pioneering study it was.

Similarly, it must be remembered that Daly is also a widely and profoundly learned writer, and like Beauvoir a careful and passionate exposer of the absurdities and outrages perpetrated upon women (and the earth) by patriarchy. Whatever one's reaction to the wildly imaginative, radical-feminist aspect of her writing, it should in no way mitigate for the reader the force of Daly's research into and presentation of the many forms of oppression of women—from footbinding and witchburning to rape as a weapon of modern warfare to repeated efforts even in our own time to turn back the clock on women's equality and rights.

One of the striking things about Daly's books is that she really employs two styles of writing, each appropriate to her purpose: 1) straightforwardly prosaic, thoroughly researched and referenced, investigations of examples of patriarchal oppression, which are powerful precisely in their prosaic, factual revelations; and 2) thoroughly poetic and metaphorical, wildly imaginative ontological explorations of women's nature, condition, and future, in which she engages in ceaseless linguistic play. For those who find it difficult to follow Daly in the fantastic voyage she charts using the second style, it's nevertheless important to take with absolute seriousness and to be troubled by her indictment of the world created by patriarchy—to allow oneself to be haunted precisely by the question why Daly is so "extreme." Is it possible that she, and other radical feminists like her, have peered into the abyss and seen dimensions of the past and present world order that most of us—even liberal feminist women and sympathetic men—find too deeply disturbing to contemplate?

– 5 –

Existentialism and the Problem of Freedom: Viktor Frankl

Viktor Frankl's otherwise illuminating psychological interpretation of concentration camp behavior in *Man's Search for Meaning* (1963) is marred by his theoretical model of free will and responsibility. It's a model which categorically asserts that human beings are always and in every situation free and therefore responsible for everything they do. This "high"existentialist definition of free will and responsibility—associated most familiarly with Jean-Paul Sartre—flies squarely in the face of ordinary moral and legal discourse, the weight of psychological opinion based on clinical observation and therapeutic intervention, and philosophical consensus about the meaning of the terms. The discrepancy is evident in Frankl's own inability consistently to sustain his absolutist theory throughout his account of camp behavior. After analyzing the problems in Frankl's theory of freedom I will propose a more realistic alternative model rooted in Kierkegaard's thought.

I want to preface my discussion, however, by saying that at one important level Viktor Frankl's testimony is unimpeachable. He was a survivor of one of the most appalling hells ever devised for human degradation and torment, and before his personal witness and the triumphant nobility of his values we can only stand with a kind of awed respect. Frankl's account of concentration camp life in *Man's Search for Meaning* is surely a classic of Holocaust literature, managing to be both clinical and humanly moving; and its impact upon me at first reading is one I shall never forget.

Likewise Frankl made important and original contributions to psychological theory and psychotherapy, as for example his illumination of the motivational importance of what he called the "will to meaning" and his development of such therapeutic techniques as paradoxical intention. The existentialist model of human nature and behavior that Frankl shared with Rollo May, Carl Rogers, Abraham Maslow, and others who at one time were collectively regarded as a "third force" in psychological theory and therapy (the other two being psychoanalysis and behaviorism), contributed a more holistic and multi-dimensional approach to human behavior without denying the partial validity of neurophysiological, psychoanalytic, and behaviorist perspectives. At the same time, however, it was precisely in its central preoccupation and affirmation—human freedom and responsibility—that the existentialist-psychological model was prone to apriorism, vagueness, unwarranted generalization, and incoherence. Frankl's version of the model clearly illustrates these deficiencies.

1. Frankl's analysis of freedom and responsibility

Freedom of will is the first of what Frankl calls the "three pillars" of logotherapy, the name he coined for his version of existential analysis and psychiatry; the other two are the *will to meaning* and the *meaning of life*. He says essentially the same thing about these three foundations of his approach in all his writings. I will describe Frankl's analysis of freedom chiefly on the basis of his essay "Metaclinical Implications of Psychotherapy" in the collection of his essays entitled *The Will to Meaning* (Frankl 1969), because it is the most systematic presentation of his ideas on free will and responsibility.

Frankl was an unrelenting critic of that aspect of scientific reductionism which he called "pan-determinism": the various attempts in the natural and social sciences to explain all human behavior entirely in terms of instinctual drives, genetic predispositions, and environmental conditioning. Drawing chiefly on phenomenological analysis of the intentionality of human consciousness, bolstered somewhat by the general systems theory of Bertalanffy and others who describe human organisms as "open" rather than "closed" systems, Frankl believed that human beings are uniquely and essentially characterized by *self-detachment* and *self-transcendence*.

In *The Will to Meaning* Frankl characterizes the human capacity for self-detachment as follows:

> By virtue of this capacity man is capable of detaching himself not only from a situation but also from himself. He is capable of choosing his attitude toward himself. By so doing he really takes a stand toward his own somatic and psychic conditions and determinants. . . . seen in this light, a person is free to shape his own character, and man is responsible for what he may have made out of himself. What matters is not the features of our character or the drives and instincts per se, but rather the stand we take toward them. And the capacity to take such a stand is what makes us human beings (17).

Self-transcendence is manifested chiefly in the human phenomena of love and conscience:

> . . . Man transcends himself either toward another human being or toward meaning. Love, I would say, is that capacity which enables him to grasp the other human being in his very uniqueness. Conscience is that capacity which empowers him to seize the meaning of a situation in its very uniqueness, and in the final analysis meaning is something unique (18-19).

We might call the human capacity for self-detachment our "openness to the self" and our capacity for self-transcendence our "openness to the world." Together they constitute what Frankl calls the "noological dimension" (from the Greek *nous*, mind), the uniquely human dimension of human existence which transcends the biological and psychological dimensions. The noological is thus the sphere of human freedom and meaning.

It is the capacity for self-detachment that concerns us here; it is the primary key to Frankl's analysis of freedom and responsibility in the death camps. The freedom of self-detachment, we have seen, is the ability to "choose my attitude" toward myself and my situation, to "take a stand" toward the factors that condition me. Frankl was quite clear in insisting that this freedom is an essential, permanent human capacity. In his collection of essays entitled *Psychotheraphy and Existentialism* he wrote: "There is nothing conceivable that would condition a man wholly, i.e., without leaving to him the slightest freedom" (Frankl 1967, 60). Hence, as he had earlier stated in *Man's Search for Meaning*, "every human being has the freedom to change at any instant" (Frankl 1963, 207). These dicta apply even to psychopathologies: ". . . a residue of freedom, however limited it may be, is left to man in neurotic and even psychotic cases. Indeed, the innermost core of the patient's personality is not even touched by a psychosis" (211). From all this it follows that every person is responsible for her life and actions.

How did Frankl apply this understanding of freedom to concentration camp behavior as he observed it? The inmates' freedom of action was obviously severely limited; and as Richard Rubenstein (1975), Terence des Pres (1980), and other commentators on the camps have pointed out, they were subjected by the SS to a thorough and systematic conditioning process expressly designed to dehumanize—to strip them of all those things we normally consider necessary to our status and dignity as human beings. In this situation Frankl's notion of freedom primarily as the inner capacity to take a stand or choose one's attitude toward one's conditions, rather than as freedom to choose alternative courses of action within the context and amid the usual supports of the "normal" human world, would seem to be peculiarly applicable. At the same time, it is clear from his account that we are not to construe the freedom of self-detachment in purely "inner" terms. Obviously the attitude a person adopts toward his or her nature and circumstances manifests itself in that person's behavior, and concentration camp behavior was no exception. But it is also clear that there were many situations that must be described as almost entirely passive in terms of the inmate's possibilities of action: e.g., when she was ill or dying, or summarily and arbitrarily motioned to the right (work) or the left (the gas chamber). Frankl himself was the object of several selection processes during his incarceration, and his survival seemed as arbitrary and whimsical as the roll of dice. He deals with these situations of almost complete passivity in his discussion of the value of suffering:

> Whenever one is confronted with an inescapable, unavoidable situation, whenever one has to face a fate that cannot be changed, e.g., an incurable disease, such as inoperable cancer, just then is one given a last chance to actualize the highest value, to fulfill the deepest meaning, the meaning of suffering. For what matters above all is the attitude we take toward suffering, the attitude in which we take our suffering upon ourselves (Frankl 1963, 178).

And, of course, everyone in such a situation is entirely free to choose the "deepest meaning" of her or his suffering.

Notice now the apparent logic of Frankl's generalizations concerning freedom so construed as he thought he observed it in the camps. I have italicized certain crucial words and phrases in these passages from *Man's Search for Meaning*:

> There were enough examples, often of a heroic nature, which *proved* that apathy could be overcome, irritability suppressed. Man *can* preserve a vestige of spiritual freedom, of independence of mind, even in such terrible conditions of psychic and physical stress (103-104).

> We who lived in concentration camps can remember the men who walked through the huts comforting others, giving away their last piece of bread. *They may have been few in number, but they offer sufficient proof* that everything can be taken from a man but one thing: the last of the human freedoms—to choose one's attitude in any given set of circumstances (104). . . .

> Even though conditions such as lack of sleep, insufficient food and various mental stresses may suggest that the inmates were bound to react in certain ways, in the final analysis *it becomes clear* that the sort of person the prisoner became was the result of an inner decision, and not the result of camp influences alone. *Fundamentally, therefore, any man can, even under such circumstances, decide what shall become of him* (105). . . .

> Of the prisoners only a few kept their full inner liberty and obtained those values which their suffering afforded, but *even one such example is sufficient proof* that man's inner strength may raise him above his outward fate (107).

Frankl's line of reasoning in such passages is both misleading and fallacious. It is misleading in suggesting that his affirmation of human freedom is simply an inference drawn from empirical observation of camp behavior. In fact, Frankl's belief in freedom was the result of a theoretical model of human behavior developed before the war which he considered the most adequate interpretation of human behavior, and he interpreted concentration camp behavior on that theoretical basis and as its confirmation. Within the context of the misleading suggestion that belief in freedom is a kind of simple inference from empirical observation Frankl's reasoning was also plainly fallacious. When he repeatedly says that the noble behavior of a few prisoners or even one is "sufficient proof" that everyone could have behaved that way, or that it is "clear" that every prisoner's behavior resulted from an inner decision and not simply from the camp environment, we must reply that on Frankl's apparent empirical grounds such inferences are obviously unwarranted. But of course what looks like his appeal to empirical observation is only apparent and not real. Frankl was observing camp behavior in the light of the presumption of self-detachment as a universal and permanent human capacity; thus noble behavior and inner strength on the part of a few constituted what he should have described as *instances* of what he believed was possible for all—certainly not "proof" for an empirical proposition.

The difficulty of carrying out the logic of this "high" existentialist doctrine of freedom in one's actual appraisal of human behavior can be seen in what certainly look like inconsistencies at various points in Frankl's account, when he lapses into explanations based on causal or determining factors in behavior. For example, he tells us that "among the [camp] guards there were some sadists, sadists in the purest clinical sense" (Frankl 1963, 134). Were these "pure sadists"—genuinely pathological cases—free to choose not to be sadistic? On Frankl's analysis, they clearly were: not only has he laid down the generalization that all human beings are free at every moment to choose their attitude, but he has explicitly applied it to neurotic and psychotic persons. Yet he mentions these "pure sadists" only briefly and in a separate category, as if merely to classify them as pathological were sufficient to explain their behavior.

Interestingly, Frankl discusses the freedom of the guards to be kind or cruel only with reference to guards who were not to be described clinically as "pure sadists." In this connection he remarks that "it was a considerable achievement for a guard or foreman to be kind to the prisoners in spite of all the camp's influences" (Frankl 1963, 136). Such a statement suggests that there are degrees of freedom among human beings depending upon the weight of their conditioning factors, and a moral meritoriousness attached to the person whose exercise of freedom must struggle harder against biological and environmental resistance. Frankl clearly suggests this in the previously-quoted statement that "a residue of freedom, however limited it may be," exists even in the severe mental bondage of psychosis. But surely if every human being is free in every instant, under any conditions, and therefore fully responsible for her actions and life regardless of circumstances, then what sense does it make qualitatively to differentiate among free acts on the basis of the varying "resistances" offered by conditioning factors? On what grounds are we justified in talking about a "residue" of freedom in a person, or a very "limited" freedom? This is a central point on which "high" existentialist theories of freedom such as those of Frankl and Sartre tend to display conceptual incoherence and an inability to make sense of our ordinary observations about differences among people's capacities to act freely.

Another example of the same sort of inconsistency can be found in Frankl's description of inmates' behavior after their release, which was for obvious reasons a traumatic experience for all of them. Frankl observes that "people with natures of a more primitive kind could not escape the influences of the brutality which had surrounded them in camp life. Now, being free, they thought they could use their freedom licentiously and ruthlessly"(Frankl 1963, 143). How could such persons be helped? "Only slowly could these men be guided back to the commonplace truth that no one has the right to do wrong, not even if wrong has been done to him" (144). In the first of these two statements the conditioning factor of a "primitive nature" is treated as a determining factor: such persons "could not escape" being brutalized by camp life. The second statement indicates that to overcome such brutalization was a gradual therapeutic process of—

how else can we put it?—moral reconditioning. All this makes perfectly good sense from the standpoints of both common observation and most psychological theory. Unfortunately, it does not make sense in the light of the aprioristic analysis of free will that Frankl considers one of the pillars of his theory. If I am free at every moment to choose my attitudes and actions, then my "primitive nature" and victimization by brutality neither explain nor excuse my being beastly in turn to other people as soon as I have the chance. Here again we have a case of Frankl's psychological observations being better than and in conflict with the volitional absolutism of his theory.

An illuminating constrast to Frankl's approach is provided by the work of the British philosophical indeterminist C. A. Campbell, as in his book *On Self-hood and Godhood* (1957). What makes Campbell especially illuminating is the fact that, like Frankl, he believed that the only legitimate data for the defense of free will were the internal data of consciousness, and pursued a phenomenological method; but unlike Frankl, he would have considered utterly unwarranted the sweeping, categorical identification of intentionality, or the human capacity for self-detachment and self-transcendence, with free will. That is because Campbell placed his analysis squarely within the general philosophical consensus on the meaning of free will, in which the term specifically refers to human decisions which are not only (1) in principle not sufficiently explicable as flowing simply and causally from a person's character, but also (2) deliberative rational-moral acts, in contrast to random or spontaneous acts. Thus a defense of free will based upon the internal phenomena of consciousness requires an examination, not of structures of consciousness generally, but of the specific experience of moral decision-making and its relation to the problem of character.

While I don't think that Campbell's own defense of free will finally succeeds, his careful analysis exposes how far removed from both our ordinary moral and legal talk about freedom and the standard meanings of the term "free will" in the philosophical tradition is a "high" existentialist doctrine such as Frankl's. Frankl opposed to "pan-determinism" a "pan-indeterminism" which is at least as aprioristic: the human capacity for self-detachment is categorically interpreted as the actual ability of every person at every moment to choose her attitude. This merely asserted ability is in turn identified with "free will," and of course the correlative assertion of our complete responsibility for all our decisions flows from it. We have seen that in his description of concentration camp behavior Frankl could not consistently maintain such a doctrine. There he allowed for deterministic explanation and exoneration in certain cases, and suggested that there are degrees of freedom among persons depending upon the weight of their conditioning factors—neither of which is compatible with his theory of free will and responsibility.

I have said that some of Frankl's observations about human behavior in the camps are better than and irreconcilable with his theory of freedom. Likewise I strongly suspect that his actual therapeutic practice with his clients was better than and in tension with his theory. Indeed, I see no connection between the cases he reports in his books and his doctrine of freedom and responsibility.

What Frankl's commitment to an aprioristic model of freedom did was to prevent him from exploring alternative models of behavior that affirm human possibility without sacrificing either theoretical or experiential coherence. To appeal, for example, to the never-fully-known potentialities of a client, or to pose to the client possibilities she has not entertained before, is not the same thing as recognizing something called "free will" at work in all her behavior. It does not require, nor is it helpfully clarified by, calling it the latter. Similarly, to bring a client to the point where she assumes responsibility for her behavior neither demands nor is it adequately illuminated by the explanation that such a person is inherently possessed of "free will" and therefore in fact responsible for all her attitudes and actions. But of these things more shortly.

An illuminating footnote to Frankl on behavior in the death camps is the contrasting testimony of a fellow survivor, the distinguished Jewish novelist and essayist Elie Wiesel, author of *Night* (Wiesel 1958). On the one hand Wiesel calls to account with searing moral passion not only a Germany that permitted Nazism but also those other governments and persons who were accomplices by their silence and inaction. Over the decades since World War II he has spoken out and acted against continuing manifestations of oppression, for which he won the 1986 Nobel Peace Prize. He challenges each of us relentlessly for our easy historical forgetting and ongoing complicity in crimes against humanity. But on the other hand, when Wiesel concretely considers those who were involved in the Holocaust's machinery of death whether as persecutors or as prisoners, he has repeatedly stated that he cannot really fathom their behavior. In his book *A Jew Today* he writes, "I understand neither the killers nor the victims" (Wiesel 1979, 14).

Of particular relevance is Wiesel's reluctance to pass judgment on the widely differing behaviors—the "choices," if you will—of the victims. In a passage affording striking contrast to Frankl's emphasis on the ability of inmates to transcend their conditions, Wiesel observes the power of that systematic degradation to overwhelm and reduce human beings. In *One Generation After* he observes: "At Auschwitz . . . a crust of bread was worth more than divine promises, a bowl of soup transformed a sensitive human being into a wild animal. Principles, disciplines and feelings only feebly resisted the implacable laws of Majdanek" (Wiesel 1970, 55). The Nazi persecutors, Wiesel goes on to say, assumed the role of God, creating a total system in which their fiendish rules and whims determined good and evil. How can we presume really to understand and evaluate the many different responses of the doomed souls enslaved within the "kingdom of night" created by such omnipotence?

> Prisoners of such a system, many deportees chose the easy path of abdication. How is one to judge them? I do not. I cannot condemn anyone who failed to withstand trials and temptations. Guilty or not, the ghetto police, the kapos, may plead extenuating circumstances. They arouse pity more than contempt. The weak, the cowardly, all those who sold their soul to live another day, another anxious night, I prefer to include them in the category of victims. More

than the others, they need forgiveness. More and in other ways than their companions, they deserve compassion and charity. Their guilt reflects on their tormentors (55-56).

"All questions pertaining to Auschwitz," Wiesel concludes, "lead to anguish" (56).

I suggest that in these reflections of the novelist-survivor we find more psychological accuracy and realism with regard to the springs of human behavior—that complex and hidden interplay between necessity and possibility—than we find in those of the psychiatrist-survivor Frankl. Unhampered by a systematic and absolutist theory of free will, gifted with a keen sensitivity to the nuances and frailties of the labyrinth of the self, and permeated by a sense of the ultimate elusiveness and inexplicability of existence inherited perhaps from his Hasidic tradition, Wiesel manages to be more convincing psychologically as a participant-observer. Significantly, it is just those passages of *Man's Search for Meaning* in which Frankl's theoretical framework is in the background and he is simply the engaged and perceptive describer of events and persons that I find the most persuasive and moving.

Of course Wiesel writes as an artist and moralist, not as a psychologist. His language is concrete and imprecise, and he is not concerned to place his observations within a general theoretical framework. Those of us who are interested in the problem of human behavior as psychologists or philosophers are obliged, like Frankl, to explore the problem with greater precision and on the basis of the most adequate theoretical models we believe we can come up with. I have argued that Frankl's version of an existentialist model is inadequate. But why I find Wiesel's judgments psychologically—and thus existentially—more satisfactory requires explanation in the light of an alternative model. In the remainder of my essay I would like to sketch in the bare outlines of such an alternative.

2. Freedom and responsibility: an alternative model

"Free will" is a concept whose supposed referent is thoroughly problematic and elusive, and a source of endless linguistic confusion and equivocation as well. It must be strictly distinguished from our ordinary empirical uses of the words "free" and "freedom"—about which, when we disagree, we at least know perfectly well how to go about adjudicating our disagreements: as when we speak of released prisoners as free, or of a free society, free inquiry, freedom from want, and the like. Most of our talk about individual human behavior being "free" is really of this empirical sort. We speak of someone's being free to come and go as she pleases, of the person who is forced to rob a store at the point of a gun as not acting freely, of the psychologically mature, autonomous, well-integrated person as being freer than the neurotic. Even when we refer to the classical model of free decision-making, the rational selection from among carefully considered alternatives, there is no compulsion to describe the phenomenon in other than empirical terms. To a very large degree, when we apply the terms "free" and "freedom" to individual behavior we refer to the relative absence of various sorts of external and internal coercion. And, as the "soft" determinists have long noted, these ways of speaking of freedom are perfectly compatible with causal explanations of behavior.

It's often forgotten that among the existentialists, who are collectively but wrongly identified with the "high" doctrine of freedom, Camus preferred to stay within the boundaries of the empirical uses of "free" and "freedom" that I've described and refused to take a position on determinism and free will. In *The Myth of Sisyphus* he wrote, "I have nothing to do with the problem of metaphysical liberty. . . . The only conception I can have is that of the prisoner or the individual in the midst of the State. The only one I know is freedom of thought and action" (1942, 56). To be sure, Camus goes on to develop a phenomenology of the consciousness of freedom of the "absurd man" (58-60), but again, this is a broadly psychological description of a state of mind.

But in fact we have to go beyond Camus and hazard the metaphysical precisely in order to make sense of the existentialist emphasis on freedom in such a way as to avoid the "libertarian absolutism" of Frankl and Sartre. While both determinism and indeterminism are metaphysical assumptions the debate between which is unresolvable, I agree with William James that indeterminism is the presupposition that makes better sense of human experience and indeed of the universe-process. But to espouse indeterminism is not the same thing as to affirm free will, as James saw clearly in his classic and neglected essay "The Dilemma of Determinism." In his characteristically metaphor-rich prose, he wrote:

> Indeterminism . . . denies the world to be one unbending unit of fact. It says that there is a certain ultimate pluralism in it; and, so saying, it corroborates our ordinary unsophisticated view of things. To that view, actualities seem to float in a wider sea of possibilities from out of which they are chosen; and, somewhere, indeterminism says, such possibilities exist, and form a part of truth (James 1897, 151).

The world so described is one characterized by *chance* and not simply necessity: ". . . indeterminism is rightly described as meaning chance; and chance . . . means only the negative fact that no part of the world, however big, can claim to control absolutely the destinies of the whole" (159). James equates chance with possibility, and prefers the word "chance" to "freedom."

> . . . there are two words which usually encumber these classical arguments [determinism vs. indeterminism], and which we must immediately dispose of if we are to make any progress. One is the eulogistic word *freedom*, and the other is the opprobrious word *chance*. The word "chance" I wish to keep, but I wish to get rid of the word "freedom" (148-9).

James wanted to set aside the term "freedom" because those he called "soft" determinists were insisting that determinism and "freedom" were compatible—by which of course they meant the empirical senses of freedom and not the full libertarian notion of free will. He believed that this was a kind of linguistic sleight-of-hand, trading on the deep and obfuscating ambiguity of the term. James believed that the case for indeterminism needed to be made independently of the concept of "freedom."

All that indeterminism requires, said James, is the general assumption that the world, and human beings as part of it, are characterized not only by necessity but also by genuine and not merely apparent *possibilities*—by what James also calls, provocatively and perhaps not altogether helpfully, "chance." It is the view that causal determination governs very largely but not absolutely; that in the complex concatenations of events that make up the world-process there are elements of unpredictability, such that some out of a real range of options are actualized and some are not. (Alfred North Whitehead and Charles Hartshorne would develop this idea into a full-scale metaphysics.) By contrast, the doctrine of free will presumes to identify a specific category of acts of human consciousness as causally underdetermined by the agent's character. I want to suggest that possibility is a much more useful metaphysical category in characterizing human behavior than free will.

Interestingly, the use of the term "possibility" in describing the dynamics of human behavior can be found at the roots of the existentialist tradition. In his very influential book *The Concept of Anxiety*, writing under the pseudonym Vigilius Haufniensis, Kierkegaard described the human self as a dialectical synthesis of necessity and possibility. Through an astonishingly fresh and original psychological "exegesis" of the Adam and Eve story in Genesis 2-4, he characterized the dawn of the awareness of choice in each human being as an inchoate, anxious realization of "the possibility of possibility"—of the sense that "I can," "I am able to...." Out of that awareness, although not determined by it, comes the "leap," the choice and the consequent responsibility for it, that defines human subjects as what Kierkegaard called "spirit" ([1844]1980, 43-44). To be sure, Kierkegaard goes on in *The Concept of Anxiety* and other books to speak of possibility also as "freedom," but when he describes the human self as a synthesis of dialectical opposites, as he does more fully in *The Sickness Unto Death*, he continues to use the term "possibility" ([1849]1980, 35-42). In the characterization of possibility that follows I don't want to be limited to Kierkegaard's analysis, although I will shortly make an explicit connection. I simply want to point out that the language of possibility to talk about human behavior has solid roots in the origins of existentialism.

So at the level of the hidden springs of human decision and action, I find it much more illuminating to speak not about free will but rather about possibilities. The human personality is a highly complex reality constantly responding to a social and physical environment that is also highly complex and always changing. While our basic individual behavior patterns can be extensively illuminated and predicted through psychological investigation, in virtually all particular situations the full range of our repertoire of possible responses is at least partly hidden both from ourselves and from others. For certain individual personalities and in certain sorts of contexts the range of such potentialities is doubtless severely limited; for other personalities and in other sorts of situations it may be quite broad. My point is simply that neither the agent nor the observer/interactor knows, except in terms of general parameters of behavior, the complete repertoire at any given time. All that constitutes the self is never completely transparent, and the environmental factors to which the self responds are always fluid and novel. For the person who is actually in the concrete situation of decision-making and for those who are interacting with or observing that person, the texture of possibilities—the realm of "chance"—is genuinely open in however limited a degree.

It seems reasonable to think that the fact that humans are subjects and not only organisms-in-environment plays the key role in this indeterminacy: our individual self-awareness, with its transcendence of everything it is aware of both externally and internally. The existentialists, beginning with Kierkegaard and of course including Frankl, have been quite right to see in subjectivity the matrix of uniquely human possibilities, and of course we have seen that Kierkegaard himself described that subjectivity in terms of possibility. Frankl preferred to speak of the subject's capacity for "self-detachment" and "self-transcendence," which also highlights structural aspects of subjectivity. It is just that Frankl (together with Sartre) pushed these characteristics of subjectivity to a needlessly extreme and untenable theory of free will.

But our behavioral possibilities are to an indeterminately large degree shaped by our nature and nurture and environment, and are always circumscribed by that framework. The force of deterministic analyses of behavior does not depend upon their deterministic assumptions but upon their clear recognition of this large measure of behavioral determination. Even C. A. Campbell argued that the great majority of human decisions and actions can be understood simply as products of character determination. Our very partial knowledge of our repertoires of possibilities is a function of the great complexity and fluidity of the configuration human-subject-responding-to-environment; it is not an argument for radical indeterminacy, and certainly not for anything as specific as "free will."

The moral challenge that seems to me to be posed by the recognition of both the determinateness and the possibilities in human behavior is to achieve a delicate balance in our relationships with and understanding of persons. It is to respond compassionately to the unknowably large biological-environmental "givenness" in my own and others' behavior, while at the same time nurturing and challenging the often unknown and surprising possibilities that are ours as subjects within those givens. This is admittedly a difficult balance to strike because of our deep-rooted assumptions about free will, our very imperfect knowledge, and the conscious and unconscious needs we bring to our involvement with and interpretation of other persons. Nonetheless, it is just such a balanced response to persons that is demanded of those who are able to respond—and of course none of us knows whether and to what degree we can so respond until we actually make a serious and repeated effort. The hiddenness of our possibilities as subjects within a heavily determined personality structure should make us charitable in our judgments of persons; but it is those possibilities that render persons responsive to circumstances and to moral challenge and accountability in never-fully-predictable ways.

I trust it is now clear why I find Wiesel's general assessment of concentration camp behavior more persuasive than Frankl's. Using as his theoretical model of human behavior a dubious categorical interpretation of the dubious concept of free will, Frankl appears to know what I believe he does not really know about the hidden sources of human attitudes and conduct. It is a model which, if carried out consistently, is also unrelievedly and unrealistically harsh; among the existentialists Sartre at least has the merit of seeing this clearly when he says that we are "without excuse"—for everything. Fortunately but revealingly, Frankl's psychological and moral judgments about people's behavior are usually much better than and inconsistent with his theory of freedom. When he compassionately explains the savage behavior of released prisoners as the result of their brutalization by camp life, expresses his admiration and wonder over guards who could be kind or a notorious camp physician who later underwent a moral conversion, or challenges his clients to understand and act upon their situation in a new way, he speaks the language of most sensitive and informed observers of human behavior. I suggest that it is a language that finds its natural and appropriate theoretical framework in the unfathomable interplay of necessity and possibility rather than in a "high" doctrine—or indeed any doctrine—of free will.

– 6 –

Three Philosophical Autobiographies: Rousseau, Mill, and Camus

The autobiographies of philosophers can be of interest and value from a philosophical as well as from a literary and a biographical standpoint. Philosophers sometimes reveal or clarify a point of view or set forth arguments in their autobiography that we do not find in their straightforwardly philosophical writings, at least not in the same form. Such autobiographies can also be philosophically illuminating as first-person accounts of sources of and influences on a philosopher's thought. Finally, at an existential level, philosophical autobiographies can show us not only the philosopher at work but also the important role that life-experiences and social context play in the shaping of that person's ideas. We need not be psychological reductionists to recognize, for example, that for an individual philosopher in a particular environment certain hypotheses are, as William James said, "live" and others are "dead" (James 1979, 14).

I want to examine a few features of the autobiographical writings of three influential philosophical writers: Jean-Jacques Rousseau's *Confessions*, John Stuart Mill's *Autobiography*, and Albert Camus's personal essays included in *Lyrical and Critical Essays*. A common thread running through the three authors will be the relationship of each to modern romanticism and how it affected their lives and ideas: Rousseau at the fountainhead of the romantic movement, Mill in the years of its flourishing, and Camus in the post-romantic era. The common elements include the romantic emphases on feeling and imagination, the human relationship to nature, and individual self-expression. In the late eighteenth and early nineteenth centuries Rousseau, child of the Enlightenment, came to enjoy immense intellectual and moral authority as an important influence not only on the ideology of the French Revolution but also on the romantic movement that emerged in the latter part of the century. Mill, growing up amid the social and political challenges of early-nineteenth-century industrial capitalism in the home of the Industrial Revolution, became a major figure in modern Anglo-American moral and political thought who incorporated elements of romanticism into his Utilitarian philosophy. Born into working-class poverty the year before the outbreak of the First World War, Camus the French Algerian *colon* came of age during the decades of philosophical and artistic disillusionment following the war and emerged to prominence at the end of the Second World War as a leading figure of the French existentialist movement, a moral spokesman of the Cold War era, and—I would suggest—a new style of romantic for an unromantic age.

The literature of personal confession, reminiscence, and reflection is so familiar to us that it is good to be reminded that the word "autobiography" was invented only about two hundred years ago, study of autobiography as a form of literature did not arise until the beginning of the twentieth century, and its recognition as a respected literary genre has come about only since World War II. People were of course telling their stories for centuries before the word was invented, with Augustine's *Confessions* (397-398) the prototype of autobiographical writing in the West. Like Augustine's, many autobiographical writings before the eighteenth century were confessional in nature, narratives in Christian spirituality such as St. Teresa's *Life of Herself* and John Bunyan's *Grace Abounding to the Chief of Sinners*, although there were notable exceptions such as Benvenuto Cellini's autobiography. It was in the eighteenth century that "modern" autobiography arose, and Rousseau's *Confessions* is arguably its first influential articulation.

"I should not talk so much about myself," wrote Henry David Thoreau on the opening page of *Walden*, "if there were anybody else whom I knew as well" (Thoreau 1981, 3). Thoreau here gives voice to the unique value of autobiography. There is simply no substitute for my telling my own story, since other persons can never know either the details of my life or my inner self as well as I do. On the other hand, and obviously, autobiography raises in a singular way issues such as motivation, honesty, accuracy, and self-knowledge. Hence autobiography is an invaluable source, but only one source, for knowledge of the author. Equally important is the work of the biographer, who normally brings to her portrayal a perspective, an objectivity, and a wider examination of evidence that are absolutely necessary to a complete picture.

Autobiographies raise interesting questions that likewise seem to be unique to the genre. In working with autobiographies in my courses, I ask my students to imagine writing their own autobiography. I raise questions such as the following: What would be your purpose in writing your story? What would be the "right" time in your life to tell your story? Who would be your audience, and what value do you think your story would have for them? Would you see in your life a unifying theme or perspective from which to tell your story? How would you organize your story? How would you decide what was important and what was not—what you should put in and leave out? How honest, how frank, do you think you could or should be in telling your story? Would you be concerned about checking the accuracy of what you wrote by consulting documents and other people? What account would you take of the role that your gender, race, and class have played in shaping your identity and your life? Closely related is the question, what significance would you give, in telling your story, to the larger social and historical context in which you have lived your life—as, for example, an American and a Kansan in the late twentieth and early twenty-first centuries?

In his book *The Forms of Autobiography: Episodes in the History of a Literary Genre* (1980), William Spengemann distinguishes among historical, philosophical, and poetic autobiography. While recognizing that the three types are not to be sharply distinguished, he characterizes them as follows: (1) *Historical* autobiography is primarily self-explanation, the recounting of one's life as a narrative of events. (2) *Philosophical* autobiography emphasizes self-examination or self-analysis in relation to larger philosophical issues and implications. (3)

Poetic autobiography is marked particularly by self-expression or self-invention, typically in artistic and sometimes in indirect or disguised form. Spengemann discusses Benjamin Franklin's *Autobiography* as an example of historical autobiography. With his *Confessions* Rousseau pioneered philosophical autobiography, which became important in the nineteenth century. The recognition of poetic autobiography, Spengemann argues, has come about in recent decades as we have expanded our notion of autobiography to include novels, poems, essays, journals, and letters. Spengemann discusses Dickens' *David Copperfield* and Hawthorne's *The Scarlet Letter* as examples of the autobiography of self-expression.

Spengemann's typology is somewhat problematic but has some limited usefulness. Since many autobiographies are a blend of "types," we should probably think in terms of emphasis rather than of distinct categories. Our three authors' autobiographies are clearly "philosophical" in Spengemann's sense, but the earliest and the latest also embody elements, respectively, of historical and poetic autobiography. Rousseau's *Confessions*, as a pioneering eighteenth-century effort in philosophical autobiography, also stands in the tradition of historical autobiography as he seeks to explain himself by recounting in detail all the events in his life he can remember. Mill's *Autobiography* is perhaps the "purest" example of philosophical autobiography, carefully focusing the recitation of life-events in the light of wider reflections on philosophy, politics, and education. Camus's essays exhibit in their approach and style many characteristics of poetic autobiography. They are works of lyrical self-expression as well as of self-analysis and philosophical reflection, not "autobiography" in the traditional sense, but personal essays that reveal aspects of Camus's early life and adult experiences.

1. **Jean-Jacques Rousseau's *Confessions*: the birth of modern autobiography**

Rousseau (1712-78) wrote the first six books of *Les Confessions*, which described his life down to 1741, during his exile in England in 1766. He resumed working on it after returning to France in 1767 and completed it in 1770. Although he held readings of excerpts for various groups, he did not have his autobiography published during his lifetime; it appeared in 1782.

With the following few lines from the first page of his *Confessions* Rousseau articulated an important aspect of his impact on the modern Western world:

> ... my purpose is to display to my kind a portrait in every way true to nature, and the man I shall portray will be myself. Simply myself. I know my own heart and understand my fellow man. But I am made unlike any one I have ever met; I will even venture to say that I am like no one in the whole world. I may be no better, but at least I am different (Rousseau [1782]1953, 17).

While he did not invent romantic individualism—*le moi romantique*—he was almost surely one of the most influential exponents of this new sense of the self that became part of the modern movement we call romanticism and has continued to contribute to our understanding of what it is to be an individual. Romanticism is notoriously difficult to generalize about, encompassing a range of emphases some of which stand in tension and even contradiction with one another. I'm focusing here on only one strand—albeit I think an important one—which I call "romantic individualism." In discussing romanticism in connection with Mill and Camus I will focus instead on the romantic emphases on feeling and imagination and the human relationship to nature.

Romantic individualism as it found expression in Rousseau's thought, and above all in his autobiography, emphasizes—indeed celebrates—the uniqueness of every human self: "I am different." It grounds that uniqueness in nature, and typically distinguishes between the "natural" or "real" self—"true to nature"—and the "artificial" self that is a creature and captive of society. The core of the natural or real self is internal and private, not external and public: a subjectivity to be discovered and explored only by introspection and personal expression. At that core are feelings, needs, desires, intuitions, and imaginings—"my own heart"—which are our profoundest connections with reality. When Rousseau resumes his narrative in 1768 with Book Seven he writes:

> I have only one faithful guide on which I can count; the succession of feelings which have marked the development of my being. . . . I may omit or transpose facts, or make mistakes in dates; but I cannot go wrong about what I have felt, or about what my feelings have led me to do; and these are the chief subjects of my story (262).

For some of Rousseau's romantic successors, the human individual so understood accordingly requires of her social and political environment a maximum of personal freedom of thought, action, and "lifestyle" in order to actualize the self's unique and creative potentialities. As we will see in the next section, John Stuart Mill, while not a romantic, was importantly influenced by romanticism in arguing for just such an environment in *On Liberty*.

In different ways, traditional senses of self were relative to a larger public context, whether as a member of family and civil society and cosmic order with a certain role to play, a sinful participant in a universal religious community, or a fellow of a universal fellowship of reason. With Rousseau and the romantics there emerges a new sense of the self's natural or inherent uniqueness, inwardness, solitariness, creativity, freedom, and goodness. In this romantic individualism the self that is each person's true inner being is more fundamental than society, church, or reason; it is a little universe unto itself. The feelings, desires, and needs with which it is naturally endowed are in themselves good, and the human predicament is the result not of original sin but of flawed human institutions. Reason is integral to human life, but to isolate and idolize it distorts and neglects the vital role of feeling, intuition, and imagination in knowing, and truncates the wholeness that is the self. We must change human institutions—familial, political, social, economic, religious, educational—so that they serve to liberate rather than to stifle and corrupt the natural self and its creative possibilities.

The *Confessions* of Augustine, written at the end of the fourth century, is the prototype of autobiography and confessional literature in the Western world. In it Augustine revealed much about himself that we would regard as intensely private and personal, including remarks about his struggle with his need for sex that can titillate or amuse the modern reader. But the Augustine who wrote the *Confessions* was a bishop of the early Catholic Church. He addresses his confession of sin and of faith to God, as a kind of extended prayer, and his purpose in writing it was to use his own path from creation to fall to redemption as an illustration to his fellow believers of the universal human drama of creation, sin, and salvation within the eternal purpose of God. He set his own brief story firmly within the context of the cosmic story of God's dealings with his creation, as in the extended meditation on the Genesis creation story in Books 11-13 that is the climax and framework of the *Confessions*. While it was probably Christianity, through its intense preoccupation with spiritual self-examination, and specifically Augustine's *Confessions*, that sowed the seed that would eventually produce the exotic flower of modern romantic individualism, Augustine is centuries away from Rousseau not only in time but also in his sense of self.

Rousseau's *Confessions* expressed and helped create a very different way of thinking about the individual, one in which the self is sovereign, self-absorbed, and essentially solitary. It is surely one of the most extraordinary literary documents of the eighteenth century. He wrote as a man with a strong need to explain and justify himself and his life—no longer before God, a very benign deity who dwelled in a deist heaven and played no role in the story, but, as Rousseau said, before other human beings: "So let the numberless legion of my fellow men gather round me, and hear my confessions" (17). Rousseau announced that he would try to be completely honest in baring his soul, not holding anything back however private, unflattering, or unsavory:

> Since I have undertaken to reveal myself absolutely to the public, nothing about me must remain hidden or obscure. I must remain incessantly beneath his [the reader's] gaze, so that he may follow me into every least corner of my life (65).

As his biographers have demonstrated, Rousseau did not live up to those intentions. In addition to memory lapses about times, places, and persons, which might be considered innocent mistakes, we know that in the *Confessions* he also suppressed some things about himself and interpreted other things self-servingly.

But when all due allowances are made, what strikes us is just how compulsively revealing Rousseau *could* be about himself, describing in meticulous detail and with unusual candor every episode in his life he could think of, from sexual habits to social behavior. Rousseau thus became a pioneer in the modern transformation of what would previously have been considered inordinate self-preoccupation and vulgar exhibitionism into something we take for granted as normal. A culture shaped by popular psychotherapy, "tell-all" autobiographies of the rich and famous, tabloids, and television talk shows should find Rousseau's *Confessions* perfectly understandable.

In telling his story, Rousseau reflected a great deal on the fundamental role that feelings and imaginings had played in shaping his life, and he displayed insight regarding the passional aspects of human life that had an important influence on the development of romanticism. Like all good romantics, Rousseau also had a deeply aesthetic and even mystical sense of the natural world which he could express quite beautifully in the *Confessions*. He believed that the individual stood in a direct relationship to nature, through body, senses, and feelings, and that this was the primary relationship in the light of which society and its institutions were to be evaluated.

Six hundred plus pages of *Confessions* were not enough confessing for Rousseau. Between 1772 and 1776 he wrote *Rousseau juge de Jean Jacques: Dialogues* (*Rousseau Judges Jean-Jacques: Dialogues*), in which his internal dialogue is joined by a third person whom he calls, generically, "Le François." In 1776 he began his last book, *Les Rêveries du Promeneur Solitaire* (*Reveries of a Solitary Walker*), in which he continued his exhaustive meditations on himself. He worked on it until April 1778, three months before his death, and never finished the tenth and final *Promenade*. Indeed, it has been said that all of Rousseau's books are at heart autobiographical. In all of them he translated his personal experience into universalizations about human nature and human origins, the problem of civilization, politics and political economy, and the education of children. A good example is the *Discourse on the Origins of Inequality*, where Rousseau speculated about what humans were like in an original state of nature, and traced the corrupting development of organized human society out of that original condition of animal innocence. He described the individual human being in the state of nature as "wandering in the forests, without industry, without speech, without dwelling, without war, without relationships, with no need for his fellow men" (Rousseau 1987, 57). Now look at Rousseau's description in the *Confessions* of the day he worked out the ideas for the essay. Temporarily free of responsibilities, in the countryside on a beautiful day, Rousseau wrote, "For all the rest of the day, wandering [alone] deep in the forest, I sought and I found the vision of those primitive times, the history of which I proudly traced" (362).

But how enormously fruitful did Rousseau's habit of seeing everything through the lens of his own subjectivity turn out to be! And that is precisely the mark of his genius. His writings are marked by grand speculative assertions and confident but often dubious assumptions and arguments, and his life stands in poignant tension with the loftiness of his ideals. But his singular personality, his fertile imagination, and his literary gifts created a fresh and powerful vision of what humans are and what they might become that has attracted and inspired political revolutionaries, moral and political philosophers, novelists and poets, and educators. Out of his acute sensitivity to his own experience, he used the language of the Age of Reason to forge a new picture of what it is to be a human being, a portrait of the self that flowered as romantic individualism. With all its deformities as well as its glories, it is a picture that has contributed to the shaping of modern Western consciousness.

2. John Stuart Mill's *Autobiography*: the results of a famous education

John Stuart Mill (1806-73), with the editorial guidance of his wife Harriet Taylor Mill (1807-58), began writing his *Autobiography* probably in 1853, working on it after her death (1858) until 1861. He made final additions and revisions in the winter of 1869-70, and the *Autobiography* was published the year of his death.

Mill tells us that he wrote an autobiography for three reasons: (1) to describe his remarkable education, planned and directed by his father, for a nation and an age in which education had become an important issue, (2) to chronicle the critical development of his mind as a progressive thinker and actor in a rapidly-changing time, and (3) most importantly, to pay tribute to those persons to whom he believed his intellectual and moral development owed everything (Mill [1873]1989, 25-26).

I think that for many readers, after being impressed by Mill's modest account of his remarkable education and his early involvement with the Utilitarian circle around Jeremy Bentham, the most interesting part of his *Autobiography* is his discussion of what he called "a crisis in my mental history," which was to transform his life and, I would argue, his philosophy as well. In the midst of a busy and outwardly gratifying life the young Mill in 1826 entered a long period of severe depression. He related that "the whole foundation on which my life was constructed fell down. . . . I seemed to have nothing left to live for" (112). Mill realized that his upbringing had emphasized the intellect, and particularly the habit of critically analyzing everything, and almost entirely starved the emotions.

After about six months of serious depression Mill was moved to tears by reading the memoirs of an eighteenth-century French writer, Jean-François Marmontel, which made him realize that deep personal feelings were not completely dried up in him. This experience started him on the road to a much more "whole" and satisfying life. In a profoundly revealing passage he wrote that the opening up of his feelings had two important effects on him. One was that

> they led me to adopt a theory of life, very unlike that on which I had before acted. . . . I never, indeed, wavered in the conviction that happiness is the test of all rules of conduct, and the end of life. But I now thought that this end was only to be attained by not making it the direct end. Those only are happy . . . who have their minds fixed on some object other than their own happiness; on the happiness of others, on the improvement of mankind, even on some art or pursuit, followed not as a means, but as itself an ideal end. Aiming thus at something else, they find happiness by the way. . . . This theory now became the basis of my philosophy of life (117-118).

Mill's insight demanded a significant departure from the central Utilitarian assumption that humans act primarily out of self-interest, pursue pleasure, and avoid pain. He always affirmed the principle of utility (the greatest happiness for the greatness number) as the criterion for evaluating moral and social behavior, but he adopted a quite different psychology of human motivation that contributed to his reinterpretation of Utilitarianism. So far as I know, we do not find this philosophical shift explicitly indicated in Mill's purely philosophical writings.

The second result of Mill's "recovery" experiences was that he began to emphasize that the full development of the inner life of the individual is as essential to human well-being as the improvement of society. He realized, further, that that development should not be one-sidedly intellectual, as his own had been, but the nourishing of all sides of the person in a harmonious and balanced way. (We can see this realization reflected in, for example, chapter 3 of *On Liberty*, "Of Individuality, as One of the Elements of Well-Being.") Thus it was that Mill's mental crisis and its resolution liberated him to indulge his passions for music and for nature, and to read and enjoy the romantic poets and novelists. While continuing to write his philosophical works in the carefully argued prose he inherited from the British Empiricist and Utilitarian traditions, Mill's personal life and general perspective were enlivened and enriched by a heritage traceable in part to Rousseau.

Mill was particularly affected by the poetry of William Wordsworth. He appreciated Wordsworth's love of natural beauty, but, he wrote, "What made Wordsworth's poems a medicine for my state of mind, was that they expressed, not mere outward beauty, but states of feeling, and of thought coloured by feeling. . . . In them I seemed to draw from a source of inward joy, of sympathetic and imaginative pleasure, which could be shared by all human beings" (121). Mill was also influenced by Goethe and the German romantic writers, and by the two British writers who were much influenced by German philosophy and literature, Samuel Taylor Coleridge and Thomas Carlyle.

Mill and Carlyle eventually became good friends, and two more different writers can scarcely be imagined. Carlyle wrote in a very colorful romantic prose, and he tended much more to sound like a preacher or prophet, proclaiming things as true in a somewhat Olympian manner rather than arguing for them. By contrast, for all his influence by romanticism, Mill's writings were always very sober, and as one who carried on the tradition of Locke and Hume he tried to be careful not to say more than he thought there was good evidence for saying. In the *Autobiography* Mill describes his intellectual relationship to Carlyle in this way:

> Instead of my having been taught anything . . . by Carlyle, it was only in proportion as I came to see the same truths, through media more suited to my mental constitution, that I recognized them in his writings. Then, indeed, the wonderful power with which he put them forth made a deep impression upon me, and I was during a long period one of his most fervent admirers; but the good his writings did me, was not as philosophy to instruct, but as poetry to animate (138-9).

I think that Mill's remarks about Carlyle may be taken as representative of the impact that romantic literature generally made on him.

The changes in Mill's life indicated above probably played an important role in his finding the love of his life, Harriet Taylor, with whom he had a long and passionate friendship and to whom he was eventually married. Associated with the "Unitarian Radicals," she was both a student of romantic literature (especially Shelley) and persistently more of a radical on women's rights than was Mill. They met in 1831, when he was twenty-five and she was twenty-three. Taylor was married with children when they met, and remained married until her husband's death in 1849. The London circles in which they moved regarded their relationship as scandalous. They spent as much time together (including travelling together) as they could, and for a short period Taylor and her husband agreed on a trial separation. Harriet and John were married in 1851, and her daughter Helen Taylor became both his consolation and an active co-worker with him after her mother's untimely death in 1858.

Harriet Taylor's influence on Mill, he related in his *Autobiography*, was enormous—not only on his life but, he insisted, on his thought. She brought about what he described as a second transformation in his intellectual development. Mill's praise of her intellect and character in his autobiography is so extravagant that traditionally interpreters have assumed that he was blinded by his devotion to her and have discounted her influence on him. More recently, however, scholars examining the issue from a feminist historical perspective have argued that perhaps we should take Mill at his word. The evidence for Taylor's substantial involvement in all the writings, beginning with *Principles of Political Economy* in 1848, is considerable. That involvement included contributing significant amounts of material, going over manuscripts line by line with Mill, and exercising a strong editorial hand. In all aspects of the writing and editing process Mill entirely deferred to her judgment. (Rossi 1970; Jacobs 2002) In 1998 Jo Ellen Jacobs and Paula Harms Payne published *The Complete Works of Harriet Taylor Mill*, which includes previously unpublished writings on ethics, religion, socialism, and other topics. Presumably the availability of Taylor's writings in published form will assist in further evaluating her own thought and comparing it to the works she co-authored with Mill.

In the *Autobiography* Mill called Taylor "the most admirable person" (145) he had ever known. He praised her "all but unrivalled wisdom" (Dedication to *On Liberty*), and described her moral character as "the noblest and best balanced which I have ever met with in life" (147). "What I owe, even intellectually, to her," he went on to say, "is, in its detail, almost infinite" (148). Taylor was passionately committed to liberal social reform and was less cautiously antireligious than he; she also taught Mill, he says, a healthy skepticism about his conclusions. Mill described Taylor as his collaborator in all that he wrote during the years of their friendship and marriage: "all my published writings were as much her work as mine; her share in them constantly increasing as years advanced." He went on to say that "the most valuable ideas and features in these joint productions . . . originated with her" (184). Mill saw his own contribution as more abstract, and attributed to Taylor whatever originality and humanity these writings possessed. He saw her as harmonizing, much better than he could, intellect and passion, reason and imagination.

Of all the books they worked on together, Mill wrote, *On Liberty* "was more directly and literally our joint production than anything else which bears my name" (188). He regarded *On Liberty* as "his" finest book and the one most likely to have a lasting influence, and he attributed its excellence to Taylor's involvement in it. She died when they were mostly through with the writing, and Mill published the book a year later, in 1859. The Dedication, of course, honors Taylor's memory and her contribution as his co-author. As a tribute to her influence, Mill later wrote *The Subjection of Women*. He wrote the first draft in 1860 and later, with the help of his stepdaughter Helen Taylor, made some changes and published it in 1869.

It seems to me that Mill's claims about the substantive influence of romanticism and of Harriet Taylor on his thought need to be seriously examined and evaluated. For me at least, reading his *Autobiography*, and particularly his account of these influences, sets at least some of his most widely-read philosophical writings in a new and illuminating context.

3. Albert Camus's lyrical essays: the invincible sun and the responsibilities of our time

Camus (1913-60) published three small volumes of "lyrical" essays. In 1935-36 he wrote five essays which he published in 1937 under the title *L'Envers et L'Endroit* (*The Wrong Side and the Right Side*) in a limited edition. They were republished in 1958 with a new Preface by Camus that is one of his most personally revealing writings, and it will be included as an autobiographical document. Camus worked on four additional essays in 1936-37 which he published, again in a very limited edition, in 1938 under the title *Noces* (*Nuptials*). They were republished in 1950. All the essays in these volumes were written in Algeria and reflect Camus's childhood and young adulthood. By contrast with the first two collections of essays, the essays published in 1954 as *L'Été* (*Summer*) were written over a much longer period of time (1939-53) and in a variety of places, and some were initially published separately. While written in a personal style, most of these later essays are not directly autobiographical and will not be considered here. The one essay from *Summer* that I will mention, "Return to Tipasa," is a profoundly autobiographical, post-war "sequel" to his early essay "Nuptials at Tipasa" from *Nuptials*. In 1967 Ellen Conroy Kennedy translated and Philip Thody edited a volume in English that brought together the three collections of "lyrical" essays and a number of Camus's "critical" essays. It was published in 1968 by Alfred A. Knopf as *Lyrical and Critical Essays*.

In awarding Camus the 1957 Nobel Prize for Literature, the Nobel Committee cited his influential role in illuminating "the problems of conscience in our time." By the end of the Second World War he was acknowledged as a leading French novelist, essayist, and playwright who had likewised distinguished himself in the French Resistance movement. Despite his protestations, he rightly came to be seen as one of the leading figures in post-war French existentialism, along with Sartre, Beauvoir, and Merleau-Ponty. During the years of the Cold War, Camus became a fiercely independent moralist who spoke out on behalf of human liberty whether in Fascist Spain or the Soviet Union. His severe criticisms of Marxism, as in his book *The Rebel*, together with his mediating position on the bloody Algerian Revolution of the 1950s, earned him the lasting enmity of many of his fellow French intellectuals but the admiration of those (including the Nobel Committee) who appreciated his integrity and his witness against extremism and violence.

Despite his eclipse, following his untimely death, by the newer French literary and philosophical movements of structuralism and post-structuralism, Camus's reputation has enjoyed repeated revivals, beginning with the revolutionary student movements of the late 1960s, and again in the 1970s and the 1980s. (He remains Gallimard Publishers' most popular author.) International attention again focused on Camus with his daughter's publication of his unfinished novel *The First Man* (1995) and the appearance of Olivier Todd's substantial biography *Albert Camus: A Life* (1997). Camus's novel is thoroughly autobiographical; only the names were changed (Camus in the novel is "Jacques Cormery"). *The First Man* is a beautiful and extraordinarily revealing narrative. At the same time, it is a very rough draft, not the book Camus would have submitted for publication had he lived. The two earlier books of lyrical essays and "Return to Tipasa," together with his deeply personal Preface to the 1958 edition of *The Wrong Side and the Right Side*, represent finished pieces, published as Camus wanted them published. As first-person essays, they are also direct rather than indirect portrayals of his life from childhood to his thirties. Finally, the essays are more overtly philosophical than *The First Man*, with Camus reflecting both coolly and passionately on basic issues of existence, meaning, and morality as they arise for him out of his experiences.

Camus grew up in the period of widespread disillusionment following the First World War, and his vision of life belongs to the existentialist sensibility and reasoning that emerged to prominence in Europe during the 1930s and 1940s. But he occupies an unusual position among the European writers of that period. "Even my revolts," he wrote of his childhood in the 1958 Preface to *The Wrong Side and the Right Side*, "were brilliant with sunshine" (6). A colonial Algerian of French and Spanish ancestry, Camus grew up in poverty on the fringes of European civilization in the North African Mediterranean world of dazzling sunlight, desert places, and the vast sea. His childhood in a working-class section of Algiers amid the splendor of the natural environment provided him with two of the central themes of his writing: the human relationship to the beauty and indifference of nature, and the moral imperative to speak out against injustice for the sake of human happiness. "Poverty kept me from thinking all was well under the sun and in history; the sun taught me that history is not everything. I wanted to change lives, yes, but not the world which I worshipped as divine" (7).

In the first volume of lyrical essays, *The Wrong Side and the Right Side*, Camus presents vignettes from his childhood about important persons in his life such as his mother and grandmother. Here we can already see him exploring the theme of absurdity with which he was to become identified: the incommensurability between the life of the individual human being, with her open and secret longings to make overall sense of her life and of human life and its cosmic context, and the "unreasonable silence" of the natural world. The young Camus writes sensitively of human loneliness, misunderstanding, "fatedness," and death within the context of an often-beautiful but also grandly indifferent nature. In an essay entitled "Irony," he writes of his dying, not-much-loved grandmother and of an uncomprehending encounter between an old man and young men: "A woman you leave behind to go to the movies, an old man to whom you have stopped listening, a death that redeems nothing, and then, on the other hand, the whole radiance of the world.... Here are three destinies, different and yet alike. Death for us all, but his own death to each. After all, the sun still warms our bones for us" (29).

In the essays in *Nuptials* Camus celebrates his intoxicated, almost mystical union with the beauty of the Mediterranean world in North Africa, Spain, and Italy. These essays reveal the most fully Camus's "existentialist romanticism" and also his relationship to the Western mystical tradition. Camus the romantic writes, in "Nuptials at Tipasa": "Everything seems futile here except the sun, our kisses, and the wild scents of the earth.... Here, I leave order and moderation to others. The great free love of nature and the sea absorbs me completely" (66). Camus the "nature-mystic" relates his experiences at times in terms that are familiar from the vocabulary of the Christian mystic: erotic love, experienced grace, ineffable union. In "The Wind at Djemila" he writes, "I was a portion of the great force on which I drifted, then much of it, then entirely it, confusing the throbbing of my own heart with the great sonorous beating of this omnipresent natural heart" (75). Camus's early intellectual interest in the Neoplatonic mystic Plotinus (whom he mentions in another essay) seems to be related to his own mystical propensities. As in the first essays, however, his experience of the natural world becomes a source of philosophical pondering on the absurdity of the human condition that sets him apart from both the romantics and the mystics. In "The Desert," he tells of climbing to the top of the Boboli Gardens in Florence and gazing out at the beautiful sweep of hills south of the city. He reflects:

> Millions of eyes, I knew, had gazed at this landscape, and for me it was like the first smile of the sky. It took me out of myself in the deepest sense of the word. It assured me that but for my love and the wondrous cry of these stones, there was no meaning in anything. The world is beautiful, and outside it there is no salvation (103).

All of Camus's writings are permeated with ideas and images whose roots are to be found in this early life-world of light, color, sea, sky, and large open spaces. His idea of *lucidity* has its natural matrix and symbol in light and the sun; of *freedom*, in the sea and the sky; of *absurdity*, in the disproportion between human wants and hopes and the silent magnitude of what the poet e. e. cummings called this "sweet spontaneous earth"; of an *ethics of limits*, in our solidarity as human creatures sharing a physical environment.

There is one essay from the later volume, *Summer*, that is worth mentioning here. In 1953 Camus returns, in December, to Algeria, to Tipasa with its Roman ruins where he had spent many happy days as a boy and young man. Now, having lived through most of the war in France as a reader for Gallimard and editor of a Resistance newspaper, he reflects on all that has happened. He reaffirms his dual commitment to love of the earth and human justice in such a way as to make clear that for him the strength to struggle for the latter is grounded in the former:

> In order to prevent justice from shriveling up, from becoming nothing but a magnificent orange with a dry, bitter pulp, I discovered one must keep a freshness and a source of joy intact within, loving the daylight that injustice leaves unscathed, and returning to the fray with this light as a trophy. Here, once more, I found an ancient beauty, a young sky, and measured my good fortune as I realized at last that in the worst years of our madness the memory of this sky had never left me. It was this that in the end had saved me from despair. . . . In the depths of winter, I finally learned that within me there lay an invincible summer (168-9).

In the lines following Camus enunciates a kind of credo that we have seen rooted in his earliest experiences: "I have not been able to deny the light into which I was born and yet I have not wished to reject the responsibilities of our time" (169).

Camus lived and wrote in an era when the romanticism that defined Rousseau and influenced Mill (together with the optimism that often accompanied it) was decidedly out of favor in literature, the arts, and philosophy. Yet the existentialist movement has its roots partly in romanticism's emphasis on the individual person in her concreteness and freedom, and on the foundational importance of feelings and intuitions in human life, taking up these themes and developing them in new ways. Camus himself, while emphasizing the importance of reason, of "lucidity," in human communication and consideration of issues, manifests in many of his writings the legacy of the older romanticism, as in his early tendencies toward a kind of "nature-mysticism." A romantic sensibility is always just beneath and sometimes on the surface of his irrepressible lyricism, suitably sobered and chastened by his existentialist sense of absurdity and forlornness. In this Camus stands in striking contrast to Sartre.

I have tried in this essay to suggest that philosophical autobiographies can be philosophically illuminating, by focusing on three influential figures from the eighteenth, nineteenth, and twentieth centuries. My frustration has been that of having to select a small number of themes and textual illustrations out of many. Rousseau's *Confessions* seems to me uniquely to illuminate the sources of the romantic individualism he pioneered and his tendency to transpose his own experiences into universal observations. In the case of Mill's *Autobiography* we see, on his own account, what appears to be the substantial influence of romanticism and of Harriet Taylor on his ideas, including in the former case a statement of his views on how romanticism altered his thinking, that I do not find elsewhere. Camus's lyrical essays reveal not only important aspects of his early life, but also their intimate relationship to what would become his characteristic emphases and elements of a romantic passion for life and the beauty of nature that remained at the core of his thought.

Pascal's Wager, Past and Present

> When I consider the brief span of my life absorbed into the eternity which comes before and after ... the small space I occupy and which I see swallowed up in the infinite immensity of spaces of which I know nothing and which know nothing of me, I take fright and am amazed to see myself here rather than there: there is no reason for me to be here rather than there, now rather than then. Who put me here? By whose command and act were this time and place allotted to me? (Pascal, 48)

Pascal's famous "Wager" was one of a number of strategies in his impassioned efforts, through Christian apologetics, to rekindle vital Christianity among the worldly sophisticates of his class in Catholic France during the seventeenth-century Scientific Revolution. It was in no sense an argument for the existence of God, which Pascal didn't believe could be demonstrated by argument, but rather an appeal to people to "bet their life" in faith on the existence of God as interpreted by Christianity, on the grounds that the choice is absolutely momentous (heaven or hell if God exists) and even if the "bettor" turns out to have been wrong she would have lost nothing significant in the living of this life.

I want to suggest that in our time Pascal's Wager is illuminating, no longer as an exercise in Christian apologetics, but as a kind of existential parable of the character of reflective theistic faith in modern Western cultures. In a world shaped by serious intellectual criticism of religion and a plurality of more or less plausible religious and secular worldviews, the thoughtful, educated believer is aware at some level that her faith and the living of her life in its light are a kind of "wager" that reality is ultimately something like what is glimpsed and affirmed in her religious tradition. I'm using it as a case study of the view that "classic" texts have an original meaning in their historical context that is normally accessible to us, but that what makes such texts "classic" is that they also generate meanings and implications for later historical generations and contexts that would not have been available to the original author or audience.

To understand the Wager in its historical context it's useful to know something about Pascal's life. Blaise Pascal (1623-62) was born in Clermont-Ferrand, the son of a government official who later moved the family to Paris. Motherless at three, a sickly child who would be plagued by ill health throughout his life, Pascal was educated by his father. Pascal was a scientific and mathematical genius, inventing a calculating machine before he was twenty and going on to develop the theory of probability and to demonstrate the relation between atmospheric pressure and altitude using Torricelli's vacuum tube. When Pascal was twenty-three his entire family were converted to Jansenism, a movement within French Catholicism that reaffirmed in all its vigor the Augustinian vision of original sin and irresistible grace and called Christians back to an austere life centered in devotion, self-sacrifice, simplicity, and charity. During his twenties Pascal was mainly occupied with studies and research in physics and mathematics and moving in fairly worldly circles, and he remained torn between the life he was leading and the demands of Jansenist Christianity.

On November 23, 1654 Pascal had a famous mystical experience, which transformed his life and which he recorded on sheets of paper sewn inside his coat that were found after his death. The memorial he wrote of the experience contains the familiar line "God of Abraham, God of Isaac, God of Jacob, not of the philosophers and scholars." As David Roberts wrote of the experience in *Existentialism and Religious Belief*: "Here, in direct encounter, Pascal experiences the difference between reason and the heart. The efforts of his own mind to solve the problem of human existence have left him in a bondage like that of the children of Israel in Egypt. The pathway of science and philosophy has led to a dead end, and the pathway of worldly ambition has brought only misery" (1959, 21). Following his experience Pascal associated himself more closely with the convent of Port-Royal, the center of Jansenist piety and activity, where his sister Jacqueline had been a nun since 1651. In 1655 he wrote and anonymously published *The Provincial Letters*, a brilliant and elegantly written defense of Jansenism and Port-Royal against the increasing attacks of the ecclesiastical establishment and especially of the Jesuits. The *Letters* were condemned by Pope Alexander VII in 1656. For the rest of his life Pascal, who always wanted to be a loyal son of the church and believed that Jansenism was not only not heretical but a positive purification of Catholic doctrine and life, was uneasily involved in the tension.

During the last years of his short life Pascal worked on a project that he called an *Apology for the Christian Religion*. What survives of that project is a somewhat miscellaneous collection of notes that were published posthumously (first in 1670) as the *Pensées* and constitute the philosophical and theological legacy by which Pascal is mainly known. The order in which these fragments should be arranged has long been debated, and widely varying editions have been published over the three centuries since their original publication. As in the case of Nietzsche's *Will to Power*, there is also the question whether Pascal would even have used all the material in the notes, at least in the form in which we have them. There is a kind of rough consensus among scholars in recent decades in following what is called the First Copy, which in turn agrees with the plan of the *Apology* which Pascal presented to the Port-Royal community in 1658 as recorded by Filleau de Chaise. In that plan the *Apology* was to consist of two main parts: 1) human wretchedness apart from God and 2) human happiness when restored to God.

The notes, particularly those characterizing human unhappiness apart from God, include penetrating analyses of human life that have caused Pascal to be regarded as a forerunner of existentialism. Particularly resonant, for those of us who inhabit a world so thoroughly transformed by the Scientific Revolution to which Pascal contributed in its early stages, are those passages such as the one with which I began this essay: passages that juxtapose human beings in their frailty and need for meaning and the "silent" universe of modern science with its unimaginable temporal and physical vastness.

As I said at the beginning, "The Wager" seems clearly intended as part of a strategy in Christian apologetics directed to the worldly, intellectually sophisticated, nominally Catholic world Pascal knew well. It is a rational argument, but not an argument for the existence of God. Pascal maintains that "We are . . . incapable of knowing either what . . . [God] is or whether . . . [God] is." God is by definition infinite, and if God exists there is an infinite gulf between the divine existence and our finite existence and understanding. Christians "know" that God is and something of what God is only through faith in revelation, not by reason—and that is just what shows that "they are not without sense" (Pascal 150), since such matters are intrinsically beyond the scope of reason. Since that is our human situation *vis-a-vis* the question of God, what we believe and how we live our lives on that basis comes down to a toss of the coin: heads God exists, tails God doesn't exist.

Pascal goes on to point out that we have no choice about wagering or not, but only about which belief we will bet on: willy-nilly, we are already betting on one or the other. Pascal is trying to show why it makes more sense to risk the wager on God than on no-God. If you wager that God exists, he argues, then "if you win you win everything, if you lose you lose nothing. Do not hesitate then; wager that he does exist." Since we're "playing" for infinite stakes (an infinite God who offers us finite beings the prospect of eternal happiness), we are "renouncing reason" if we don't stake our life on such a possibility of infinite gain (151). Pascal tries to convince the reader that since this is a case in which the odds are even, 50-50, a gambler would be rational in staking everything on the infinite gain. Pascal concludes by making what is surely a crucial point, that even if you were to bet your life on the existence of God and an eternal happiness and it turned out that you were wrong, "[i]t is true you will not enjoy noxious pleasures, glory and sensual delights [délices], but will you not have others? . . . . you will gain even in this life (153) . . . ."

There has been a lot of criticism of Pascal's Wager over the past three hundred years. If we look at nineteenth- and twentieth-century developments in Christian theology, we have to say that the argument depends upon theological assumptions that are simply no longer generally acceptable in critical forms of "mainstream" theology—assumptions such as the exclusive truth of Christianity and the reality and everlastingness of hell. The most widespread criticism of the Wager, however, has been that it appeals crassly to the mentality of gambling and calculation when faith is nothing of the kind. Within Pascal's own religious and intellectual milieu, I think that the sympathetic interpretation is that he was trying earnestly to win people by any means he could. He certainly knew that real faith was something far more than calculating the odds, but he seems to have believed that someone who began even with a wager would, by doing the things faith does—praying, making confession, attending mass, trying to practice charity—learn to have faith.

What I want to suggest, contrary to much of the criticism of Pascal's Wager, is that it is precisely the "wagering" feature of the argument that makes it particularly valuable—but now as an illuminating parable of the situation of reflective, self-critical theistic faith in the modern West rather than in its original intent and context. Three centuries of the advance of scientific knowledge, critical reflection on religion, and an increasing plurality of worldviews both religious and secular have made the thoughtful believer keenly aware that her and her faith community's interpretation of the world and life-commitment is one among many possibilities and that the world is such as to bear a variety of plausible descriptions. As the philosophical theologian John Hick has said, the universe is ambiguously susceptible to both theistic and nontheistic interpretations, and there is no evidence conclusively to adjudicate the matter this side of the grave (Hick 1990, 80-81). Rudolf Bultmann used to describe faith as a dialectical "because of" and "in spite of": one believes as a Christian, for example, because of certain things in one's experience and in spite of others that seem to tell against it (Bultmann 1958, 60-85). Hence the reflective theist is indeed in the situation of Pascal's "bettor," although usually not so consciously or dramatically. For modern critical forms of theistic faith, then, I suggest that Pascal's Wager functions as a dramatic illumination of the phenomenological structure of belief rather than as a weapon in the armory of Christian apologetics.

In an interesting twist on Pascal's Wager, I sometimes ponder the uncounted numbers of Jews, Christians, and Muslims (not to mention believers of other faiths centered in service to the gods and hope beyond death) who have actively lived out their faith in word and deed. From the critical and pluralistic standpoint of modernity, I wonder whether they have they staked their lives and ultimate hopes on illusions. If they have, their illusions are forever incorrigible although their lives may have been admirable and beneficial to others. By contrast—and in the light of the more universalistic and forgiving tendencies of recent theologies rather than the stringent and exclusivistic Catholic and Protestant theologies of the seventeenth century—if theistic interpretations of God and human destiny turn out to be true, then we have the odd result that the person who stakes her life on this world, as an unbeliever, may be in a position to have her illusions corrected hereafter and thus "win" as surely as the believer!

– 8 –

Evolution, Theism, and Naturalism

Despite the fact that creationism and its most recent and sophisticated variant, "intelligent design," are scientifically untenable, for at least three reasons some of my students—and, according to surveys, a substantial percentage of Americans generally—consider them a genuine alternative to evolutionary theory and believe they should be taught as science in biology classrooms. The first reason is ignorance of what science is: what sorts of questions it tries to answer, its presuppositions and methods, its scope and limitations. The second is ignorance of the fact that there has been a long and lively tradition of Christian and Jewish acceptance of evolution, ably represented by "mainstream" Catholic, Protestant, and Jewish theologians and scientists and officially recognized by major denominations. The third reason is student and public awareness that the writings of some of the leading scientific popularizers of Darwinism and biology textbook authors identify evolutionism with a naturalistic or atheistic worldview—an identification that creationists and intelligent design proponents fully exploit in their writings as a foundational flaw in evolutionism. (By "naturalism" here I mean the view that nature, the universe, comprises all that there is.) In this essay I will address these three issues, and argue that the only serious theological debate regarding evolution is between *theistic and naturalistic versions of evolutionism*. The belief that the issue is "biblical creationism" or "intelligent design" versus "godless, materialistic evolutionism" is based on ignorance and false premises. In my presentation of theistic versions of evolutionism I will pay special attention to an influential existentialist theological approach to the relationship between science and religion.

The focus of my remarks is the late Stephen Jay Gould's essay "Nonoverlapping Magisteria" in the March 1997 issue of *Natural History*. (Gould 1997). He went on to expand what he said there into his book *Rock of Ages: Science and Religion in the Fullness of Life* (Gould 1999). Although the main elaboration in the book consists of historical discussion and not new arguments, I will refer to it later in the essay. The *Natural History* essay is a lively discussion of Pope John Paul II's "Message on Evolution" to the Pontifical Academy of Sciences on October 22, 1996, in which he defended the evidence for the theory of evolution and affirmed its consistency with Catholic doctrine. A good bit of Gould's essay is a close comparative study of the texts of John Paul's statement and Pope Pius XII's 1950 encyclical *Humani generis*, which also dealt with evolutionary theory positively but much more tentatively.

But what makes Gould's essay fascinating and, I think, significant is that he provides a context for his exegesis of the papal documents by sharing his own views on science and religion and presenting a theory of the relationship between the two. Gould was always infectiously engaging and characteristically very broadly informed, but in this essay he additionally shares his lively personal interest in and respect for religion as a "Jewish agnostic." His approval of John Paul II's straightforward endorsement of the compatibility of evolution and Catholicism is enthusiastic. The theory of the relationship between science and religion that Gould uses to discuss the papal pronouncements is what he calls "nonoverlapping magisteria" or NOMA, borrowing the term *magisterium*, teaching authority, from the Catholic Church. Gould describes the "NOMA principle" as follows: "The net of science covers the empirical universe: what is it made of (fact) and why does it work this way (theory). The net of religion extends over questions of moral meaning and value. These two magisteria do not overlap, nor do they encompass all inquiry (consider, for example, the magisterium of art and the meaning of beauty)" (Gould 1997, 19-20).

What interests me about the *Natural History* essay is that it shows Gould as a leading evolutionary scientist and a foremost popularizer of science who considered himself—in sharp contrast to, say, Richard Dawkins—a genial skeptic and good friend of religious faith. In the essay Gould relegates creationism to the status of a peculiarly American and parochial movement and fully recognizes that the Catholic Church and most major Protestant and Jewish bodies have for decades accepted critical-historical interpretation of the Bible and affirmed evolution as compatible with theistic faith. At the same time, a close look at Gould's friendly "NOMA principle" on the relationship between science and religion subtly reveals Gould's own equation of evolutionism with naturalism. In the remainder of this essay I will present a brief history of the responses of Christian theology to evolutionary theory, present a typology of theological responses to evolution, and finally examine Gould's NOMA principle more closely within the context of interpretations of evolution that equate it with an atheistic or naturalistic worldview.

1. Theistic evolutionism

In 1896 Andrew Dickson White published a two-volume work entitled *A History of the Warfare Between Science and Theology*. Over a hundred years later it still seems to be a common assumption that the relationship between science and religion is a "warfare" or "conflict," a matter of science *versus* religion. This is a considerable oversimplification and distortion of a much more complex and subtle relationship. Even the terms "science" and "religion" need refining and clarifying, since we're normally talking only about what has constituted mainstream "modern science" since the sixteenth and seventeenth centuries, and about Christian (and to some extent Jewish) thought. When I lecture on Charles Darwin (and also on Galileo) I always give the students what I call my "little homily" on the so-called "conflict between science and religion." I point out that historically the great paradigm shifts in science—notably the Copernican theory and Darwin's theory of evolution through natural selection—have always divided both the scientific and the religious communities. In response to both Copernicanism and Darwinism there were scientists who opposed and resisted the new ideas and theologians who accepted and affirmed them. I add that most of the great scientists of the sixteenth through the eighteenth century were themselves believers, some of them, such as Copernicus and Newton, devoutly so.

When Darwin published *The Origin of Species* in 1859, there were indeed church leaders and theologians who argued that there could be no compromise: we must choose *either* the Bible (the Genesis creation stories) *or* Darwinism—both cannot be true. Leading the attack in England was Anglican Bishop Samuel Wilberforce, who, at a meeting of the British Association in June of 1860, flippantly played upon the sentimental Victorian idealization of women to ask: "If anyone were willing to trace his descent through an ape as his grandfather, would he be willing to trace his descent similarly on the side of his grandmother?" Unfortunately for Wilberforce, his opponent in the meeting's debate was the young Thomas Henry Huxley, who whispered to his neighbor, "The Lord hath delivered him into my hands," stood up, and replied that "If there were an ancestor whom I should feel shame in recalling, it would rather be a man, a man . . . who . . . plunges into scientific questions with which he has no real acquaintance, only to obscure them by an aimless rhetoric, and distract the attention of his hearers from the real point at issue by eloquent digressions and skilled appeals to religious prejudice." Another opponent of evolution was Philip Gosse, a prominent but religiously conservative naturalist (in the older sense of someone who avidly and systematically studies aspects of nature) who bizarrely speculated that God had distributed fossil remains on the earth in such a way as to make plausible an evolutionary interpretation, simply to test people's faith.

But with the emerging acceptance of Darwinism among many scientists, a growing number of Protestant theologians accepted evolutionary theory as entirely compatible with belief in a creator God and specifically with Christian doctrine. Paving the way for this acceptance was the increasing influence of critical-historical study of the Bible in the early and mid-nineteenth century. German scholars, most of them Protestant Christians, led the way in applying the methods of historical study to both the Hebrew Bible and the New Testament, shedding a great deal of new light on the biblical authors and texts in their historical and cultural setting and on the meaning and purposes of the language they used.

Critical-historical study of the Bible brought about a reinterpretation of the meaning of biblical inspiration and authority on the part of not only liberal but also often more traditional theologians as well. Many Protestant theologians and biblical scholars came to accept that there are factual errors and conflicting accounts in the biblical writings; to distinguish between the enduring religious ideas expressed in, say, the Genesis creation stories and the ancient Israelite cosmology or worldview in terms of which they were historically expressed. They interpreted the Genesis stories as symbolic, mythological affirmations of God as the source of all things and the dependence of the universe and human life upon God, not as literal history or science. As with earlier scientific discoveries, these Protestant scholars believed that the theory of evolution provides us with a vastly expanded and corrected knowledge of just *how* God creates and sustains the universe and an enlarged understanding of the biblical emphasis on the creatureliness of humankind. Over time this became and has remained the outlook of "mainstream," non-fundamentalist Protestant theologians and churches to the present day: evolution through natural selection is as well-grounded a scientific theory as gravitation or relativity, and faith and reason are compatible in the case of evolution just as they are in other branches of scientific knowledge.

Something similar happened among nineteenth-century Roman Catholic theologians and biblical scholars. While officially the Church was slow to accept evolution, in time it acknowledged the evolution of the human body and brain from animal ancestry while affirming the special creation of each human soul by God. In the twentieth century there were the two important papal documents addressing evolution to which Gould devotes his article on "Nonoverlapping Magisteria": Pope Pius XII's encyclical *Humani generis* in 1950, and Pope John Paul II's "Message on Evolution" to the Pontifical Academy of Sciences in 1996. Pius cautiously affirmed that evolutionary theory was compatible with Catholic teaching as long as it did not deny the special creation of the human soul. Building on the statements of his predecessor, John Paul went further. Referring to a variety of twentieth-century developments in evolutionary biology, he said: ". . . new knowledge has led to the recognition that the theory of evolution is more than a hypothesis. It is indeed remarkable that this theory has been progressively accepted by researchers, following a series of discoveries in various fields of knowledge. The convergence, neither sought nor fabricated, of the results of work that was conducted independently is itself a significant argument in favor of the theory" (Quoted in Gould 1997, 60). Modern Catholic scholars have long accepted historical-critical study of the Bible and do not interpret the Genesis stories literally. In their affirmation of the compatibility of faith and reason with regard to modern science, they stand squarely in the tradition of Augustine and Thomas Aquinas.

This "mainstream" approach in both Protestantism and Catholicism (and also in Reform and Conservative Judaism) that arose in the nineteenth century in response to Darwin's theory may be called *theistic evolutionism*. Since then the serious intellectual debate has not been between evolutionists and "creationists," but between *theistic* evolutionists and *naturalistic* or *non-theistic* evolutionists.

Following the 1859 publication of Darwin's *Origin of Species*, a group of thinkers and writers of the Church of England wrote articles and books defending Darwinism and arguing its compatibility with Christian belief. They were among the earliest theistic evolutionists. The Anglican priest Charles Kingsley, who was also a popular novelist, championed evolution, as did theologians such as Aubrey Moore and J. R. Illingworth and the eminent poet, critic, and lay theologian Matthew Arnold. Aubrey Moore made this striking statement in his book *Science and the Faith*:

Evolution as a theory is infinitely more Christian than the theory of 'Special Creation.' For it implies the immanence of God in nature, and the omnipresence of his creative power. Those who opposed the doctrine of evolution in defense of a 'continued intervention' of God seem to have failed to notice that a theory of occasional intervention implies as its correlative a theory of ordinary absence. . . . Anything more opposed to the language of the Bible and the Fathers can hardly be imagined (Livingston 1971, 232). . . .

Both Moore and Illingworth were contributors to an important and controversial volume of essays entitled *Lux Mundi* ("Light of the World"; Gore 1890). The contributors to the book, all of them Anglican clergy, were not "liberals." They were high-church Anglicans who saw themselves as standing fully in the tradition of classical Trinitarian Christianity. Illingworth's *Lux Mundi* essay, called "The Incarnation and Development," was a restatement of the Christian doctrine of the Incarnation (the belief that Jesus of Nazareth is fully God and fully a human being) in the light of the new knowledge of human origins and development from evolutionary theory. He viewed the theory of evolution as simply the latest in a centuries-old series of intellectual revolutions that the churches had assimilated, taking the best thought of every age "captive to Christ" and reinterpreting ancient truth in the light of the new knowledge. Building on the early identification, in the first chapter of John's Gospel, of Christ with the *logos* or universal divine ground of rationality in the universe, Illingworth wrote that "In the incarnation . . . there was provided the key for understanding the continuity of God and nature, of nature and man, of man and Jesus Christ and of Jesus Christ and God" (Gore, 187).

At this point it should be observed that, like almost all non-scientist interpreters of evolution (and also many scientists) in the nineteenth century, most theologians interpreted evolution as a progressive, purposeful development of life on earth from simple life-forms to its culmination in the human species. They found irresistible the identification of evolution with progressive development in both the natural and the human spheres, which conveniently cohered with the optimistic and progressivist interpretations of the divine purpose or the historical process that dominated the age. In other words, most people thought of evolution in positive metaphysical and moral terms—which contributed to making it attractive both to many Christian theologians and to secular humanists. The various forms of Social Darwinism were part of this wider response. As Darwin clearly recognized, these were philosophical and theological interpretations, *not* the scientific theory of evolution, which simply seeks to explain change over time through natural selection without inferring that the whole process has some ultimate direction, meaning, or goal. We see here an early example of the compatibility of evolutionary theory with a variety of metaphysical interpretations. However, in the twentieth century most leading theological and secular interpreters of evolution came fully to recognize the distinction between scientific evolution and philosophical and theological ideas of cosmic purpose and meaning.

In the United States, as in Britain, a number of nineteenth-century Christian intellectuals from liberal to orthodox endorsed evolutionary theory as true and entirely compatible with Christian teaching. On the liberal side were people such as Lyman Abbott, a prominent Congregationalist minister, writer, and editor. He wrote two books, *The Evolution of Christianity* (1892) and *Theology of an Evolutionist* (1897), in which, typically, he thought of evolution as a universal and progressive process of development in both the natural and the human orders. Among theologically conservative adherents of evolution, notable was Asa Gray, the Harvard biologist who was the main champion of Darwinism in America. Gray was a Calvinist Presbyterian and thoroughly orthodox in his Christian beliefs. James McCosh, president of Princeton Theological Seminary and a prominent Presbyterian leader, argued that God had established the initial design of the whole evolutionary process but continues to work through what appear to us to be "spontaneous" (random) changes in the process. Interestingly, as Calvinists, both Gray and McCosh had a deep sense of struggle and tragedy in human existence and throughout nature; they had no problem with the theory of natural selection, which just seemed to reinforce the dark Calvinist view of an earth in the grip of original sin. Many commentators have observed social, cultural, and economic influences on the nineteenth-century discussion, dominated as it was by the metaphors of "struggle" and "competition" for survival and lyrically rendered by Tennyson in his poem *In Memoriam* as "nature red in tooth and claw." It was the philosopher Herbert Spencer, writing in 1851, who gave us the phrase "survival of the fittest," which Darwin later used.

What we call "fundamentalism" did not arise until the early twentieth century. It was a new movement, and not the same thing as traditional Christian orthodoxy. Fundamentalism arose specifically as a reaction against "modernism" in all its forms: it condemned historical-critical study of the Bible, evolutionary theory, and various other developments in modern knowledge. The movement originated in a series of pamphlets, *The Fundamentals*, published in 1909. The specific fundamentalist doctrines were a literalistic interpretation of biblical inerrancy, an emphasis on Jesus' atoning death and second coming, and the sudden conversion of the believer in accepting Jesus as personal savior. While in previous centuries Christian orthodoxy had held that the biblical writings were the fully inspired Word of God, this had not been tied to a literalistic interpretation of the biblical texts. In the twentieth century it has been fundamentalists, not "mainstream" orthodox Christians, who have aggressively opposed evolutionary theory with creationist views based upon a literalistic interpretation of the opening chapters of Genesis, treating them as if they were a textbook of science and history. (It surprises me that to my knowledge no critic of creationism has pointed out that a *truly* literal interpretation of Genesis 1 would have to accept the ancient Israelite cosmology it expresses: creation as God's moulding a primeval watery chaos into an ordered cosmos [not creating "out of nothing," as in classical Christian doctrine], making a "firmament" or translucent dome to divide the watery chaos and make a space for earth and life, and establishing the earth as a disk with sun, moon, planets, and stars fixed on the firmament. We don't have even a Ptolemaic, much less a Copernican, universe here!)

Summing up, we may say that the picture of Christian theological responses to Darwinism in the nineteenth century is a complex and subtle one. Those responses ran the gamut from full acceptance, by both liberal and many orthodox Christian thinkers, to complete rejection by fundamentalists. Out of the positive responses emerged the "mainstream" Protestant and Catholic affirmations of evolution in the twentieth century, a broad consensus that I have called "theistic evolutionism." It has been represented by theologians and theologically-informed scientists who have been fully aware that scientifically evolution does not mean progressive development culminating in *homo sapiens*. I will mention only some of the major figures: among them scientists who were also theologians, such as Pierre Teilhard de Chardin, C. A. Coulson, Arthur Peacocke, John Polkinghorne, and Ian Barbour; and theistic philosophers from A. E. Taylor, F. R. Tennant, and Alfred North Whitehead in the early twentieth century to Charles Hartshorne, Richard Swinburne, and John Haught more recently. To these thinkers who have worked specifically on the issues raised by evolution we may add virtually all the "famous names" of twentieth-century theology—Karl Barth, Paul Tillich, Rudolf Bultmann, Jürgen Moltmann, Karl Rahner, Bernard Lonergan, Hans Küng, and many others—who have accepted evolutionary theory within the context of a variety of understandings of the relationship between science and faith. My point here is that there is a long and highly respected tradition of theistic evolutionism which has in fact come to define "mainstream" Catholic and Protestant thinking on the issue; that there is a good deal of serious literature by experts who thoroughly examine evolutionary theory and creatively rethink the philosophical and theological issues surrounding the relationship between God and the world.

2. **Types of theological interpretation of evolution**

Ian Barbour is a physicist and theologian and one of the world's leading authorities on science and religion and the history of their relationship. In his book *Religion and Science: Historical and Contemporary Issues*, drawn very largely from his 1989-91 Gifford Lectures, Barbour presents a typology of four approaches to the relationship between science and religion: conflict, independence, dialogue, and integration (Barbour 1997, 77-105). Here I will briefly define the four approaches, reserving a more extended discussion only for an influential existentialist version of the view that science and religion are independent of each other.

Conflict is the view that where they disagree, science and religion are simply incompatible and necessarily in conflict. Both Christian fundamentalists and some scientific naturalists hold this view, but of course from opposite directions. According to the former, the Bible (or rather a certain literalistic way of interpreting it) is infallibly true, and that includes its statements about nature such as the creation stories; thus Darwinism must be false. According to the latter, the whole realm of religion consists of false beliefs about the world and human life; only through reason, and specifically through science, can we obtain whatever knowledge we can get. So-called "creation scientists" represent the "conflict" model from the Christian side; a scientist such as Richard Dawkins, who actively argues for atheism, represents it from the other side.

The interpretation of science and faith as *independent* of each other has probably been the most popular theological response since the middle of the twentieth century. On this view, as Barbour says,

> Each has its own distinctive domain and its characteristic methods that can be justified on its own terms. . . . there are two jurisdictions and each party must keep off the other's turf. . . . Each mode of inquiry is selective and has its limitations. . . . the languages of science and religion serve very different functions in human life (84).

This is the response that has characterized existentialist-inspired theologies, which dominated twentieth-century Protestant thought, and also those theologies informed by language philosophy and specifically by Ludwig Wittgenstein's later reflections. In his later lectures and writings Wittgenstein developed a functional analysis of linguistic meaning. There is no universal verificational norm to which language must conform in order to be meaningful (as he had earlier believed). Humans "play" a variety of "language games," each with its own appropriate vocabulary and rules giving linguistic expression to one of the many "forms of life" or modes of social behavior in which we are involved. Applied to the present issue, the language of science and the language of religion perform very different functions in human life and thought, each with its distinctive and autonomous ways of speaking. I will return to a consideration of the existentialist model of independence after summarizing the other two types of approach to the science-religion relationship.

The third type of theological interpretation of the science-religion relationship is *dialogue*. As the name suggests, this refers to theological discussions of general features of scientific and theological knowledge-claims directed toward engagement with scientists and philosophers of science. Barbour sees dialogue going on in three areas: 1) questions about the presuppositions and limits of scientific knowledge and their relationship to theological claims; 2) methodological parallels between scientific and theological inquiry, such as the use by both of models and metaphors; and 3) the exploration by theologians of a "nature-centered" spirituality grounded in but transcending the contemporary scientific synthesis about the nature of the universe developed by physics, chemistry, and biology. Several prominent Roman Catholic philosophers and theologians of the twentieth century, including Ernan McMullin, Karl Rahner, and David Tracy, were active in exploring these three areas, as were Protestant theologian Wolfhart Pannenberg and Anglican scientist-theologian John Polkinghorne. It is worth noting that the "dialogue" has been conducted almost entirely among religious philosophers and theologians, not with scientists.

Representatives of the fourth type of approach to the science-religion relationship, *integration*, as the label suggests, believe that it is possible to develop a synthesis between scientific and theological knowledge. Barbour distinguishes among three subtypes of the integration model: 1) Natural theology is the continuation in modern form of the long tradition of efforts to demonstrate philosophically some of the assertions of Christianity (above all the existence and something of the nature of God), fully incorporating but transcending the work of science. A prominent contemporary representative is the British philosopher Richard Swinburne. 2) "Theology of nature" is the reformulation of traditional Christian doctrines in the light of modern scientific knowledge. Probably the best-known and most influential theologian of nature in the twentieth century was the Jesuit scientist-theologian Pierre Teilhard de Chardin. 3) "Systematic synthesis" is the construction of a comprehensive metaphysics embracing and unifying science and religion. Clearly the most important and influential version of systematic synthesis has been process philosophy, grounded in the philosophy of Alfred North Whitehead and articulated most prominently by Charles Hartshorne and John Cobb. These extraordinarily creative attempts at integrating science and religion at a metaphysical level require the overcoming of continued widespread skepticism among philosophers, scientists, and indeed many theologians about the possibility of theoretical knowledge of putative realities beyond the spatio-temporal universe.

To return now to a fuller discussion of the "independence" model of understanding the relationship between science and religion, which as I have said has been the dominant approach especially in Protestant theology. Existentialism, as we've seen in previous essays, carried forward Kant's distinction between theoretical and practical knowledge— reinterpreted as the difference between our knowledge as theoretical inquirers and as concretely existing subjects—and also Kant's skepticism about the possibility of purely theoretical knowledge of anything apart from the world of sense experience and nature. Theologians informed by existentialism have argued that religious faith is a mode of relationship to reality that arises out of and takes its appropriate forms of expression from our lives as concrete subjects-in-relation involved with issues of meaning and value. On this view it is only through the various forms of faith—trust in and openness to unseen and invisible realities grounding and sustaining the world's and our existence—that we have knowledge of anything beyond nature. The sciences, by contrast, are the proper mode of obtaining generalized objective knowledge of physical nature and of ourselves as biological organisms (including the psychosocial behaviors arising from our biological nature). Scientists seek natural explanations of natural phenomena by formulating hypotheses that are repeatedly and thoroughly questioned and tested as accounts of the relevant data according to agreed-upon protocols of procedure. Out of this process of scientific investigation and debate emerge established theories that become the scientific paradigms for interpreting the universe unless and until they are displaced by theories that come to be accepted as more adequate by the scientific community. Undergirding the scientific enterprise are presuppositions about nature, prominent among them uniformity and causality, and the bedrock assumption that the physical universe is "rational" in the sense that it is susceptible to reasoned inquiry and explanation. These presuppositions and procedures define both the scope and the limits of science.

Although it's perhaps obvious, it should be noted that in order to work, the theological account of science and religion as independent spheres of meaning and discourse must interpret both spheres in such a way that there is no possibility of conflict between the two. That eliminates any sort of biblical literalism and requires a fully historical-critical hermeneutics of the biblical writings, according to which, for example, the creation stories in Genesis are to be understood as mythological rather than historical or scientific. From a theological point of view it also eliminates every form of scientism, or naturalism, the absolutizing of scientific knowledge into an all-sufficient metaphysics or worldview. What's interesting is that Gould's NOMA principle clearly belongs to the "independence" model of the relationship, but as we shall see, he makes it work by defining religion in terms of "morals and meanings," reductionistically interpreted as ways of talking about human feelings and relationships, and by surreptitiously equating science with a metaphysical naturalism.

Probably the single most important figure who worked out an existentialist approach to the relationship between religion and science was a leading Christian theologian of the twentieth century, Rudolf Bultmann. Bultmann's important contribution to twentieth-century theology was to insist that the hermeneutical task must be undertaken systematically, consistently, and thoroughly. He also argued that the theologian must be clearly and consciously guided by a modern philosophical analysis of "lived" human existence in terms of which the enduring message of Christianity can be illuminated and distinguished from the traditional mythology in which it expressed itself. Bultmann found such a philosophy in the existential analysis of Martin Heidegger (for a time his colleague at the University of Marburg) in his revolutionary 1927 book *Being and Time*.

Bultmann called his hermeneutical approach to biblical texts and Christian theology "demythologizing" (*Entmythologisierung*). In his programmatic 1942 essay, "New Testament and Mythology," he articulated its main ideas (Bartsch 1953, 1-44). In the biblical writings the Christian proclamation of creation, sin, and redemption is expressed largely in terms of the mythology of first-century Judaism: a three-story universe comprised of heaven, earth, and hell, hierarchies of angels and devils, possession of humans by evil spirits, miracles abounding, and vivid and detailed apocalyptic expectations of the imminent end of the world. Bultmann defines what he means by "mythology" very specifically: "Mythology is the use of imagery to express the other worldly in terms of this world and the divine in terms of human life, the other side in terms of this side. For instance, divine transcendence is expressed as spatial distance"(10). Thus in the New Testament God is pictured as "dwelling" in heaven, hell has a location in which human torments are described in physical terms, and the evils in the world are ascribed to Satan as the ruler of this world and to evil spirits as malevolent beings who go about possessing people and making them mentally and physically ill.

But mythologies have a purpose that can be distinguished from the mythologies themselves. "The real purpose of myth," Bultmann writes,

> is not to present an objective picture of the world as it is, but to express man's understanding of himself in the world in which he lives. *Myth should be interpreted not cosmologically, but anthropologically, or better still, existentially.* Myth speaks of the power or the powers which man supposes he experiences as the ground and limit of his world and of his own activity and suffering. . . . Myth is an expression of man's conviction that the origin and purpose of the world in which he lives are to be sought not within it but beyond it—that is, beyond the realm of known and tangible reality. . . . Myth is also an expression of man's awareness that he is not lord of his own being. . . .myth expresses man's belief that in this state of dependence he can be delivered from the forces within the visible world" (10-11; italics added).

This existential interpretation of what is enshrined in myth is not itself mythological; it is the permanent foundational element in what Bultmann believed to be the Christian message—an understanding that he believed is fully compatible with modern science. Here Bultmann also makes clear that by demythologizing (a term which he himself considered both useful and inadequate) he did not mean eliminating Christian mythology but reinterpreting it in existentialist terms.

According to Bultmann, to the extent that the Christian message is uncritically proclaimed as inseparable from its original mythological "clothing"—which has continued to dominate Christian language and imagery down to the present day—it is simply incredible in the light of modern scientific knowledge. He writes, in "New Testament and Mythology," "Man's knowledge and mastery of the world have advanced to such an extent through science and technology that it is no longer possible for anyone seriously to hold the New Testament view of the world—in fact, there is hardly anyone who does" (4). The physical universe as understood by the sciences is governed by causal relations that are in principle if not already in fact explainable. In a statement that became famous among students of Bultmann's theology, he asserts:

> It is impossible to use electric light and the wireless [radio] and to avail ourselves of modern medical and surgical discoveries, and at the same time to believe in the New Testament world of daemons and spirits. We may think we can manage it in our own lives, but to expect others to do so is to make the Christian faith unintelligible and unacceptable to the modern world (5).

Especially in the light of the rapid growth and influence of conservative forms of Christianity in our time, Bultmann's remarks may seem naïve. Obviously, one might observe, many people do in fact continue to hold fullblown beliefs in traditional Christian mythology even in an age that has been dramatically shaped by science and technology. But Bultmann clearly recognized, in the 1930s and 1940s, that many Christians, Catholic, Orthodox, and Protestant alike, still affirmed the full mythology in their creeds, worship, and discourse. He simply believed that in the post-Enlightenment world—and especially among better-educated believers—such affirmations manifest self-deception or (to use Heidegger's language) "inauthenticity." The modern Christian who continues to profess belief in the mythological worldview of the New Testament is either compartmentalizing her knowledge and her faith, or subtly and often unconsciously demythologizing: reinterpreting, in a more or less haphazard way, aspects of the mythology to make it compatible with modern knowledge. In other words, according to Bultmann, believers only *think* they fully believe the mythology and at the same time live fully as inhabitants of the world of Darwinism, quantum mechanics, electric lights, and modern technologies of communication; they don't really. No one in the twentieth (or the twenty-first) century can actually function as if she were living in the first century.

However, "there is nothing specifically Christian in the mythical view of the world as such. It is simply the cosmology of a pre-scientific age" (3). The Christian message is that the "authentic life" is "a life based on unseen, intangible realities. . . . the abandonment of all self-contrived security. . . . faith that the unseen, intangible reality actually confronts us as love, opening up our future and signifying not death but life" (19). In his later book *Jesus Christ and Mythology*, Bultmann explained that to speak existentially of God, the "unseen, intangible reality," as active in the world and our lives, "confronting us as love," is not to speak mythologically but *analogically*:

> . . . when we speak in this manner of God as acting, we conceive God's action as an analogue to the actions taking place between men. . . . we conceive the communion between God and man as an analogue to the communion between man and man. It is in this analogical sense that we speak of God's love and care for men, of His demands and of His wrath, of His promise and grace, and it is in this analogical sense that we call Him Father (Bultmann 1958, 68-69).

Bultmann is arguing that even in a world explained by the sciences, it is legitimate to speak of an unseen, non-physical reality that grounds, sustains, and is active in the world. That is because science is limited to natural explanations of physical phenomena, while human beings as self-transcending subjects also inhabit a world of meanings and values through and in terms of which transcendent reality manifests itself to them. As Bultmann says, "my self, my personal existence, my own personal life, is no more visible and capable of proof than is God as acting" (65). The appropriate language for speaking of the reality and activity of the unseen God (and here there is overlap between the existentialist and the language-philosophy approaches) is metaphors taken from our experience as subjects dwelling together with other subjects in a common human world of interrelationships. God confronts humans as individual subjects in the context of their lives together, and God's activity is experienced and responded to only in that existential milieu. Bultmann did not consider this way of talking about God as mythological as he defined mythology: the objectifying of the transcendent God and the divine activity in images and stories that represent God as a this-worldly, anthropomorphic being presiding over the cosmos from heaven, commanding ranks of angelic beings whom he sends to earth on various missions, doing battle against Satan and his legions, and producing miracles that interrupt and suspend the normal workings of nature.

Central to Bultmann's existentialist interpretation of Christianity is that the only authentic affirmations about God are those that express the speaker's own experience of the divine presence and activity: ". . . only such statements about God are legitimate as express the existential relation between God and man. Statements which speak of God's actions as cosmic events are illegitimate" (69). "God's action generally, in nature and history," Bultmann says, "is hidden from the believer just as much as from the non-believer" (64), apprehended only in personal trust here and now based on the Christian message as historically and prototypically witnessed in the biblical writings.

Bultmann summarizes his version of the existentialist approach to the independence of science and religion as follows:

> In faith I realize that the scientific world-view does not comprehend the whole reality of the world and of human life, but faith does not offer another general world-view which corrects science in its statements on its own level. Rather faith acknowledges that the worldview given by science is a necessary means for doing our work within the world. Indeed, I need to see the worldly events as linked by cause and effect not only as a scientific observer, but also in my daily living. In doing so there remains no room for God's working. This is the paradox of faith, that faith "nevertheless" understands as God's action here and now an event which is completely intelligible in the natural or historical connection of events. . . . This "nevertheless". . . is inseparable from faith. Only this is real faith in miracle. He who thinks that it is possible to speak of miracles as of demonstrable events capable of proof offends against the thought of God as acting in hidden ways. He subjects God's action to the control of objective observation (65-66).

It goes without saying that Bultmann's view of modern science encompassed evolutionary theory, and that he regarded the Genesis creation stories as mythological expressions of an understanding of human existence that can be expressed non-mythologically. A good example of his treatment of the subject is his 1936 essay "The Meaning of the Christian Faith in Creation" (Bultmann 1960, 206-225).

3. Naturalistic evolutionism

The real issue, then, is the fact that evolution may be interpreted within either a theistic or a naturalistic metaphysical framework. Underlying his many criticisms of aspects of evolutionary theory, what really agitates Phillip Johnson, the author of *Darwinism on Trial* and a guru of creationists and intelligent design advocates, is the identification of scientific evolutionism with a reductionistic philosophical naturalism by many of its leading proponents (Johnson 1993). A case in point is Douglas Futuyama, author of a widely used college textbook in evolutionary biology. In the book, *Evolutionary Biology*, Futuyama writes: "By coupling undirected, purposeless variation to the blind, uncaring process of natural selection, Darwin made theological or spiritual explanations of the life processes superfluous" (Johnson 1995, 19). This seemingly "scientific" statement in a college textbook contains "loaded," nonscientific language and naturalistic philosophical assumptions. A more elegant example is to be found in Richard Dawkins' *The Blind Watchmaker*, where, both admiring and rejecting William Paley's "watchmaker" argument from design as an explanation of adaptation in nature, he writes:

> .... All appearances to the contrary, the only watchmaker in nature is the blind forces of physics. ... A true watchmaker has foresight: he designs his cogs and springs, and plans their interconnections, with a future purpose in his mind's eye. Natural selection, the blind, unconscious, automatic process which Darwin discovered, and which we now know is the explanation for the existence and apparently purposeful form of all life, has no purpose in mind. It has no mind and no mind's eye. It does not plan for the future. It has no vision, no foresight, no sight at all. If it can be said to play the role of watchmaker in nature, it is the *blind* watchmaker (Dawkins 1986, 5).

Dawkins' metaphor of the "blind watchmaker" and assertion of "what we now know" is "the explanation" of things is, like Futuyama's remarks, naturalistic metaphysics, not science.

At this point I return to Stephen Jay Gould, a naturalistic evolutionist who, unlike scientists like Futuyama and Dawkins, offered a theory that he believed reconciles and maintains the integrity of both science and religion. As I have indicated, he said he genuinely had "enormous respect for religion," and believed "with all his heart" in "a respectful and even loving concordat" between religion and science. In terms of Barbour's typology, Gould's approach, the "NOMA principle," clearly sees science and religion as *independent* of each other, each legitimate in its own sphere and coming into conflict only when one claims to pronounce authoritatively on something that is properly within the other's sphere. After describing and criticizing Gould's approach I will return briefly to Barbour's typology by way of calling attention to Gould's willful ignoring of virtually the entire twentieth-century theological discussion of evolution.

When we look closely at Gould's fleshing out of the NOMA principle, we see that he seems generally to interpret religion as "the search for proper ethical values and the spiritual meaning of our lives" (Gould 1997, 18), as dealing with "questions of moral meaning and value" (19). There is a long tradition of interpreting religious claims functionally as moral claims, from Spinoza to Einstein, which conveniently leaves science and indeed naturalism the undisputed claimant to the epistemological and ontological realms. Gould, reminiscent of Einstein, happily defers to religion as the proper source of moral values and also, somewhat vaguely, as answering people's need for meaning to their lives. But surely this is a severely truncated characterization of religion that would not be acceptable to most believers. We've seen, in examining Bultmann's existentialist version of the "independence" model, that our human existence as subjects in a realm of intersubjectivity opens up to us genuine dimensions of reality that are simply not reducible to moral values or the human need for meaning.

Somewhat inconsistently with the above, Gould occasionally recognizes that religion makes certain distinctive epistemological and ontological claims, and he specifically mentions the existence of the soul. But even here, he says, "My world [science] cannot prove or disprove such a notion, and the concept of souls cannot threaten or impact my domain." He then offers his own humanistic interpretation of language about souls: "I surely honor the metaphorical value of such a concept both for grounding moral discussion and for expressing what we most value about human potentiality: our decency, care, and all the ethical and intellectual struggles that the evolution of consciousness imposed upon us"(62). What Gould apparently will not allow for is the possibility that concepts such as the soul might point to a competing epistemological and ontological framework for which scientific descriptions of the universe have the status of essential but selective abstractions from a wider and deeper range of knowledge and reality. Anyone who has read his books or heard any of his popular lectures knows that Gould also attacked the traditional belief in purposiveness in nature with a zest and attentiveness which clearly implied that a metaphysical naturalism is the proper context of interpretation and ruled out non-naturalist alternatives.

In his book *Rocks of Ages* Gould cavalierly omits almost any mention of the entire literature of theistic evolutionism since the end of the nineteenth century (he was well informed on aspects, but only aspects, of the nineteenth-century discussion). He contents himself, at the end of the book, with briefly presenting what he calls the "syncretic school"—what Barbour would call the "integration" model of the relationship between science and religion. Gould caricatures it as "the claim that science and religion should fuse to one big, happy family, or rather one big pod of peas, where the facts of science reinforce and validate the precepts of religion, and where God shows his hand (and mind) in the workings of nature" (Gould 1999, 212). His only references are articles in *The New York Times* and *The Wall Street Journal*, from which he quotes in order to ridicule, for example, the Templeton Foundation's sponsorship of a 1998 conference on "science and the spiritual quest" that received much media attention. What his remarks reveal is that Gould had no patience whatever with—and probably little if any knowledge of—any sort of philosophical efforts at integrating scientific knowledge into a larger and more comprehensively reasoned vision of the cosmos. The possibility that modern theistic philosophers and philosophical theologians, such as Whitehead, Teilhard, Hartshorne, and Haught, might think of God and the divine activity in new ways that recover neglected aspects of the Christian tradition of theism and make theological sense of evolution, even if at all known to Gould, would have been completely irrelevant and uninteresting to him. The phenomenon of scientists who are also theologians, such as Barbour, Polkinghorne, and Peacocke, likewise failed to arouse his curiosity. The NOMA principle, which consigns the entire realm of religion with convenient vagueness to providing humans with "meaning and moral values," leaves Gould's metaphysical naturalism—which he though of simply as "science"—firmly in charge of the epistemological and ontological questions. And, of course, he confidently believed that NOMA is the only legitimate player in the field on the matter of science and religion.

3. Summing up

At bottom, then, what really troubles those who reject evolution in favor of creationist theories (for which the only "evidence" is a disingenuously literalistic reading of the first chapters of Genesis) is that they believe that evolutionary theory is equivalent to atheism—or, as I have been describing it, naturalism, the belief that there is simply nature, the physical universe, and nothing more. But naturalism is not science, but a metaphysical theory or worldview based on science. Simply to equate evolutionary theory with atheism or naturalism is to equate science with a particular worldview: scientific assumptions, methods, and knowledge are selective and abstractive and compatible with a variety of perspectives on the ultimate character of reality. It may be that naturalism is true, but it needs considerably more than simple assertion and assumption presented as science. On the issue of distinguishing between scientific theory and metaphysical theory the theistic evolutionists, for perhaps obvious good reasons, seem more critically aware of the necessary distinctions.

Creationists raise questions and criticisms that have been satisfactorily answered over and over again—while offering no scientific evidence for their views—but at bottom is the fear that to accept evolution means to espouse a "godless, secular atheism": one simply cannot be a Christian, or even a theist, and also an evolutionist. Proponents of intelligent design, whose arguments are typically more sophisticated than those of creationists, believe that the complexity of organic life on earth cannot be fully explained by evolutionary biology, and argue that we must posit an "intelligent designer" in order to provide a full explanation. The problem is that hypotheses such as an intelligent designer are simply outside the purview of science; they stand in the tradition of natural theology and specifically of the teleological argument or "argument from design" for the existence of God. From a philosophical or theological point of view, one may legitimately question whether evolutionary theory completely "explains," in some ultimate and total sense of explanation, organic life on the planet. But evolutionary biology explains what it does within the framework and limits of science. What further explanation might be called for is not within the realm of science.

Science by definition seeks natural explanations for natural phenomena. An "intelligent designer" is a supernatural explanation, and thus beyond the boundaries of science. To argue that the only explanation for the complexity of nature is an intelligent being outside of nature is to call an arbitrary halt to the quest for scientific explanation by invoking a supernatural explanation, which contradicts the very essence of the scientific enterprise. Such efforts in the past, appealing to what is often called the "God of the gaps," have uniformly failed. They represent the mentality that says "Well, science may be able to explain x, but it will never be able to explain y"—whether y was the force that holds the planets in their orbits, the origin of life out of non-life, or the origin of human beings. It's also disingenuous of adherents of intelligent design, in their public presentations and debates, not to use the term "God" to refer to the intelligent designer, since it's clear from their writings and personal remarks that they clearly mean "God"—and not simply "God" but the God of the Bible as interpreted by a very conservative version of Christianity. Indeed, some of the leading proponents of intelligent design, such as Phillip Johnson and Stephen Meyer, are by their own admission creationists who have found in intelligent design what they consider a more publicly palatable way to get their views presented in the biology classroom.

As a strictly scientific theory explaining the origins and development of life, Darwinism is compatible with a variety of metaphysical beliefs, including both theism and atheism. This is the genuine, intellectually significant issue, in the light of which creationism and intelligent design should be viewed as the spurious alternatives they are.

The Faith of a Heretic: Walter Kaufmann

In this essay I want to recall and recognize the legacy of the distinguished twentieth-century American philosopher, Walter Kaufmann, as a philosopher of religion. I believe that philosophers and theologians can continue to learn and benefit from Kaufmann's understanding of the philosophical enterprise, his vigorous critique of the whole enterprise of theology, and his richly developed analysis of what he calls the "essential ambiguity" of the idea of God. I also want to suggest that his understanding of the task and scope of philosophy was very "existential" in nature, and that despite his own strictures against labelling or "isms" and his specific criticisms of existentialism, his own religious perspective—what he called "the faith of a heretic"—represents a kind of purely existentialist stance toward religious questions.

In order to appreciate more fully the breadth of learning and intense personal engagement Walter Kaufmann brought to the study of religion, it may be helpful to say something about his background. He was born in Freiburg, Germany in 1921. All four of his grandparents had been Jewish, but Grandmother Kaufmann had urged her sons to take a familiar path to full social acceptability and become Christians. Kaufmann was raised a Lutheran until, at the age of eleven, he decided to return to the Jewish heritage of his grandparents and eventually brought his father and brother along with him, during the early and middle 1930s precisely when things were starting to become increasingly difficult for Jews in Germany. Kaufmann points out that he took both the Christian and the Jewish faiths absolutely seriously (he was inclined to Orthodoxy as a Jew) until critical questions drove him out of both traditions, and he remained to the end of his life a skeptic with a passionate absorption in religion. He also acquired a good classical humanistic education in Germany which laid the foundations for the later direction of his scholarly interests.

In 1939 Kaufmann's parents got him out of Germany and to the U.S., where he entered Williams College. He majored in philosophy as an undergraduate and won a scholarship to do graduate study at Harvard. His doctoral study was interrupted by four years in the U.S. army. He returned to Harvard and completed the Ph.D. with a dissertation on "Nietzsche's Theory of Values" in 1947. For many years a distinguished scholar and popular teacher at Princeton, Kaufmann died in 1980.

To understand Kaufmann's philosophical outlook it is essential to realize that his thought was informed by a remarkable breadth of learning and sensibility, and that he understood philosophy and its methods in a very large-minded way. He was a thoroughgoing *humanist*, in both of the usual senses of the term: by education and interest immersed in the humanities, and entirely devoted to exploring the human condition. Kaufmann was fully at home in philosophy, religion (especially Judaism, Christianity, and Buddhism), classical and modern literature, and psychology in the Continental tradition. He was a published poet and photographer, and travelled and studied throughout the world. He brought to the study of Judaism and Christianity a knowledge of the original languages and of the biblical texts and theological literature that rivalled that of many scholars in those traditions.

A sampling of titles from Kaufmann's many books provides a good indication of the range of subject matters and topics encompassed by his intellectual passions. I think many people know of Kaufmann only as a leading translator and interpreter of Nietzsche, and perhaps also for his widely-used anthology *Existentialism from Dostoevsky to Sartre* (1956). But he was also a translator of Goethe, numerous other modern German poets, and Martin Buber, and a substantial and original interpreter of the whole modern German tradition in philosophy, literature, and psychology. Kaufmann's last and most comprehensive project was a three-volume series with the general title *Discovering the Mind* (1980). Volume I was on Goethe, Kant, and Hegel; volume II on Nietzsche, Heidegger, and Buber; and volume III on Freud, Adler, and Jung.

Among Kaufmann's other books are *From Shakespeare to Existentialism* (1959), *Religion from Tolstoy to Camus* (1961), *Hegel: A Reinterpretation* (1965) and *Hegel's Political Philosophy* (1970), *Tragedy and Philosophy* (1968), *Religion in Four Dimensions: Existential and Aesthetic, Historical and Comparative* (1976), and a series of books of photographs and text with titles such as *Life at the Limits*, *Man's Lot*, *Time is an Artist*, and *What is Man?* While his chief expertise and interest lay in Continental thought, Kaufmann also read and appreciatively critiqued British empiricism, positivism, and analytic philosophy, and he had considerable respect for Wittgenstein. Although he had also read James, Dewey, and Whitehead, he shows virtually no appreciation of what we have come to think of as the distinctive contributions of American pragmatism and of process philosophy.

In presenting Kaufmann's discussions of philosophy, "-isms," theology, and God, I will confine myself to the two books in which he devotes sustained attention to these issues: *Critique of Religion and Philosophy* (CRP, 1961) and *The Faith of a Heretic* (FH, 1963).

1. Philosophy as a quest for honesty

Kaufmann's presentation of philosophy—like his approach to most subjects—was comprehensive and many-sided. But he made clear that he considered the most important task and achievement of philosophy to lie in its tradition of critical questioning. For philosophy, "no man has authority, except provisionally: all opinions are subject to critical examination, though some may prevail even after acid tests" (FH, 21). Kaufmann called philosophy at its best "the quest for honesty" (23), which often takes the form of "heresy" or skepticism in relation to prevailing assumptions and conventions. In characterizing the methods by which philosophy carries out its critical task, he emphasized, without restricting it to, "a search for truth that involves following arguments and evidence, without recourse to authority, wherever they may lead (17). . . ." This is in fact the method Kaufmann himself used and frequently invoked, albeit in a very expansive way appropriate to the subject matters with which he mainly deals—religion, art, and morality.

Kaufmann also argues that philosophy "at its best" addresses itself to the central and perennial issues of human life, and changes the life of the person who comes under its influence—and here he seems to me to have been squarely aligned with the existentialist tradition. Art, religion, and philosophy all involve this existential engagement; but what distinguishes the philosopher is living in the tension between criticism and engagement. The idea of philosophy as a way of life as well as a critical humanism is of course an ancient one, and Socrates is its patron saint. Socrates was indeed Kaufmann's patron, "the unexamined life is not worth living" was his motto, and Kaufmann clearly saw himself as philosophizing in a Socratic mode appropriate to the twentieth century. For philosophy so conceived there can be no dichotomy between reason and passion, but only a passion channeled and corrected by critical reason and a reason that is not blind to the realities of passion in oneself and in the human situation.

> In its inception . . . philosophy is a way of life and, as the Greek word suggests, a kind of love and devotion. It is the life of reflective passion—penetrating experience, unimpeded by accepted formulas. . . . That was what philosophy meant to Socrates, and if we want to bring philosophy down to earth again, it can mean nothing less than that to us (CRP, 98).

We should not be surprised by this point to find that Kaufmann, like Nietzsche, also considered both playfulness and polemics to be not only legitimate but eminently desirable characteristics of the philosopher. He believed that among the things Socrates taught us is that "playfulness is quite compatible with seriousness."

> . . . the philosopher's seriousness need not consist in the unhumorous insistence that he must be right. He need not even attach ultimate significance to right opinions. He may be serious in his determination to change other men by making them less irrational, and in his willingness to be changed himself in the course of his inquiries (CRP, xv).

Self-transcending humor can of course be a valuable element in correcting one's own tendencies to intellectual dogmatism and solemnity, while forms of humor such as irony and satire can in appropriate contexts be very effective rhetorical devices in the critical exposure of error. Kaufmann, like Nietzsche, mainly employed the latter—quite ably and at times to devastating effect. Arguing for the importance of discussing views one rejects, Kaufmann also suggested that "Polemic recaptures the excitement of the search for truth" (xx). He engaged in it vigorously in discussing philosophy, religion, and theology. Brilliant and extremely well-read, Kaufmann, it must be said, as a polemicist could at times be unfair and ungenerous and occasionally downright nasty.

Playfulness and polemics are also closely connected with literary style, and Kaufmann considered questions of style important to philosophical writing, as his own prose style and imaginative experimentation with a variety of literary forms attest. His immersion in literature and questions of literary style as important to philosophy places him more closely with the existentialists than with any other group of modern philosophers.

2. **The trouble with "isms"**

Kaufmann's understanding of philosophy made him suspicious and critical of labels or "isms." He saw them as inherently in tension with the comprehensively critical task of philosophy, and as functioning to constrict people's intellectual horizons and originality.

> Perhaps the single best example of the common lack of high standards in questions of honesty is our tendency to think in labels. Terms like existentialism, pragmatism, and empiricism . . . are, more often than not, so many excuses for not considering individual ideas on their merits and for not exposing oneself to the bite of thought. . . . These labels have some uses that are perfectly legitimate, but frequently they function as an aid to thoughtlessness and permit people to appear to *think* when they are merely talking (FH, 27).

Kaufmann's portrayals of analytic philosophy and existentialism in *Critique of Religion and Philosophy* afford us concrete models of his analysis of philosophical "isms" (CRP, 20-61). He showed (writing in the late 1950s and early 1960s) how both movements had created their own philosophical subculture: with leaders who shaped things not only by their approach to philosophy but also by their personality, followers whose "discipleship" could look to the outsider a lot like slavishness and idolatry, a vocabulary that became an identifying in-group jargon, a self-serving interpretation of the history of philosophy, and a self-limiting perspective on philosophical questions and problems—all of which, Kaufmann argued, give expression implicitly or explicitly to a vision of what it is to be human.

In his sketch of G. E. Moore, one of the fathers of British language philosophy, and in sections entitled "The British Vision of Man" and "Donnish Doubt," Kaufmann exposed what he believed to be the limited view of philosophy and of the human that characterized analytic philosophy, as when he observed:

> One of the most important functions of philosophy is to scrutinize beliefs and arguments, and to exercise a certain skill in showing up fallacies. From Berkeley and Hume to Broad and Ryle, British philosophy has excelled in this work . . . . The charge against this tradition should not be that it has been too critical . . . but that it has avoided an awareness of its relevance to experience, or indeed of the nature of the experiences to which various beliefs and arguments owe their significance. In this they have been un-Socratic and aloof (CRP, 43).

But while he believed the existentialists were much more attuned to experience and "holistic" in their views of what it is to be human, Kaufmann criticized existentialism for errors that lay at the opposite pole from those of analytic philosophy: ". . . First, it tends to ignore the ordinary for the extraordinary and to mistake the uncommon for the rule. Secondly, it does not demand of itself, let alone achieve, the greatest possible clarity of which its often difficult subject matter is capable" (47).

These criticisms of analytic and existentialist philosophies need themselves to be criticized, especially in the light of forty years of further development in both traditions. In them Kaufmann correctly highlighted certain tendencies in both traditions but elevated them into all-defining characterizations, failing to take into account the diversity and nuance within the two schools of thought. However, with his characteristic comprehensiveness, Kaufmann had praise for both traditions and high praise for individual exemplars such as (the later) Wittgenstein and Sartre. His general point that for all their virtues, philosophical "isms" exhibit tendencies to narrowness and partiality that are fundamentally at odds with philosophy's commitment to an open and critical approach to knowledge, remains a cautionary reminder.

3. Against theology

Despite some shortcomings that I will mention, Kaufmann's critical reflections on theology—and within that context on the problem of the word "God"—are both provocative and valuable. I have simply taken the title of a chapter of *The Faith of a Heretic* as my title for this section of my essay, and it expresses quite succinctly Kaufmann's attitude toward the whole theological enterprise. He considered theology, understood as an intellectual enterprise—which he always distinguished from religion—to be inescapably dishonest. (Since Christianity early and explicitly appropriated Plato's term and has been probably the most theological of all religions, when Kaufmann spoke of "theology" he almost always meant "Christian theology.")

At one point Kaufmann summarized succinctly his three general objections to theology: ". . . First, theology is of necessity denominational. Second, theology is essentially a defensive maneuver. Third, it is almost always time-bound and dated quickly" (CRP, 221).

Kaufmann borrowed the political term "gerrymandering" to characterize theology, by which he meant interpreting everything in such a way as to give one's own position an unfair advantage. "Unlike historical and philological scholarship in the employ of conscientious efforts at interpretation, the theologian's method is not designed to uncover the original intent and meaning of the quoted passages" (FH 106). The reason theologians gerrymander is that "They set themselves an impossible task that cannot be solved with sound methods: to present to us 'the message' of the New Testament, indeed of the whole Bible" (109). Kaufmann documented these characterizations by examining and quoting substantially from theologians from Augustine and Aquinas to Tillich, Bultmann, and Reinhold Niebuhr. He was particularly effective in exposing the distortions in standard Christian theological interpretations of the Hebrew Bible and the Jewish tradition.

Kaufmann rejected the enterprise of classical natural theology (for example, the philosophical "proofs" of the existence of God) with familiar arguments:

"From the facts of nature one can infer further facts of nature, but one cannot with any certainty infer anything beyond nature, not even with probability" (FH 91). In the final analysis, furthermore, natural theology always falls back on dogmatic theology: ". . . it is never really the facts of nature that determine what is invoked [in the conclusions to the classical arguments], but some preconceived ideas mediated by religion" (92).

In distinguishing theology from religion, Kaufmann insisted that a great deal of religion is anti-theological, and his favorite examples of anti-theological religion were the Hebrew prophets, Job, and what he saw as a dominant impulse in the Jewish tradition. He explained what he meant by "anti-theological" in the following passage: "In the Prophets and in parts of the New Testament—though certainly only in parts—love, justice, and humility appear to be all that is asked of man, and questions of belief entirely peripheral, while precise formulations about God . . . are altogether out of the picture" (FH 128). Clearly, then, he did not mean by "theology" any and every expression (to use H. Richard Niebuhr's phrase) of "faith reasoning." Rather he meant (1) a central emphasis on (correct) beliefs, and (2) the disciplined endeavor to systematize and rationalize such beliefs. Christianity, according to Kaufmann, is an inescapably theological religion—and that is exactly its main problem. ". . . [A] Christian may choose to reject theology. . . . But in that case he gives up Christianity, though in some laudatory senses of the word he may be a better Christian than some theologians" (130).

In "A Dialogue Between Satan and a Theologian," Satan, speaking for "devil's advocate" Kaufmann, makes a single statement that reveals much about Kaufmann's characterization of theology, his distinction between religion and theology, and (to anticipate) his approach to the problem of God and his own relationship to religion. Sounding very much like Matthew Arnold in *Literature and Dogma*, Satan remarks that *"Theology is a misguided attempt to make poetry scientific, and the result is neither science nor poetry"* (CRP, 238).

While acknowledging that much theology has historically exhibited such defects, the contemporary critically-minded theologian may well, and quite reasonably, object to important features of Kaufmann's overall description of theology, and further contend that Kaufmann's *identification* of theology with these characteristics (like his brief descriptions of analytic and existentialist philosophies) unfairly generalizes about and hypostasizes what has been a demonstrably self-correcting intellectual endeavor. But the strength of Kaufmann's portrayal is precisely that it *is*, to a documentable and somewhat dismal extent, an accurate description of most theology as it has articulated itself for 1900 years. Furthermore, Kaufmann goes to some lengths to try to show that modern *liberal* forms of theology have been just as guilty of "gerrymandering" as classical and conservative forms.

Theology has historically been a form of Christian reflection—"faith seeking understanding"—but even if we universalize the term beyond Christianity and think of it as systematic reflection on the grounds, meanings, and implications of any religious tradition by one who stands within that tradition, we are still left with the fact that historically and to the present day theology is by definition "denominational"—a form of "ism." It is the self-understanding of a religious tradition, with all the tendencies to narrowed focus and self-serving exegesis and argument which that has almost inevitably involved. Within Christianity, over the centuries, that has of course further subdivided into Roman Catholic and Orthodox and Protestant theologies, and further into Lutheran and Calvinist and Methodist theologies.

What would a "non-denominational"—a religiously "global" or "ecumenical"—theology be? Do not these juxtapositions simply produce an oxymoron? If they do not, then the person who believes in the possibility of such a redefinition of theology must describe it and show how it differs from the philosophy of religion. This seems to me to be an especially acute question for liberal theologians, who see themselves as engaged in constructive theology but who want to be truly universal in scope. They achieve it, as for example George Lindbeck in *The Nature of Doctrine* (1984) and Sallie McFague in *Models of God*,(1987), by being frankly pluralistic and postmodern, not claiming any "higher" truth or justification for Christianity and thereby implying that their adherence to that religious tradition reduces to personal and cultural factors.

At a still deeper level Kaufmann raises the issue of the whole point of theology as he conceives it. Theology not only distorts, it "de-existentializes" religion, draining the lifeblood from what are imaginative outpourings of human experience. In a number of places Kaufmann expresses things in such a way as to suggest a large measure of agreement with Martin Buber's famous statement in *I and Thou* (which Kaufmann translated) that God "may properly only be addressed, not expressed." Kaufmann's discussion of the Book of Job in a section of *Critique of Religion and Philosophy* entitled "Suffering and the Bible," to which I will refer in the conclusion of my essay, is an excellent example of his rejection of theology on this point. Furthermore, Kaufmann contended that theology as an intellectual enterprise is massively irrelevant to what actually goes on in religion—even in Christianity—and that among most believers it is politely tolerated but not of interest. The first of these judgments demands a reasonable accounting of the commitment to redescribing existential religious expressions in the more abstract vocabulary of theology. The second raises the embarrassing and usually tacit question, If theology serves the church (however broadly defined), to whom are theologians talking except to one another?

In the light of the revival and contemporary dominance in America of evangelical Protestantism and specifically of fundamentalism beginning in the 1980s, would Kaufmann's judgments here need to be revised or rejected? When he—and I—talk about "theology," we typically have in mind what in the twentieth century we used to think of as "mainstream": critically sophisticated forms of theology represented influentially by figures such as Barth, Bultmann, Tillich, and the Niebuhr brothers. Certainly conservative evangelicalism and fundamentalism are highly theological, and lay members of such groups are supposed to understand and appropriate that theology in a very existential way. But fundamentalist theologies seem to be made up largely of "canned" and aprioristic positions on doctrine and morality based on the denominational tradition involved and articulated in biblical prooftexting, while their lay adherents appear to place the most stock in personal experience rather than in thoughtful consideration of doctrine.

4. The essential ambiguity of "God"

It is in a chapter of *Critique of Religion and Philosophy* entitled "God, Ambiguity, and Theology" (173-227) that Kaufmann most fully develops his analysis of the meaning of "God" and what it means to say that "God exists." His approach bears similarities to the sort of analytic philosophy of religion, inspired by the later Wittgenstein, that we see in books such as D. Z. Phillips' *Faith and Philosophical Enquiry* and Paul van Buren's *The Edges of Language*. (As many interpreters have noted, Wittgenstein's later approach to the analysis of language in terms of "language games" expressive of different human practices or "forms of life" has important links to existentialism.) The foundation of Kaufmann's discussion is the fact that everyone raised in the Jewish or Christian traditions, or in the cultures dominated by them, learns the meaning of "God" almost entirely from the Jewish and Christian scriptures as mediated by those communities of interpretation. In the biblical literature "God" is a proper name for a highly complex individual who appears and acts in quite varied ways in "widely different contexts and . . . radically divergent situations" (173), who speaks and is spoken to in visions, dreams, prayer, and worship—all related in widely diverse writings that span 1200 years of religious history and development.

Hence "statements about God belong to a universe of discourse which has its own characteristic conventions" (175)—the biblical writings and, deriving from them, the Jewish and Christian traditions of interpretation—and we can determine correct and incorrect usage within this universe of discourse:

> Much discourse about God is therefore meaningful and even verifiable in an important sense without implying that God does in fact exist. In some kinds of discourse statements about God are legitimately verified by references to the Bible, or found false because they are in conflict either with express assertions or with implications of some passages in Scripture. In other kinds of discourse statements about God are found to be true or false by referring back to the traditions of a religious community or denomination. In both cases, disagreement may be frequent. . . . For all that, there is an area of agreement, and some propositions about God would be considered true by almost everyone brought up against the background of the Bible, others false. All this is independent of the question whether God exists (176).

But what *about* the question, Does God exist? Given the rich polyvocality of "God" in the biblical realm of discourse whence we all learned to use the name—a polyvocality compounded by centuries of Jewish and Christian biblical interpretation—Kaufmann suggested that the question whether God as so understood "really" exists "has no clear meaning" (177). Elsewhere he says that the reason is precisely that the word is "overcharged with meaning" (180) in its original and historic contexts. Theological definitions of God and proofs for God's existence inevitably abstract out certain features from the complex and ambiguous mosaic portrayed in the biblical literature. While these developments have been understandable and in a sense inevitable, they have created a situation in which the questions of not only the nature but also the existence of God are highly ambiguous and the answers given to them misleading.

One of Kaufmann's main criticisms of modern theologians is that they reinterpret traditional religious language to mean something quite different from its historic usages, and then either practice "doublespeak" between classroom and congregation or else claim that what *they* mean is what the language *really* meant all along. Kaufmann characterizes—many would say he caricatures—this hermeneutical strategy in the context of a critical discussion of Paul Tillich's *Dynamics of Faith*:

> ... he redefines such terms as faith and heresy, atheism and revelation. It turns out that the man who accepts the ancient beliefs of Christendom, the Apostles' Creed, or Luther's articles of faith may well be lacking faith, while the man who doubts all these beliefs but is sufficiently concerned to lie awake nights worrying about it is a paragon of faith (FH, 118).

Kaufmann makes a discerning and perhaps uncomfortable observation when he describes the continuing attachment to theology of liberal theologians such as Tillich in terms of "childhood associations":

> What one is conscious of is not a strenuous intellectual effort but rather a wealth of childhood associations that evoke a sense of fellowship with others, past and present, and the reassurance that we are far from alone. It feels fine, but is it honest? And if one has a highly sensitive intellectual conscience, does it still feel fine (32)?

Why, for example, do liberal theologians whose ontological views are essentially indistinguishable from those of philosophical naturalists or agnostics want to continue engaging in "God-talk" and trying to make sense out of the religious symbols and traditions? Does this loyalty to the theological profession amount to anything more than nostalgia for and an unwillingness to let go of one's religious background? Is it simply an uneasy compromise between adhering to impossible beliefs and the full demands of intellectual honesty, motivated whether consciously or unconsciously by personal affection and respect for one's religious heritage? I have pondered this question a good deal in the light of my own experience as well as the experience of friends and acquaintances who engage in the philosophy of religion and theology. In the conclusion of my essay I will examine Kaufmann's own resolution of these issues.

It will come as no surprise by this point that Kaufmann's criticisms of theological oversimplification of "God" and "God exists" include theological redefinitions past and present:

> The use of "God" as a synonym for being-itself, or for the "pure act of being," or for nature, or for scores of other things for which other terms are readily available, cannot be disproved but only questioned as pettifoggery. The asser-

tion that God exists, if only God is taken in some such Pickwickian sense, is false, too: not false in the sense of being incorrect, but false in the sense of being misleading and to that extent deceptive (*FH*, 139-140).

In this passage Kaufmann threw down the gauntlet at the feet of theologians past and present, such as Thomas Aquinas (God as the "pure act of being"), Paul Tillich (God as "being-itself"), and some more recent process theologians (God as "nature"). His challenge—not surprisingly after his characterization of theology—is that such redefinition is univocal, stipulative, and honorific, and thus in the final analysis deceptive.

In a "Dialogue Between Satan and a Christian," Kaufmann has the Christian tell what he means when he says "God exists." The Christian plausibly—and eloquently—interprets it in terms of statements about his own existence, as for example:

> God exists—that means: life is bearable, the reality of everyday life is not the only reality. . . . our ideals, whatever they are, have authority; the passion for justice, however conceived, is no mere quixotism. . . .
> . . . God exists—that means: I shall not want, I will fear no evil, the ocean and the mountains hold no terror for me, nor does man (CRP 246). . . .

To all of which Satan/Kaufmann quite happily assents, since it simply confirms his own conclusion (reminiscent of analytic philosopher John Wisdom's celebrated essay "Gods") that "Theism is a language, a way of speaking, rather than a fact" (249). The above renderings of "God exists" translate (or reduce) God-language into a certain kind of redescription of the human situation.

The whole drift of Kaufmann's discussion of the meaning of "God" will strike some readers as problematic or wrongheaded in the extreme, and to examine the many criticisms that might be offered is beyond the scope of this essay. Recalling his emphasis on the critical, gadfly task of philosophy, however, I suggest that, whatever its overall fairness as a characterization of the theological tradition, it is valuable and provocative as a challenge to theology and the philosophy of religion. Particularly helpful, I think, is his reminding us that the biblical literature and the Jewish and Christian traditions of biblical interpretation continue to be the living context in which almost all people in our civilization learn what "God" means and how to use the term. What indeed *is* the relationship between what theologians say and the "field" on which this "game" is concretely played? Are theologians really at liberty to play the Red Queen and decree that "'God' means what I say it means"? And what if their hearers are simply mystified over why anyone would want to define what he or she has learned to think of as "God" in such a curious way?

Kaufmann's arguments that the term "God" and the statement "God exists" are essentially ambiguous in the light of the foundational and paradigmatic usage in the biblical universe of discourse—that "God" and its uses are in some primary sense "overdetermined"—also seem to me to demand serious consideration by critical theologians. Is affirming or rejecting "God" simply being able or not able to speak a certain language, to share in a particular community of discourse? Or does it also involve philosophical and theological analysis and redefinition? If the latter, what is the relationship between the analysis and redefinition on the one hand and the religious communities, with their heritage of scripture and tradition, on the other?

6. The faith of a heretic

How, finally, did Walter Kaufmann resolve his passionate but skeptical engagement with religion in his own thought and life? For the most part I will let him speak for himself, adding only my observation that in his belief and doubt—often eloquently and even lyrically expressed—he himself largely remained within and preferred the language of the biblical and Jewish traditions that were his heritage.

In a chapter of *The Faith of a Heretic* on "Suffering and the Bible," Kaufmann remarked, after a provocative examination of the Book of Job, that "The only theism worthy of our respect believes in God not because of the way the world is made but in spite of that. The only theism that is no less profound than the Buddha's atheism is that represented in the Bible by Job and Jeremiah" (FH, 168). He continued:

> Their piety is a cry in the night, born of suffering so intense that they cannot contain it and must shriek, speak, accuse, and argue with God—not about him—for there is no other human being who would understand, and the prose of dialogue could not be faithful to the poetry of anguish. In time, theologians come to wrench some useful phrases out of Latin versions of a Hebrew outcry, blind with tears, and try to win some argument about a point of dogma. Scribes, who preceded them, carved phrases out of context, too, and used them in their arguments about the law. But for all that, Jewish piety has been a ceaseless cry in the night, rarely unaware of "all the oppressions that are practiced under the sun," a faith in spite of, not a heathenish, complacent faith because (168).

Kaufmann's admiration for the Hebrew Bible and the Jewish heritage is obvious throughout his works, and in his comparative observations Christianity suffers—both for its distortions of Judaism and for its less humane and more theological character as a fellow heir and interpreter of the biblical traditions. As the passage above suggests, by comparison with Christianity Kaufmann believed that Judaism has been a notably untheological religion, its hermeneutical discussions quite different in character and typically over issues of practice.

Kaufmann the "heretic" calls himself an "infidel" in *Critique of Religion and Philosophy*, and has a section on "infidel piety," which he calls an "antitheological extension of Jewish piety." Here we find one of the most impassioned and personal of Kaufmann's "confessions" of his own "faith":

> While refusing to permit himself the least ambiguity in matters of faith, a man may nevertheless find that some kind of religious language, both in its traditional form as we find it most notably in the Bible . . . and in spontaneous

outbursts, now blasphemous, now desperate, is emotionally more adequate for him, more of a relief for an overflowing heart, than any other idiom he commands. If he could compose a first-rate poem, that might be still more adequate; but he cannot, and in his present quandary he addresses God. He does not believe anything about God and accepts no dogmas of any sort. He does not feel more tolerant of the theologians than before. He turns to God as one might turn to a Shakespearean outcry or a Negro spiritual or a walk up a mountain, without belief....

The dialogue without belief.... is an explosion of the heart, a bursting of its walls, a breakdown of inhibitions. One does not relax one's honesty; on the contrary, one does not permit one's beliefs or disbeliefs to get in the way of an honest expression of one's inmost heart. And if, more rarely, one should feel addressed, one listens first and asks questions later.

... We can keep questioning, making absolutely everything subject to critical reflection, without necessarily sacrificing our emotional life and becoming intellectual shadows. We need not choose between thinking and feeling. Nor is it true that those who think most feel least....

There are those who, without belief, find themselves addressing and addressed spontaneously, now often, now rarely, and reflect on these experiences instead of arbitrarily limiting themselves to the more usual forms of sense experience. They ... simply feel that in all honesty they must seek to do justice to them (286).

This is an extraordinary "confession of faith," and thoroughly existentialist in its approach to the problem of faith and doubt. Also worthy of comment is that here Kaufmann integrates into one sustained statement the elements I have been separately examining in this essay. This is the voice, not of a hardboiled atheism, but of a profoundly sensitive and searching—indeed, a religious and anguished—agnosticism.

Alternatively—and more prosaically and critically—Kaufmann characterized his perspective as a "tragic view of the world." Such a view, he said, includes four characteristics: first, failure is compatible with (human) greatness; secondly, greatness, like the universe itself, is in the final analysis mysterious; thirdly, failure is final; and fourthly, failure is inevitable (FH 346-350) . Kaufmann's discussions of the Western tradition of tragic drama, the incompatibility of tragedy and Christianity, and tragic elements in the thought of writers such as Freud, are characteristically rich and illuminating. Even here, in spelling out what he meant by a tragic view of the world, Kaufmann seems to me to issue a challenge to contemporary liberal theologians, both Christian and Jewish, some of whom affirm God but reject the belief in personal immortality or resurrection after death. Is not any such interpretation of the world a tragic view of life, on these terms? If not, why not? Should not such theologians be more forthcoming about it if this is indeed the case? And what advantage does such a religious perspective have over Kaufmann's? How indeed does it differ from it in any meaningful way as a religious perspective, if failure is final and inevitable on both views?

For Kaufmann's final word I return to "Suffering and the Bible," where he concludes with remarks about Job which again constitute a confession of his own "faith" and his ideal of a human life. Referring to Job's statement, "Naked I came from my mother's womb, and naked shall I return; the LORD gave, and the LORD has taken away; blessed be the name of the LORD" (1:21), Kaufmann wrote:

> In the form of an anthropomorphic faith, these words express one of the most admirable attitudes possible for man: to be able to give up what life takes away, without being unable to enjoy what life gives us in the first place; to remember that we came naked from the womb and shall return naked; to accept what life gives us as if it were God's own gift, full of wonders beyond price; and to be able to part with everything. To try to fashion something from suffering, to relish our triumphs, and to endure defeats without resentment: all that is compatible with the faith of a heretic (169).

– 10 –

Two Types of Religious and Secular World-Orientation

A commonly-held view is that religious interpretations of life are basically other-worldly, while secular outlooks on life are straightforwardly this-worldly. As a generalization about the bewildering variety of religious perspectives and practices in the world past and present, "other-worldliness" is a somewhat hazardous conjecture. Even if we limit the discussion, as I will, to the Christian religious tradition, informed participants in and observers of the wide range of Christian thought and practice know that to call this tradition simply "other-worldly" is a great oversimplification of Christian beliefs about and attitudes toward this life and this world. They are less likely, however, to question the general interpretation of secular philosophies, ideologies, and patterns of life as straightforwardly this-worldly. Furthermore, even students and critics of Christianity who appreciate its world-affirming elements often assume that there is a general correlation between orthodox or conservative forms of Christianity and a higher degree of other-worldliness, and between more liberal forms of Christianity and greater world-affirmation.

I want to suggest and explore a way of looking at these issues that I think more adequately illuminates both religious and secular forms of world-orientation. I want to propose two types of basic dispositional styles, sensibilities, or ways of being in the world. I believe that looking at belief and unbelief the way I'm suggesting can shed some perhaps unexpected light on the relationships between faith and skepticism.

The two types I want to delineate are what I call *indwelling* and *exile*, or "at home" and "not at home" in the world. The more common terms with which I began—"this-worldly" and "other-worldly"—are limited, somewhat misleading, and finally unsatisfactory ways of trying to talk about religious and secular orientations to life, as I hope to persuade the reader in what follows. Beginning with a description of the two types, I will spend the rest of the essay illustrating my main point: that these two types of world-orientation cut right across the division between religious and secular ways of life and belief. Both of these basic world-orientations—"indwelling" and "exile"—manifest themselves in both religious and secular ideas and patterns of life, and help shed light on the familiar fact that some "believers" seem to have more in common with "unbelievers" than with other "believers."

I need to make two preliminary comments before I launch into exploring the two types. The first concerns the limitations of all typologies. The very great usefulness of typologies is in helping us conceptually organize and illuminate our experience. But types are of course abstractions, ideal conceptual forms. We seldom find a concrete example that purely incarnates a type; real life is always a "mixed bag." In the context of the present topic, I intend the two types of world-orientation I'm describing to point to two contrasting sorts of governing tendencies or emphases in human personality that shape and manifest themselves in people's ways of relating to and interpreting the world. That we characteristically find the two poles mixed together, Yang/Yin-like, in real human beings should not surprise us.

My second preliminary statement is that the two world-orientations, "indwelling" and "exile," are at least in part bound up with temperament. When I speak of temperament I have in mind that cluster of dominant psychological dispositions that are the dynamic product in each of us of the finally baffling interplay of our nature, nurture, social context, and choices. This is not a case for determinism or a denial of intellectual freedom, but simply a realistic observation of the important role of our basic personality traits in shaping our patterns of life and outlooks on the world. I'm suggesting, along with the philosopher William James many years ago, that it's usually the case that we are drawn to a particular way of thinking about and imagining life because it resonates with, articulates, and confirms our own deepest inclinations. I hasten to add that the processes of personal and intellectual assimilation and rejection of different ways of interpreting the world are subtle and complex. We are corrigible, sometimes surprising, never-fully-transparent, and always-unfinished creatures. Nonetheless, when we're dealing with such fundamental human stances toward life as feeling "at home" and "not at home" in the world, I believe that careful observation of actual people (including most importantly of course ourselves) will indicate that temperament plays an important role.

Let me highlight something I said when I characterized temperament. I included "nurture" and "social context" among the shapers of temperament. Nurture and social context have to do with the particular culture a person grows up in, which includes specific forms of religion and values, and with the family patterns that are a part of that culture. I grew up a white male in a middle-class Protestant family in the Southwestern United States. Had I been born black or female—and race and gender are at least as much social constructs as they are biological givens—my cultural and family context would have given me different sorts of messages. Had I grown up in a Buddhist family and culture in, say, Thailand, my family and cultural setting would have shaped me in still other different ways. Within every culture there is a wide range of personalities and temperaments, because of the individual factors such as genetic inheritance, unique circumstances, and personal choices.

I think it's fair to say that different cultures value, emphasize, and try to produce certain types or psychological dispositions more than others—for example, aggressive or peaceful, competitive or cooperative—although of course no culture entirely succeeds in this because of the stubbornly individual factors involved in shaping what each of us is like. I raise the issue of the social factors in personality, because whole cultures dominated by, say, a particular form of Christianity during certain historical periods may have tended to produce more people exhibiting one of the two temperamental types—"indwelling" or "exile"—than other cultures or other periods. But in my remarks here I'm addressing the situation in modern Europe and the United States, which have been culturally complex and hospitable to a wide range of religious and non-religious beliefs and lifestyles.

In dealing with the social factors influencing people's basic orientation toward the world, I also don't think we can omit the sheer impact of events. To live in a nation at war, as in present-day Iraq, Congo, or Sudan, is entirely different from living in conditions of peace, and it seems to me that these are things that contribute to shaping our sense of our environing world and its possibilities and limitations. Phenomena such as economic depression, famine, and brutally oppressive political rule must likewise affect people. But people respond in a variety of ways to these negative forces, again exhibiting the important role that individual factors play within the social context.

To turn now to a characterization of the two types: The very terms "indwelling" or "at home" and "exile" or "not at home" are almost self-descriptive in their evocations and connotations. To feel at home or "rooted" in the world is to feel that one really belongs in the world. It is to possess a basic sense of harmony with one's social and physical environments as one's "natural" habitat. "At home" people are inclined to be at least soberly optimistic about the world's possibilities, confident in their own earthly powers, and involved in the practical affairs of the society around them with a robust eagerness. All this is entirely compatible with (although it also may be lacking in) a deep sense of the unfinality and transiency of the world and the limitations and tragedies of human life. Nor are such persons necessarily lacking in longings for and dreams of the never-more and the might-be. It's just that "indwelling" persons do not "dwell-on" these things. If they take them seriously into account, they do so and then get on with the business of doing what they can while they can. Thus they're inclined to be unsentimental about life and fully "present" in and to it.

By contrast, to be "not at home" in the world is to be characterized by a keen sense of estrangement from, of incongruity with, one's environment. The world's "exiles" tend to be afflicted and at times overwhelmed by doubt, pessimism, *Angst*, and despair over the earth and the human situation. They are often possessed of a heightened—sometimes an excruciating—sensitivity to the ephemerality, fragility, and pain of life. Those for whom the world does not feel like home are restless with the nostalgia of which religion and literature are full: inexpressible longings for long ago and far away, golden ages and celestial cities, ultimate perfection and fulfillment. Exiles may be quite active in the world (although they also may not): striving affirmatively and energetically for earthly goals, capable of quite practical calculation and execution. But at the core of their being gnaws the worm of alienation and pathos which ever and again produces a dyspeptic sense of worldly futility.

Here is a little chart that quickly summarizes these general descriptions of the polar emphases of the two types in their orientations to the world:

Indwelling	*Exile*
belonging	estrangement
harmony	incongruity
optimism	pessimism
confidence	uneasiness
present-ness	nostalgia

Now I want to turn to some modern examples of the two types, reminding the reader again that we won't find pure representatives but rather mixtures with one element or the other predominating. Central to my purpose, as I've said, will be to illustrate that the two types of orientation to the world are to be found along the spectrum of both religious and secular outlooks. Naturally in what follows I'll be focussing on prominent and articulate expressions of indwelling and exile: well-known persons who have wittingly or unwittingly revealed much about themselves and their views of life in their writings. But it should go without saying that the two types of world-orientation are played out daily by all sorts and conditions of human beings—high and low, ordinary and extraordinary, reflective and unreflective. In fact, if the typology I'm exploring is at all useful, an important aspect of its usefulness will be to illuminate not only our theologies and philosophies but more broadly and basically ourselves and the people and social currents around us.

1. "Indwelling" and "exile" as religious ways of being in the world

To feel an exile in the world—a "stranger and pilgrim" as the New Testament Letter to the Hebrews has it—is the stereotypical Christian mentality. Texts seeming to ground and support such an attitude are abundant throughout Christian literature from the beginnings to the present. In a variety of metaphysical ways, "exile" forms of Christian world-orientation are connected with the distinction between this created universe and God its creative Ground, Context, and Goal. Contrasted with the transcendent realm this world is seen—not without a certain obvious and persuasive "logic"—as inferior, relativized, temporary, and fallen. To use some time-honored metaphors, for the "exilic" Christian outlook this world is a river to get across, a vale of tears and soul-making, a testing-ground for eternity. The world is the realm mysteriously held captive to Satan, the sphere of deep bondage as well as of radical contingency.

Examples of world-estrangement abound in popular Christian piety, both Catholic and Protestant, down to the present time. Among well-known modern Christian thinkers and writers Søren Kierkegaard provides a good reflective illustration. Although his writings contain abundant evidence of spirited, sensitive immersion in the actualities of daily and cultural life and a richly affirmative aesthetic appreciation, at bottom there is the persistent melancholy and the longing for eternal peace with God. After his strikingly world-affirming characterization of the "knight of faith" in his pseudonymous book *Fear and Trembling* (Kierkegaard [1843] 1983, 38-41) early in his writing career, Kierkegaard came more and more, in the light of public ridicule and his increasingly vigorous attack on the Danish Lutheran Church, to believe that authentic Christian existence in this fallen world inescapably takes the form of suffering. Only in that eternal fellowship with God for which the human self is created will it find the fulfillment of its confused and restless longings and thus become what it truly is (Kierkegaard [1848] 2000, 479-481).

There are prominent examples of Christian world-skepticism from the twentieth century as well. The novels of Graham Greene, such as for example *The Power and the Glory* (2003), *The End of the Affair* (2004), and *A Burnt-Out Case* (1992), are permeated by what is often called an "Augustinian" pessimism about human motives and possibilities, with heavily ironic, mock-heroic, ambiguity-riddled deaths as their characteristic climax. Sharing the subtlety of Greene's world-pessimism (but lacking his fine sense of ironic humor) was Simone Weil, the mystic and unbaptized Catholic convert who was surely one of the most unusual and provocative Christians of the twentieth century. When all due qualifications have been made in the light of her powerful affirmations of creaturely existence and of our concrete fellowship with one another as common citizens of the world, pervading Weil's writings is an "exile" mentality which is closely related to the solitariness and suffering in her own life. Her letters and essays in *Waiting for God* ([1951] 1973), and her miscellaneous meditations in *Gravity and Grace* ([1947] 1952), are revealing in this regard. In the case of Weil it's necessary, I think, to look behind the content of her world-affirmative remarks to the austere language of suffering and estrangement with which they're surrounded. An even more explicit and intense pessimism, bordering on the Manichaean, underlay the religious and autobiographical writings of British journalist and critic Malcolm Muggeridge. In a book like *Jesus Rediscovered* (1979), Muggeridge used his acerbic wit and keen powers of observation relentlessly to expose the utter bondage and futility of all human and earthly enterprises. The divine grace primarily saves us wretched sinners out of this world in which all is vanity.

But among many modern Christian theologians and writers, it has long been considered absolutely *de rigueur* to be robustly "at home" in the world. Modern "critical mainstream" Christian thinkers share a common heritage as children of modern secularization, inheritors of the modern biblical and theological discovery of the world-affirmation of Israel's faith, disciples of Dietrich Bonhoeffer and other theological analysts and affirmers of secularization, and students of the classical Marxist critique of religion's "other-worldliness." They have been very concerned to be, and to be seen to be, just as bona fide "indwellers" as their secular comrades.

For all that, however, most modern theologians have retained the classical Christian hope that looks beyond this world for ultimate fulfillment, while interpreting the content of that hope with an appropriately "agnostic" modesty and reserve and focusing on this world and its possibilities. One of the many misunderstandings during the early years of interpretation of Dietrich Bonhoeffer's *Letters and Papers from Prison* ([1953] 1972) was the failure to appreciate that what he called "non-religious interpretation" of the Gospel was a new way of talking about the full reality of Christian faith, not a theological reductionism. This man who wrote of a new kind of "worldly" holiness, who preferred to speak of God "at the center of life" and not at all at its boundaries, was also the one who could write in very traditional language of the eternal God and the assurance that all things were embraced within the redemptive purpose of God in Christ (376, 391, 393).

At the beginning of the essay I said that "this-worldliness" and "other-worldliness" were too limited and misleading to use as general terms to characterize the two types of world-orientation I'm trying to describe and illustrate. My portrayal of contemporary theological "at-home-ness" in terms of its relationship to the traditional Christian hope of eternal life is essential to the discussion of "indwelling" and "exile" as religious attitudes, but may be similarly misleading. The crucial point here is that affirmation of eternal life does not in itself express an "exile" frame of mind. In the case of any Christian believer and writer, as Kierkegaard might have said, we must look not simply at the "what" of her views on the kingdom of God, but much more at the "how" of her total evaluation—both cognitive and affective—of the world. The pages of Bonhoeffer's *Letters and Papers from Prison* are striking in their robust and vigorous love of life and the world and their sharp criticisms of forms of Christian faith that emphasize "inwardness," suffering, and other-worldliness. Equally striking in that context, however, is Bonhoeffer's repeated affirmation of what he called the "full content" of Christian doctrine, including the hope of eternal life. (285-7, 327-9)

Just as the affirmation of eternal life is compatible with both an "exile" and an "indwelling" frame of mind, so likewise are Christian orthodoxy and liberalism. G. K. Chesterton and C. S. Lewis must both be regarded as robustly orthodox Christians: both were also robustly world-affirming persons. Chesterton's "at-home-ness" appears in his best-known theological work *Orthodoxy* (1908) as well as in his Father Brown detective series, Lewis's in his books like *Mere Christianity* (1952). Karl Barth's creative "neo-orthodox" interpretation of Christianity, with its vigorous reaffirmation of the doctrines of original sin and divine grace and sovereignty, went hand in hand with a joyous lust for life and earthy "dwelling-in" the world. By contrast, Albert Schweitzer, who early on came to a radically liberal view of Jesus and Christianity and ended his life a self-described humanist, was deeply haunted and at times almost overcome throughout his life by the suffering caused by the ceaseless competition of life with life in nature, as he recounted in his autobiography *Out of My Life and Thought* (1933). Interestingly, on the specific issue of life after death, perhaps no twentieth-century theologian wrote more on, or seemed more preoccupied with, the subject than the British philosopher-theologian John Hick, who by almost any criterion must be seen as having espoused a vigorously liberal interpretation of the Christian message and its relationship to other religious truth-claims. The liberalism is explicit in *God Has Many Names* (1982) and permeates the whole approach in *Death and Eternal Life* (1976). Not that Hick exhibits an "exile" mentality thereby; he is simply a modern Christian thinker who has believed that it's essential to the full "logic" of the faith to affirm the hope of eternal life. Again, my point is that we must look at the full content and, at another level, at the tone of theological writings, and set completely aside all a priori notions or superficial expectations. My discussion of Christian liberalism and orthodoxy further illustrates, I believe, that a typology of "indwelling" and "exile" can be illuminating in getting at root patterns of world-orientation in Christian thought and life.

2. **Secular forms of "indwelling" and "exile"**

If the sense of exile is the stereotypically Christian attitude toward the world, the feeling of "at-home-ness" is the stereotypically secular frame of mind. Historically the modern roots of this secular sensibility are foreshadowed in the Renaissance and emerge with vigor and explicitness in the eighteenth-century Enlightenment, beginning that decisive turn toward fascinated immersion in this world of human institutions, ideas, and consciousness that has dominated and defined what we call the modern world. Modern Enlightenment-inspired "indwelling" has been marked by an optimism of which two chief expressions have been the beliefs in historical progress and in human perfectibility. Its characteristic metaphysics has been a naturalism which—perhaps paradoxically—interprets the human race both entirely as the product and indweller of nature, and at the same time as the rational controller of nature.

Illustrations of this secular sense of harmony with the world are of course abundant and hardly need dwelling on. The French *philosophes* of the eighteenth century, notably Diderot and Condorcet, are the great early modern exemplars, with their call for the liberation of humankind through reason from the shackles of a superstitious other-worldliness and for the building of paradise on earth. Condorcet's *Outline of the Progress of the Human Mind* ([1795] 1955) is perhaps the supreme example of Enlightenment optimism. And the philosopher Immanuel Kant, for all his sobriety regarding human nature and his decisive critique of Enlightenment thought, was likewise dominated by Enlightenment faith in human autonomy and its utopian possibilities, as in his "Idea for a Universal History with a Cosmpolitan Intent" ([1784] 1983).

If eighteenth-century Enlightenment writers proclaimed a "gospel" of unqualified progress, many dominant voices of the nineteenth century believed it was being increasingly actualized in their time. The period from about 1850 to 1914 seemed to many in the upper and middle classes of that time a "golden age" of European culture, when the forces of oppression and ignorance, disease and war, appeared to be yielding on every hand to the march of science, democratic institutions, and education. The feelings of optimism and earthly self-confidence accompanying this rather remarkable era of the Pax Britannica widely permeated both secular and religious thought. Among secular thinkers and writers we find it in socialists like Marx and Engels, in *laissez-faire* capitalists like Herbert Spencer, in scientists like T. H. Huxley, and in writers like Charlotte Perkins Gilman, Edward Bellamy, and H. G. Wells.

In characterizing the "indwelling" orientation to life earlier, I said that it's quite compatible with sensitivity to the transiency, the tragedies, and the psychosocial distortions of human life. While many forms of eighteenth- and nineteenth-century secular world-affirmation are in retrospect fatuously optimistic, not all are. In very different ways Voltaire in *Candide* ([1759] 2000), John Stuart Mill in *Three Essays on Religion* (1874), and Friedrich Nietzsche in *Twilight of the Idols* ([1889]1968) were clear-eyed critics of the illusions of their time. And after Verdun and Hiroshima, Auschwitz and the Gulag, Cambodia and Bosnia and Rwanda, no twentieth-century versions of "at-home-ness" in the world can be taken seriously that don't stare these horrors and their implications squarely in the face. Most forms of contemporary humanism and naturalism have thoroughly rejected the superficial optimism that was prominent in eighteenth- and nineteenth-century secular thought; yet a lingering Christian stereotype of secular world-views still tends to bind them to their Enlightenment past and thereby to set up an easy "straw man" for criticism.

The second half of the twentieth century saw the continued flourishing of an only somewhat chastened Enlightenment-style optimism about the human situation and prospect. Significantly, most of the versions of this sort of humanism I can think of were to be found in the United States, the country more than any other in which eighteenth-century faith in human nature and historical progress became integral to its national ideology and in which that faith still survives at both a popular and a sophisticated level. These expressions of a thoroughly optimistic "indwelling" were all variations on the technocratic mentality: through the proper sorts of social and technological tinkering the many ills besetting us can be alleviated if not simply resolved, and we can look forward to a future bright with widespread prosperity and peace if we will only apply our rapidly advancing knowledge and techniques. The futurist Herman Kahn of the Rand Corporation was a well- known representative of this optimism, as in his book *The Coming Boom: Economic, Political, Social* (1983). Another familiar exponent was the father of operant behaviorism, B. F. Skinner, who characteristically combined a scientific naturalism and determinism with a cheerful utilitarian confidence in the possibilities of redesigning the human environment so that people would be generally happier, as in his utopian novel *Walden Two* (1976).

But what the typology of "indwelling" and "exile" as basic dispositional emphases in both religious and secular outlooks illuminates for us is the counter-stereotypical fact that there is a contemporary secular sensibility at the opposite pole from Skinner and Kahn: a profoundly tragic sense of life, an intense perception of the depths of human bondage and the indifference of nature without the consolation of redemption here or hereafter, a feeling of the ultimate futility and forlornness of the human condition. Nor is this secular sensibility simply the product of the appalling twentieth century, although it certainly achieved its most widespread forms of expression beginning with the carnage of World War I. In the nineteenth century, even Mark Twain's comedies contain much incisive and sometimes bitter satire on human folly; and such works as *The Mysterious Stranger* ([1916] 1962) and *Letters from the Earth* ([1909] 1974) are darkly and unrelievedly pessimistic about the human race and its place in the scheme of things.

But it was indeed the twentieth century—primarily and significantly in Europe—that produced whole schools of thought and art expressive of a view of the human situation as radically godless, homeless, meaningless, and hopeless. The paradigm word is "absurdity," and it manifested itself in central aspects of such artistic movements as Dadaism and the theatre of the absurd. Samuel Beckett's bleak and desperate human landscapes in such plays as *Waiting for Godot* (1954) and *Endgame* (1958) are among the best-known and most striking articulations of this "exile" mentality.

Secular forms of existentialist thought in certain of their moods and some of their themes and language tended toward a world-orientation emphasizing human "abandonment" and despair, and of course that has certainly been the popular caricature of existentialism. The young Albert Camus in *The Myth of Sisyphus* ([1942] 1955) worked out what he called the "logic of absurdity," and Jean-Paul Sartre seemed almost to relish speaking of human reality as a "useless passion" in *Being and Nothingness* ([1943] 1956). Yet humanistic existentialism is not, in the fullness of its articulation, a philosophy of exile but a call to world-affirmation through creativity, community, and ethical and political action. For all of its sometimes dramatic metaphors of human estrangement in the world, even Camus's *Sisyphus* is in the last analysis a celebration of the uniqueness and creative possibilities of human life; and his later writings, while grimly preoccupied with the horrors of the twentieth century, also argue eloquently for the enduring character of values wrested out of our human relationship to one another and to the world. As for Sartre, in his famous lecture "Existentialism is a Humanism," he replied explicitly to the popular criticism of existentialist philosophies as pessimistic and set forth with stirring brevity a radical affirmation of human freedom and responsibility.

Viewed in the full range of their themes, secular forms of existentialist thought such as we find in Camus and Sartre are examples of what I would call a "dialectical" humanism. I've previously indicated that non-fundamentalist modern Christian thought, whether conservative or liberal, holds together dialectically an "indwelling" world-orientation and the historic hope of eternal life. I want now to suggest that there are modern secular perspectives that manifest their own version of holding together two ideas that may not seem compatible: the full affirmation of life in this world as our proper and only human habitation, together with the full and sensitive recognition of the depth of human bondage and suffering and an accompanying refusal to deify humanity or the world. The dialectical Christian perspective believes that our ultimate context is beyond this present world, while affirming life here and now as good and as absolutely integral to that larger context. The dialectical humanistic outlook I've described rejects any human context other than this world, but realistically faces the implications of that world-view given the negative conditions of life, and refuses to make virtue of necessity by an idolatrous devotion to nature, society, or the individual.

The mature Camus of *The Plague* ([1947] 1948) and *The Rebel* ([1951] 1956) seems to me an outstanding exemplar of the kind of humanism of which I've been speaking. He was one of the most clear-sighted and unflinching unmaskers of the colossal crimes and tragedies of the twentieth century and the enduring ills of the human condition. At the same time, he celebrated with a passionate lyricism the natural "graces" in human life in every age: above all beauty, compassion, and the word of truth. He sought to illuminate permanent values brought to light precisely through the human experience of revolt against oppressions of every sort: human life itself, human community, justice, moderation and limits to human action. Camus was an unrelenting foe of modern ideologies which dethrone God only to put an absolutist vision of humanity in God's place, and he traced the fateful course by which the authentic rebel so often becomes the revolutionary ideologue. Deeply aware of human finitude, he affirmed our deep relationship with the natural world and would not join in those various modern tendencies completely to historicize human existence. As he wrote in *The Rebel*: ". . . the only original rule of life today [is] to learn to live and to die, and, in order to be a man, to refuse to be a god" (306).

I could cite a number of other distinguished twentieth-century secular thinkers who have likewise embodied in richly varied ways the realistic, dialectical affirmation of human "at-home-ness" in the world I've been talking about. To mention only a few: Sigmund Freud, Bertrand Russell, and Martin Heidegger as important intellectual influences of the century; and, in the second half of the twentieth century humanists such as Simone de Beauvoir, Andrei Sakharov, and Michael Harrington. Their writings also illustrate a dialectical humanism which exhibits a fully "indwelling" secular world-orientation while facing honestly all the problems and implications of such a view given the realities of human life in the world.

3. Conclusion

I've tried to show that a typology of "styles" of world-orientation—what I've called the types of "indwelling" and "exile"—enables us to transcend the usual stereotypes regarding both religious and secular forms of world-orientation and look at them in their actual complexity with fresh eyes. I hope I've succeeded in showing that the still-typical categorizations in terms of other-worldliness vs. this-worldliness and, within Christian thought, relationships between world-orientation and liberal vs. conservative views, are inadequate, inaccurate, and misleading. There are Christian writers who do indeed seem to be "other-worldly" in their outlook; but the evidence of other Christian thinkers who are robustly "this-worldly" makes it clear that the issue hangs, not on belief in or rejection of the hope of eternal life or on being "liberal" or "orthodox," but on what I've called "indwelling" and "exile" mentalities which interpret Christian faith accordingly. Among secularists we predictably find those who are vigorously and optimistically "this-worldly," but we also find deep-dyed pessimists; while what I've called the dialectical secular sensibility is a world-orientation characterized by both affirmation and realism. And again, I believe that these differences among secular writers are illuminated better in terms of the mentalities of "at-home-ness" and "not-at-home-ness" than by division along strictly theoretical or ideological lines.

At the beginning of the essay I said that looking at religious and secular outlooks in terms of the two poles of "indwelling" and "exile" has implications for our understanding of the relationships between faith and skepticism. I went on to state my thesis that these two dispositional styles cut across the division between Christian and secular world-orientations. It should be apparent by now what I had in mind in making these statements. By focussing on basic dispositions rather than simply on intellectual content in religious and secular world-views, we realize that there are "kinship lines" running across the two, such that a Christian may have more in common with some secular humanists in her deepest responses to life and on a number of issues than with some fellow Christians—and vice versa. There are Christians of an "exile" mentality who rejoice in and welcome every manifestation of pessimism and even nihilism from secular quarters. It has been a standard homiletical device of some well-known fundamentalist evangelists, although it was also fashionable, I recall, among some "neo-orthodox" scholars, clergy, and seminarians of my own theological generation of some forty years ago. By contrast, as he revealed in his *Letters and Papers from Prison*, a Dietrich Bonhoeffer working in the German resistance movement during World War II identified much more closely with his secular comrades-in-conspiracy, who risked their lives for purely human values and hopes, than he did with many other Christians (200, 281-2, 325-7, 344-6). Bonhoeffer's experience has been confirmed repeatedly by many Christians since then, especially in connection with social and political action.

To say that a person is a "believer" or a "skeptic" is only to take the first small step toward understanding how that person interprets life. In fact, because of our stereotypical expectations, it may be worse than misleading, and certainly humanly insensitive, to stay at that level. We have to go on to explore, first, the content of a person's religious faith or secular outlook—and the range and variety here are vast within both Christianity and humanism. Then, at a more fully existential level, we need also to try to discern the dispositional style that finds expression in both the form and the content of a person's world-view. In this task of clarifying and understanding basic world-orientations, I suggest that the differences between "indwelling" and "exile" styles may prove illuminating.

Bibliography of Works Cited

Abbott, Lyman. *The Evolution of Christianity*. Boston and New York: Houghton Mifflin, 1892.

_____. *The Theology of an Evolutionist*. London, 1897.

Arnold, Matthew. Literature and Dogma. [Popular Edition, 1883.] Edited, abridged, and with an introduction by James C. Livingston. New York: Frederick Ungar, 1970.

Aronson, Ronald. *Camus and Sartre: The Story of a Friendship and the Quarrel That Ended It*. Chicago: University of Chicago Press, 2004.

Augustine. *City of God*. Translated from the Latin by Marcus Dods, with an Introduction by Thomas Merton. Reprint edition. New York: The Modern Library, 1994.

_____. *Confessions*. Translated with an Introduction by R. S. Pine-Coffin. London: Penguin Books, 1961.

Barbour, Ian G. *Religion and Science: Historical and Contemporary Issues*. New York: HarperSanFrancisco, 1997.

Barnes, Hazel. *An Existentialist Ethics*. New York: Random House, 1967.

_____. *Humanistic Existentialism: The Literature of Possibility*. Lincoln: University of Nebraska Press, 1959.

_____. *The Story I Tell Myself: A Venture in Existentialist Autobiography*. Chicago: University of Chicago Press, 1997.

Barrett, William. *Irrational Man*. New York: Doubleday, 1958.

Beauvoir, Simone de. *The Ethics of Ambiguity*. Translated by Bernard Frechtman from the French *Pour une morale de l'ambiguité* (Paris: Gallimard, 1947). New York:
Philosophical Library, 1948.

_____. *The Second Sex*. Translated by H. M. Parshley from the French *Le Deuxieme Sexe* (Paris: Gallimard, 1949). New York: Knopf, 1952; Vintage, 1989.

Becker, Ernest. *The Denial of Death*. New York: The Free Press, 1973.

Beckett, Samuel. *Endgame*. Translated by the Author from the French *Fin de Partie*. New York: Grove Press, 1958.

——————. *Waiting for Godot*. Translated by the Author from the French *En Attendant Godot*. New York: Grove Press, 1954.

Bonhoeffer, Dietrich. *Letters and Papers from Prison*. Edited by Eberhard Bethge. Translated by Reginald Fuller, Frank Clarke and others with additional material translated by John Bowden, from the German *Widerstand und Ergebung: Briefe und Aufzeichnungen aus der Haft* (Munich: Christian Kaiser Verlag, 1970). New York: Macmillan, 1972.

Buber, Martin. *I and Thou*. Translated by Walter Kaufmann from the German *Ich und* Du (1923). New York: Charles Scribner's Sons, 1970.

Bultmann, Rudolf. *Existence and Faith: Shorter Writings of Rudolf Bultmann*. Selected, translated and introduced by Schubert M. Ogden. New York: Meridian Books, 1960.

——————. *Jesus Christ and Mythology*. New York: Charles Scribner's Sons, 1958.

——————. "New Testament and Mythology." In Hans W. Bartsch, ed., *Kerygma and Myth: A Theological Debate*. Translated by Reginald H. Fuller from the German *Kerygma und Mythos* (Hamburg-Volksdorf: Herbert Reich, Ev. Verlag G.m.b.H., 1948). New York: Harper & Row, 1961.

Busch, Eberhard. *Karl Barth: His Life from Letters and Autobiographical Texts*. Translated by John Bowden. Philadelphia: Fortress Press, 1976.

Campbell, C. A. *On Selfhood and Godhood*. Reprint edition. London: Routledge & Kegan Paul, 2004.

Camus, Albert. *The First Man*. Translated by David Hapgood from the French *Le Premier Homme* (Paris: Gallimard, 1994). New York: Alfred A. Knopf, 1995.

——————. *Lyrical and Critical Essays*. Translated by Ellen Conroy Kennedy and edited by Philip Thody from a variety of sources published by Gallimard. New York: Alfred A. Knopf, 1967.

_____. *The Myth of* Sisyphus. Translated by Justin O'Brien from the French *Le Mythe de Sisyphe* (Paris: Gallimard, 1942). New York: Random House, 1955.

_____. *The Plague*. Translated by Stuart Gilbert from the French *La Peste* (Paris: Gallimard, 1947). New York: Random House, 1948.

_____. *The Rebel: An Essay on Man in Revolt.* Translated by Anthony Bower From the French *L'Homme révolté* (Paris: Gallimard, 1951). New York: Knopf, 1956.

_____. *Resistance, Rebellion, and Death.* Selected essays translated and with an introduction by Justin O'Brien. New York: Knopf, 1960.

_____. *The Stranger*. Translated by Stuart Gilbert from the French *L'Etranger* (Paris: Gallimard, 1942). New York: Alfred A. Knopf, 1946.

Cavell, Stanley. *Philosophical Passages: Wittgenstein, Emerson, Austin, Derrida.* Oxford: Basil Blackwell, 1995.

Chesterton, G. K. *The Father Brown Omnibus.* New York: Dodd, 1983.

_____. *Orthodoxy*. London: The Bodley Head, 1908.

Condorcet, Jean Antoine Nicolas Caritat Marquis de. *Sketch for a Historical Picture on the Progress of the Human Mind.* [1795] Translated by June Barraclough. London: Weidenfeld & Nicolson, 1955.

Cotkin, George. *Existential America.* Baltimore: The Johns Hopkins University Press, 2003.

Daly, Mary. *Beyond God the Father: Toward a Philosophy of Women's Liberation.* Boston: Beacon Press, 1973.

_____. *The Church and the Second Sex.* Boston: With a "Feminist Postchristian Introduction" and an "Archaic Afterwords." Beacon Press, 1985.

_____. *Gyn/Ecology: The Metaethics of Radical Feminism.* Boston: Beacon Press, 1978.

_____. *Outercourse: The Be-Dazzling Voyage.* New York: HarperSanFrancisco, 1992.

_____. *Pure Lust: Elemental Feminist Philosophy.* Boston: Beacon Press, 1984.

―――――. *Quintessence... Realizing the Archaic Future: A Radical Elemental Feminist Manifesto*. Boston: Beacon Press, 1998.

――――― and Jane Caputi. *Websters' First New Intergalactic Wickedary of the English Language*. London: The Women's Press, 1988.

Darwin, Charles. *The Origin of Species*. London: John Murray, 1859.

Dawkins, Richard. *The Blind Watchmaker*. New York: W. W. Norton & Co., 1987.

Donovan, Josephine. *Feminist Theory: The Intellectual Traditions of American Feminism*. New York: The Ungar Publishing Co., Inc., 1985.

Dostoevsky, Fyodor. *Notes from Underground*. Translated from the Russian by Richard Pevear and Larissa Volokhonsky. New York: Alfred A. Knopf, 1993.

Douglass, Frederick. *Narrative of the Life of Frederick Douglass, An American Slave*. [1845] New York: Doubleday Anchor, 1989.

Frankl, Viktor. *Man's Search for Meaning: An Introduction to Logotherapy*. Third edition, revised and enlarged by the author. Part One translated from the German by Ilse Lasch. Preface by Gordon W. Allport. New York: Simon & Schuster, 1984.

―――――. *Psychotherapy and Existentialism: Selected Papers on Logotherapy*. With contributions by James C. Crumbaugh, Hans O. Gerz, and Leonard T. Maholick. New York: Simon & Schuster, 1967.

―――――. *The Will to Meaning: Foundations and Applications of Logotherapy*. New York: New American Library, 1969.

Freud, Sigmund. *Civilization and Its Discontents*. Translated and edited by James Strachey from the German *Das Unbehagen in Der Kultur* (Vienna: Internationaler Psychoanalytischer Verlag).

Gore, Charles, ed. *Lux Mundi: Studies in the Religion of the Incarnation*. London: John Murray, 1890.

Gould, Stephen Jay. "Nonoverlapping Magisteria." *Natural History* 106:2, March 1997, 16-22, 60-62.

———————. *Rocks of Ages: Science and Religion in the Fullness of Life.* New York: The Ballantine Publishing Group, 1999.

Greene, Graham. *A Burnt-Out Case.* Reprint edition. New York: Penguin, 1992.
———————. *The End of the Affair.* Reprint edition. New York: Penguin, 2004.

———————. *The Power and the Glory.* Reprint edition. New York: Penguin, 2003.

Harrington, Michael. *The Politics at God's Funeral: The Spiritual Crisis of Western Civilization.* New York: Viking Penguin, 1983.

Hegel, Georg W. F. *The Phenomenology of Spirit.* Translated by J. B. Baillie. 2 volumes. Second revised edition. New York: Macmillan, 1931.

Heidegger, Martin. "The Question Concerning Technology," in *The Question Concerning Technology and Other Essays.* Translated by William Lovitt from the German "Die Frage nach der Technik," in *Die Technik und die Kehre* (Pfullingen: Günther Neske, 1962). New York: Harper & Row, 1977.

———————. *Being and Time.* Translated by John Macquarrie and Edward Robinson from the German *Sein und Zeit* (*Jahrbuch für Phänomenologie und Phänomenologische Forschung*, 1927). New York: Harper & Row, 1962.

Hick, John. *Death and Eternal Life.* New York: Harper & Row, 1976.

———————. *God Has Many Names.* Philadelphia: Westminster Press, 1982.

———————. *Philosophy of Religion.* 4th edition. Englewood, NJ: Prentice Hall, 1990.

Ibsen, Henrik. *A Doll's House.* Translated by Eva Le Galliene. In *Western Literature in World Context.* Edited by Paul Davis et al. New York: St. Martin's Press, 1995.

Jacobs, Jo Ellen. *The Voice of Harriet Taylor Mill.* Bloomington: Indiana University Press, 2002.

James, William. "The Dilemma of Determinism" and "The Will to Believe." In *The Will to Believe and OtherEssays in Popular Philosophy.* Republication of original 1897 edition published by Longmans, Green & Co. New York: Dover Publications, 1956.

Jaspers, Karl. *The Future of Mankind.* Translated by E. B. Ashton from the German *Die Atombombe und die Zukunft des Menschen* (Munich: Piper & Co., 1958). Chicago: University of Chicago Press, 1961.

_____. *The Question of German Guilt.* Translated by E. B. Ashton from the German *Die Schuldfrage, ein Beitrag zur deutschen Frage.* New York: Dial Press, 1947.

Johnson, Phillip. *Darwin on Trial.* Downers Grove, IL: InterVarsity Press, 1993.

Kahn, Herman. *The Coming Boom: Economic, Political, Social.* New York: Simon & Schuster, 1983.

Kant, Immanuel. "Idea for a Universal History with a Cosmopolitan Intent." In *Perpetual Peace and Other Essays.* Translated, with Introduction, by Ted Humphrey. Indianapolis: Hackett Publishing Company, 1983.

Kaufmann, Walter. *Critique of Religion and Philosophy.* Garden City, NY: Doubleday Anchor, 1961.

_____, ed. *Existentialism from Dostoevsky to Sartre.* New York: World Publishing Company, 1956.

_____. *Existentialism, Religion, and Death: Thirteen Essays.* New York: New American Library, 1976.

_____. *The Faith of a Heretic.* Garden City, NY: Doubleday Anchor, 1963.

Kierkegaard, Søren. *Concluding Unscientific Postscript to Philosophical Fragments.* Vol. I: Text. Edited and Translated with Introduction and Notes by Howard V. Hong and Edna H. Hong. Princeton, NJ: Princeton University Press, 1992.

_____. *The Concept of Anxiety.* Edited and translated with Introduction and Notes by Reidar Thomte in collaboration with Albert B. Anderson. Princeton: Princeton University Press, 1980.

_____. *Either/Or.* Edited and translated with introduction and notes by Howard V. Hong and Edna H. Hong. Princeton: Princeton University Press, 1987.

_____. *Fear and Trembling/Repetition*. Edited and translated by Howard V. Hong and Edna H. Hong. Princeton: Princeton University Press, 1983.

_____. *The Point of View for My Work as an Author* [1848]. In *The Essential Kierkegaard*. Edited by Howard V. Hong and Edna H. Hong. Princeton: Princeton University Press, 2000.

_____. *The Sickness Unto Death* [1849]. Edited and translated with introduction and notes by Howard V. Hong and Edna H. Hong. Princeton: Princeton University Press, 1980.

Léon, Céline and Sylvia Walsh, eds. *Feminist Interpretations of Søren Kierkegaard*. University Park, PA: Pennsylvania State University Press, 1997.

Lewis, C. S. *Mere Christianity*. London: Collins, 1952.

_____. *The Problem of Pain*. New York: Macmillan, 1962.

Lindbeck, George. *The Nature of Doctrine: Religion and Theology in a Postliberal Age*. Philadelphia: Westminster John Knox Press, 1984.

Marcel, Gabriel. *Being and Having: An Existentialist Diary*. New York: Harper & Row, 1965.

_____. *The Mystery of Being*. Vol. I: *Reflection and Mystery*. Translated by G. S. Fraser from the French *Le mystere de l'etre*. Vol. I: *Réflexion et mystere* (Paris: Aubier, 1951). Chicago: Henry Regnery Company, 1960.

_____. *Homo Viator: Introduction to a Metaphysic of Hope*. Translated by Emma Craufurd from the French. New York: Harper & Row, 1962.

_____. "Existence and Human Freedom." Translated by Manya Harari from the French "L'Existence et la liberté humaine chez Jean-Paul Sartre" (Paris: J. Vrin, [1946] 1981). In *The Philosophy of Existentialism*. New York: Philosophical Library, 1956.

_____. *Three Plays*. Introduction by Richard Hayes. New York: Hill and Wang, 1965.

McFague, Sallie. *Models of God: Theology for an Ecological, Nuclear Age*. Philadelphia: Fortress Press, 1987.

Mill, Harriet Taylor. *The Complete Works of Harriet Taylor Mill.* Edited with an Introduction by Jo Ellen Jacobs and Paula Harms Payne. Bloomington: Indiana University Press, 1998.

Mill, John Stuart. *Autobiography.* [1873] Edited and with an introduction by John M. Robson. New York: Penguin Books, 1989.

_____. *On Liberty.* [1859] Edited, with an introduction, by Elizabeth Rapaport. Indianapolis: Hackett Publishing Company, Inc., 1978.

_____. *Three Essays on Religion.* New York: Greenwood Press, reprint of 1874 edition.

_____ and Harriet Taylor Mill. *Essays on Sex Equality.* Edited with an introduction by Alice S. Rossi. Chicago: University of Chicago Press, 1970.

Moore, Aubrey. *Science and the Faith.* London, 1889.

Muggeridge, Malcolm. *Jesus Rediscovered.* New York: Doubleday, 1979.

Murdoch, Iris. *The Black Prince.* Introduction by Martha C. Nussbaum. New York: Penguin, 2003. Original copyright Iris Murdoch, 1973.

_____. *Existentialists and Mystics: Writings on Philosophy and Literature.* Edited with a Preface by Peter Conradi. Foreword by George Steiner. London: Chatto & Windus, 1997.

_____. *Metaphysics as a Guide to Morals.* New York: Penguin, 1993.

_____. "On 'God' and 'Good.'" In *The Sovereignty of Good.* London: Routledge & Kegan Paul, 1970, 45-74.

_____. *Sartre: Romantic Rationalist.* New Haven: Yale University Press, 1953.

Murphy, Julien S., ed. *Feminist Interpretations of Jean-Paul Sartre.* University Park, PA: Pennsylvania State University Press, 1999.

Nietzsche, Friedrich. *Twilight of the Idols.* Translated, with an Introduction and Commentary, by R. J. Hollingdale. Harmondsworth, England: Penguin Books Ltd., 1968.

_____. *The Will to Power.* Translated by Walter Kaufmann and R. J. Hollingdale from the German *Der Wille zur Macht* (1901). Edited, with commentary, by Walter Kaufmann. New York: Random House, 1967.

Ortega y Gasset, José, *The Revolt of the Masses*. Authorized translation from the Spanish *La Rebelión de las Masas* (1930).. New York: W. W. Norton & Co., 1932.

Pascal, Blaise. *Pensées*. Translated from the French, with an Introduction, by A. J. Krailsheimer. Baltimore: Penguin Books, 1966.

_____. *The Provincial Letters*. Translated from the French *Les Provinciales*, with an Introduction, by A. J. Krailsheimer. Harmondsworth: Penguin, 1967.

Percy, Walker. *Lost in the Cosmos: The Last Self-Help Book*. New York: Pocket Books, 1983.

Phillips, D. Z. *Faith and Philosophical Enquiry*. New York: Schocken Books, 1971.

Pinker, Steven. *The Blank Slate: The Modern Denial of Human Nature*. New York: Penguin Books, 2002.

Quinones, Ricardo. *Mapping Literary Modernism: Time and Development*. Princeton: Princeton University Press, 1985.

Roberts, David. *Existentialism and Religious Belief*. New York: Oxford University Press, 1959.

Rousseau, Jean-Jacques. *Confessions*. [1782] Translated and with an introduction by J. M. Cohen. New York: Penguin Books, 1953.

_____. *Discourse on the Origin and Foundations of Inequality among Men*. [1754] In *The Basic Political Writings*. Translated and edited by Donald Cress, introduced by Peter Gay. Indianapolis: Hackett Publishing Company, Inc., 1987.

Russell, Bertrand. *Why I am not a Christian and Other Essays on Religion and Related Subjects*. Edited by Paul Edwards. New York: Simon & Schuster, 1957.

Sakharov, Andrei. *Alarm and Hope*. New York: Random House, 1978.

Sartre, Jean-Paul. *The Age of Reason*. Translated by Eric Sutton from the French *L'Age de raison* (Paris: Gallimard, 1945). New York: Knopf, 1947.

_____. *Anti-Semite and Jew.* Translated by George J. Becker from the French *Réflexions sur la Question Juive* (Paris: Paul Morihien, 1946). New York: Schocken Books, 1948.

_____. *Critique of Dialectical Reason.* Translated by Alan Sheridan-Smith from the French *Critique de la raison dialectique* (Paris: Gallimard, 1960). London: Verso, 1976.

_____. *Being and Nothingness: An Essay on Phenomenological Ontology.* Translated by Hazel Barnes from the French *L'Etre et le néant: Essai d'ontologie phénoménologique* (Paris: Gallimard, 1943). New York: Philosophical Library, 1956.

_____. *Troubled Sleep.* Translated by Gerald Hopkins from the French *La Mort dans l'ame* (Paris: Gallimard, 1949). New York: Knopf, 1950.

_____. *The Words.* Translated by Bernard Frechtman from the French *Les Mots* (Paris: Gallimard, 1963). New York: Braziller, 1964.

_____. *The Reprieve.* Translated by Eric Sutton from the French *Le Sursis* (Paris: Gallimard, 1945). New York: Knopf, 1947.

Schweitzer, Albert. *Out of My Life and Thought.* Translated by C. T. Campion from the German *Aus Meinem Leben und Denken.* New York: Henry Holt & Company, 1933.

Shestov, Lev. *Athens and Jerusalem.* Translated, with an Introduction, by Bernard Martin. New York: Simon & Schuster, 1966.

Skinner, B. F. *Walden Two.* New York: Macmillan, 1976.

Smith, Huston. *Forgotten Truth: The Common Vision of the World's Religions.* New York: HarperSanFrancisco, 1992.

Solomon, Robert C. *Existentialism.* Second edition. New York: Oxford University Press, 2005.

_____. *From Hegel to Existentialism.* New York: Oxford University Press, 1987.

Spencer, Herbert. *Social Statics.* London, 1851.

Spengemann, William. *The Forms of Autobiography: Episodes in the History of a Literary Genre*. New Haven: Yale University Press, 1980.

Thoreau, Henry David. *Walden*. [1854] In *Walden and Other Writings*. Edited by William Howarth. New York: Random House, 1981.

Tillich, Paul. *The Courage to Be*. New Haven, CT: Yale University Press, 1952.

_____. *Dynamics of Faith*. New York: Harper & Brothers, 1957.

Todd, Olivier. *Albert Camus: A Life*. Translated by Benjamin Ivry from the French *Albert Camus: une vie* (Paris: Editions Gallimard, 1996). New York: Alfred A. Knopf, 1997.

Twain, Mark. *Letters from the Earth*. New York: Harper & Row, 1974.

_____. *The Mysterious Stranger and Other Stories*. New York: New American Library, 1962.

Unamuno, Miguel de. *Tragic Sense of Life*. Translated by J. E. Crawford Flitch from the Spanish *Del Sentimiento Trágico de la Vida*. New York: Dover Publications, 1954.

Van Buren, Paul. *The Edges of Language: An Essay in the Logic of a Religion*. New York: Macmillan, 1972.

Voltaire, François Marie Arouet de. *Candide and Related Texts*. Translated by David Wootton. Indianapolis: Hackett Publishing Co., 2000.

Weil, Simone. *Gravity and Grace*. Translated by Emma Crawford and Mario von der Ruhr from the French *La Pesanteur et la grâce* (Paris: Librairie PLON, 1947). With an introduction and postscript by Gustave Thibon. London: Routledge & Kegan Paul, 1952.

_____. *Waiting for God*. Translated by Emma Craufurd, with an Introduction by Leslie Fiedler. New York: Harper & Row, 1973.

White, Andrew Dickson. *A History of the Warfare of Science with Theology*. Two volumes. New York: D. Appleton, 1896.

Wiesel, Elie. *A Jew Today*. Translated by Marion Wiesel from the French *Un Juif aujourd'hui*. New York: Random House, 1979.

_____. *Night*. Translated by Stella Rodway from the French *La Nuit* (Paris: Les Editions Minuit, 1958). London: Fontana Books, 1972.

—————. *One Generation After.* Translated from the French by Lily Edelman and the author. New York: Avon Books, 1970.

Wilson, A. N. *Iris Murdoch as I Knew Her.* London: Random House, 2004.

Wilson, Colin. *The Outsider.* New York: Delta, 1956.

Wilson, Edward O. *Consilience: The Unity of Knowledge.* New York: Random House, 1998.

Wittgenstein, Ludwig. *Philosophical Investigations.* Translated by G. E. M. Anscombe from the German *Philosophische Untersuchungen.* New York: Macmillan, 1953.

Index

Allen, Woody, 1
analytic philosophy, 5, 6, 45, 55, 130, 132, 136
antisemitism, 37
Arnold, Matthew, 15, 114, 134
Artaud, Antonin, 3
atheism, 4, 19, 48, 118, 126, 127, 137, 139, 140
Augustine, 7, 70, 97, 114, 133
authenticity, 1, 15, 57, 66, 68
autobiography, iv, 36, 48, 49, 62, 75, 93, 94, 95, 96, 97, 99, 101
bad faith, 15, 17, 42, 44, 46, 57, 64, 65, 70
Baillie, Donald, 6
Baillie, John, 6
Barbour, Ian, 117, 118, 119, 125
Barnes, Hazel, 6, 36, 49, 57, 61
Barrett, William, 5, 6, 41
Barth, Karl, 6, 117
Beauvoir, Simone de, iii, 1, 3, 4, 8, 15, 16, 21, 23, 25, 40, 43, 44, 57, 58, 61, 62, 63, 64, 65, 66, 67, 68, 69, 70, 71, 73, 77, 78, 79, 102, 152
Becker, Ernest, 1, 4
Beckett, Samuel, 1, 3
Brunner, Emil, 6
Buber, Martin, 3, 16, 39, 130, 135
Bultmann, Rudolf, v, 3, 4, 6, 40, 110, 117, 120, 121, 122, 123, 133, 135
Campbell, C. A, 86, 91
Camus, Albert, iv, v, 1, 2, 3, 4, 5, 7, 13, 16, 17, 19, 20, 21, 22, 39, 40, 43, 44, 47, 49, 50, 53, 55, 62, 68, 89, 93, 96, 102, 103, 104, 105, 130
capitalism, 48, 50, 51, 70, 93
Cavell, Stanley, iv
Christian apologetics, iv, 107, 109, 110

cognitive science, 1, 2, 17, 25, 26, 41
communism, 48, 50, 51
Condorcet, 71
consciousness, 4, 8, 17, 31, 33, 36, 40, 43, 44, 45, 46, 47, 48, 49, 52, 53, 54, 55, 57, 61, 63, 64, 65, 66, 67, 68, 69, 71, 77, 82, 86, 89, 90, 98, 125
courage to be, 73, 74
creationism, iv, 111, 112, 116, 127
Daly, Mary, iii, 57, 61, 71, 72, 73, 74, 75, 76, 77, 78, 79
Darwin, Charles, 112, 113, 115, 116, 124
Darwinism, 111, 113, 114, 116, 117, 118, 122, 124, 127
Dawkins, Richard, 112, 118, 124
demythologizing, 120, 121, 122
Derrida, Jacques, 33
determinism, iii, 14, 17, 25, 26, 82, 86, 89
Dickie, Edgar, 6
Dostoevsky, Fyodor, 2, 3, 5, 16, 23, 33, 40, 41, 130
Douglass, Frederick, 65
Dubuffet, Jean, 3
Eliot, T. S., 3, 33
Ellison, Ralph, 3, 6
Enlightenment, 30, 33, 34, 35, 93, 122
essentialist, 59
evolutionary psychology, 17, 25
evolutionism, iv, 111, 112, 117, 124
existential courage, 73, 74, 75, 76, 77
existential psychoanalysis, 4
existential psychology, 4
existentialist ethics, 15, 37, 68
existentialist hero, 43, 44, 52, 53
existentialist novel, 43, 51, 52, 53

feminism, 27, 37, 57, 59, 61, 71, 72
feminist existentialists, iii, 57
feminist, iii, 35, 36, 57, 58, 59, 60, 61, 62, 68, 71, 72, 73, 74, 76, 77, 79, 101
feminists, 57, 62, 69, 71, 72, 75, 79
Frankl, Viktor, iii, v, 4, 18, 81
free will, 14, 26, 43, 81, 82, 86, 87, 88, 89, 90, 91, 92
freedom, iii, 1, 4, 7, 14, 15, 19, 20, 21, 26, 38, 41, 43, 44, 46, 47, 52, 53, 57, 61, 63, 64, 65, 66, 67, 68, 77, 78, 81, 82, 83, 84, 85, 86, 88, 89, 90, 92, 96, 104, 105
fundamentalism, 116, 135
fundamentalists, 116, 117
genetics, 17, 26, 30, 41
Gould, Stephen Jay, 111, 112, 114, 124, 125
Greene, Graham, 53
Hegel, G. W. F., 1, 7, 8, 9, 58, 61, 130
Heidegger, Martin, 3, 4, 6, 8, 15, 16, 21, 22, 25, 33, 39, 40, 50, 55, 120, 130
Heim, Karl, 6
Heller, Joseph, 3
Hesse, Hermann, 3
Hick, John, 110
human nature, iii, 17, 20, 25, 26, 27, 28, 29, 32, 37, 41, 43, 47, 81, 98
humanists, 2, 27, 32, 115
humanities, iii, 25, 32, 38, 129
Husserl, Edmund, 8, 21, 22
Ibsen, Henrik, 65
ideologies, 18, 35, 37, 67, 69, 78
ideology, 36, 37, 51, 93
inauthenticity, 7, 15, 122
indeterminism, iii, 86, 89, 90
intelligent design, 111, 124, 126, 127
Ionesco, Eugene, 3
James, William, iii, v, 33, 89, 90, 93, 116, 130

John Paul II, Pope, 111, 114
Kafka, Franz, 33
Kant, Immanuel, 52
Kaufmann, Walter, iv, v, 41, 129, 130, 131, 132, 133, 134, 135, 136, 137, 138, 139, 140, 141
Kierkegaard, Søren, 25, 32, 39, 40, 41, 42, 55, 58, 59, 60, 90, 91
Kierkegaardian model, iii, 21, 22, 23
King, Jr., Martin Luther, 69
logotherapy, 82
Marcel, Gabriel, iv, 33, 39, 40, 44, 45, 46, 47, 48, 49, 50, 53, 54, 55
Marxism, 35, 36, 40, 51, 64, 67, 102
May, Rollo, 81
meaning of life, 82
Merleau-Ponty, Maurice, 61, 40, 102
Mill, John Stuart, iv, 71, 93, 96, 99, 100, 101, 105
misogyny, 59, 72, 73
modernism, 33, 35, 116
moral philosophy, 39, 55, 64
Murdoch, Iris, iii, 39, 42, 43, 44, 45, 47, 48, 49, 50, 51, 52, 53, 54, 55, 56
mystic, 39, 104
mystical novel, 51, 52, 53, 54
mystical, 51, 52, 53, 54, 98, 104, 108
mythologies, 68, 69, 78, 121
mythology, 120, 121, 122, 123
natural sciences, 25, 29, 30
naturalism, 111, 112, 120, 124, 125, 126
neuroscience, 25, 26, 41
Niebuhr, H. Richard, 134
Nietzsche, Friedrich, iv, 25, 33, 35, 40, 55, 58, 61, 130, 131
NOMA principle, 112, 120, 124, 125, 126
nonoverlapping magisteria, 112
noological, 82

ontological, 41, 42, 48, 63, 64, 65, 66, 72, 73, 75, 77, 78, 79, 125, 126, 137
Ortega y Gasset, José, 3
Other, iii, 32, 40, 68, 69, 70, 71
Otherness, 69, 70
Percy, Walker, 32, 38
perspectivism, 34
phenomenological analysis, iv, 46, 48, 82
phenomenology, 41, 44, 45, 46, 47, 49, 63, 64, 89
Pinker, Steven, 26, 27, 28, 29, 30, 31
Pius XII, Pope, 111, 114
Platonism, 35, 39, 54
possibility, iii, 46, 48, 51, 52, 57, 66, 67, 87, 88, 89, 90, 91, 92, 109, 119, 120, 125, 126, 135
postmodernism, iii, 25, 32, 33, 34, 35, 36
reductionism, iii, 26, 28, 30, 38, 82
relativism, 35, 36, 38, 47
relativism, 47
responsibility, 42, 46, 65, 66, 81, 82, 83, 86, 88, 90
revolt, 51, 67, 68
Roberts, David, 108
romantic individualism, 95, 96, 97, 98, 105
romanticism, iv, 93, 95, 96, 98, 100, 102, 104, 105
Rorty, Richard, 33
Rousseau, Jean-Jacques, iii, iv, 59, 93, 95, 96, 97, 98, 100, 105
Sartre, Jean-Paul, 25, 26, 36, 39, 40, 41, 43, 44, 45, 46, 47, 48, 49, 50, 51, 53, 55, 58, 61, 62, 63, 64, 67, 68, 81, 85, 89, 91, 92, 102, 105, 130, 133
Sartrianism, 40, 44, 49, 55
scientists, 26, 27, 32, 111, 113, 115, 117, 118, 119, 124, 126
self-awareness, 54, 63, 65, 66, 91
self-detachment, 82, 83, 84, 86, 91
self-transcendence, 82, 86, 91
skepticism, iv, 35, 101, 119, 130
Social Darwinism, 115
sociobiology, 25
Solomon, Robert, 41
Spengemann, William, 94
subjectivism, 47, 60
subjectivity, 28, 29, 31, 32, 37, 38, 60, 61, 63, 64, 65, 66, 91, 96, 98
Taylor, Harriet, 99, 100, 101, 102, 105
theism, 74, 126, 127, 139
theistic evolutionism, 114, 117, 125
this-worldly, 123
Thoreau, Henry David, 94
Tillich, Paul, 40, 73, 74, 75, 76, 117, 133, 135, 137, 138
transcendence, 38, 48, 66, 75, 82, 91, 121
Unamuno, Miguel de, 40
Utilitarian, 93, 99, 100
Utilitarianism, 100
Weil, Simone, 39
Wiesel, Elie, 87
will to meaning, 81, 82
Wilson, E. O., 30
Wittgenstein, Ludwig, 118
Woolf, Virginia, 33, 72

www.ingramcontent.com/pod-product-compliance
Lightning Source LLC
Chambersburg PA
CBHW021127300426
44113CB00006B/315